AGILIZING
THE ENTERPRISE

Collaborative Leadership, Dynamic Strategy,
and Organizational Flexibility

AGILIZING
THE ENTERPRISE

Collaborative Leadership, Dynamic Strategy,
and Organizational Flexibility

JOSEPH RAYNUS

CRC Press
Taylor & Francis Group
Boca Raton London New York

CRC Press is an imprint of the
Taylor & Francis Group, an **Informa** business
AN AUERBACH BOOK

CRC Press
Taylor & Francis Group
6000 Broken Sound Parkway NW, Suite 300
Boca Raton, FL 33487-2742

First issued in paperback 2022

© 2018 by Taylor & Francis Group, LLC
CRC Press is an imprint of Taylor & Francis Group, an Informa business

No claim to original U.S. Government works

ISBN 13: 978-1-03-247614-8 (pbk)
ISBN 13: 978-1-138-19797-8 (hbk)
ISBN 13: 978-1-315-27172-9 (ebk)

DOI: 10.1201/9781315271729

**Visit the Taylor & Francis Web site at
http://www.taylorandfrancis.com**

**and the CRC Press Web site at
http://www.crcpress.com**

Dedication

To my wife, Gail

Contents

Dedication   vii

Contents   ix

Foreword   xi

Preface   xiii

Acknowledgments   xv

About the Author   xvii

1 Meeting at the Airport   1

2 Searching for Answers in History   13

3 Searching for the Age of Agility   35

4 Searching in Change Management   49

5 Searching in Strategic Leadership   71

6 Searching for Agile Organizations   95

7 Searching for Agile Leadership Qualities   133

8 Searching for Problem Solving and Decision Making   153

9 Searching for Innovation   199

10 Moving to the Age of Agility   223

Index   237

Foreword

Joe Raynus often stops by my office, plops himself down in a chair, and with a twinkle in his eyes makes a controversial statement to see how I will respond and to get the conversation going. He loves to discuss business theories to probe what works in what context. He will argue using his vast knowledge of the theories and his industry experience. His stories usually make me laugh, but I also usually learn something new. I am happy to see that Joe has used this "approach" in his new book, *Agilizing the Enterprise: Collaborative Leadership, Dynamic Strategy, and Organizational Flexibility*—a book that tells stories but also gives information.

The book does not just discuss agility, however, but also covers how agility is tied into dynamic strategies, dynamic capabilities, organizational change, and change management. The information part of the book demonstrates how one theory cannot be used in isolation from others and then goes on to discuss how to apply them in the real world. To work, this requires deep knowledge of the pros and cons of each theory, experience to understand the challenges of implementing the theories, and empathy for human nature as to how people actually behave in organizations. Joe can do this because of his experience as both a teacher and a consultant to many organizations.

The style Joe uses in imparting this information is a story as in a novel. This allows him to romp through ancient history, philosophy, and science, as well as to use business examples. The read is breezy, easy, and fun. But, you will learn something new, just as I do in our office conversations.

— John H. Friar
Executive Professor of Entrepreneurship
D'Amore-McKim School of Business
Northeastern University
Boston, MA

Preface

Agility has become a prerequisite for organizations and companies in every industry worldwide. With digital transformations underway in nearly every industry, it is difficult for organizations to survive without the ability to adapt and change according to the world around them. The number one reason for the failure of businesses and organizations throughout the world is that they lack the ability to make the decision to renew themselves and revamp their business models and processes according to the changing environment.

Contrary to popular belief, agility is not synonymous with the stability of an organization. In fact, stability is one of the requirements for an organization to be agile. For an organization to successfully be agile, it is extremely necessary for it to have a stable foundation. What this means, in simple terms, is that even though changes in the environment and industry may require a business or organization to revise and revamp, the core of the organization should remain unshaken by any and all types of changes that are bound to occur within the industry and the organization itself.

Dynamic strategy is another aspect that is necessary for agility. Unless an organization has dynamic capabilities, it is bound to fail in the domains of responsiveness, speed, and nimbleness, all because the organization did not have the ability to move as fast as was necessary.

In this book, we will discuss the importance of agility and how it affects the solutions that are being delivered by an organization. We will also talk about how a blend of strategic innovation, visionary leadership, managed resilience, and organizational agility go hand in hand to ensure the success of an organization. Enterprise agility is not a far-fetched possibility. Once the problems of the organization are identified, with the right tools and effort, the agility, efficiency, and effectiveness of an organization, as well as the processes that the success of the organization are based on, can all be maximized.

Acknowledgments

One evening in a conversation with my wife, Gail, I complained that many professional books written today are not particularly enjoyable to read; the dry content can make these books heavy going—unless the book is a "how to" manual with a *silver bullet* solution inside, which may not work anyway.

Gail looked at me with her very serious "Gail look" and said, "Stop complaining! You are good with stories. Why don't you write one?"

So, I did.

Thank you, Gail! Without your help, support, and inspiration I would never have been able to start and complete this project.

Talking and writing on the subject of agility is easier said than done.

I want to thank my friends in industry and academia who helped me to complete my research and get this book into shape during many after-hours discussions.

I'm really thankful to Dr. John Friar. I appreciate the time he spent with me and the way he patiently expanded my understanding of the subject of agility and entrepreneurship.

Thank you, John!

I would like to thank Steve Kasmouski for his time, wisdom, and support of this project.

Thank you, Steve!

Thank you, Dr. Hans Mulder, for your guidance and for sharing your thoughts on innovation and organizational structure with me. Your input into this book has been invaluable.

Thank you, Hans!

Thank you, Marje Pollack (DerryField Publishing Services), my copy editor and typesetter, for keeping me focused. Thank you for your diligence and attention to minor details. It has been an incredibly rewarding learning experience working with you.

Thank you, Marje!

Dr. John Wyzalek (Senior Acquisitions Editor, Taylor & Francis), you published my first book 20 years ago, and you have supported all of my projects, including this one. Thank you for your enthusiasm and support.

Thank you, John!

It was a long and challenging journey that would have been impossible to complete without many people who helped me to shape the content and gave me the opportunity to communicate my thoughts and implement my methodology.

THANK YOU ALL!!!!!!!!!!!!!!

About the Author

Joseph Raynus is a speaker, author, trainer, and consultant who brings a unique blend of practical hands-on experience with innovative ideas and solutions to deal with the real-world challenges of complex environments.

He is a recognized expert in strategic program management and performance improvement. He has facilitated large-scale organizational change, designed and led comprehensive training programs, managed multi-million-dollar technology projects, and mentored different levels of management.

Joseph teaches a variety of undergraduate and graduate courses at the D'Amore-McKim School of Business at Northeastern University, in Boston, Massachusetts. He is a founder of the consulting company, ShareDynamics, Inc., providing training and consulting services to enable enterprise agility and facilitate the development of roadmaps that align value delivery at both strategical and tactical levels.

He is a frequent speaker at industry events and is the author of several books, including *Software Process Improvement with CMM* (Boston, Artech House, 1998), which is also available in the Japanese and Chinese languages.

Joseph's book, *Improving Business Process Performance: Gain Agility, Create Value, and Achieve Success* (New York, Taylor & Francis, 2011), was recognized by the KPI Institute as one of the top 10 books in the Business Performance Management and Operational Performance Management categories in 2013.

Chapter 1

Meeting at the Airport

There I was, sitting and watching TV in one of the bars at Newark Liberty International Airport. The weather forecast was not really promising, which is why many flights were delayed or cancelled. My flight back to Boston, too, was delayed—a typical mid-February day in the Northeast.

For the last four hours, I had been waiting for my flight to Boston to be announced. A lot had happened in these four hours—a gate change, announcements of flight delays, losing my seat once due to an overbooked flight. Having already finished all of the reading material I was carrying, it's fair to say that I wasn't having one of the best days of my life.

I decided to buy a new book at the airport's bookstore to kill time without ruining my IQ by mindlessly watching TV. Who knew how long it would be before my flight back home would be announced? As soon as I got up to head to the bookstore, a commercial came on the TV. It was one of those commercials that paid a lot of money for 30 seconds of air time. The kind of commercials that are aimed at convincing executives to invest millions in a technological product that would act as an elixir of sorts to get their company out of all of the problems that it has ever seen.

I love watching commercials that target business audiences. In this TV commercial, a group of C-level executives are sitting around the conference table during the wee hours of the night with piles upon piles of papers before them. It is implied that these executives, along with their CEO, are trying to decide how they can save money and cut the budget.

To make things worse, the CEO makes a statement that they will not leave the room until the crisis is resolved. Agony and defeat is evident on the faces of these executives. Exhausted and disheveled, these executives look at each other in search of answers—each of them more tense and tired than the other.

Suddenly, the focus shifts to one of the more senior-looking executives, who looks like a revelation just dawned on him.

"What about this?" he asks, pointing at the pile of papers. "They cost millions!"

And in that very instant, the solution was found. The next thing you see is signs of relief on the faces of the executives who were worried sick just a few moments ago.

Another crisis is resolved. Everybody can go home now. See you next time when another crisis hits. The elephant was swallowed in one bite. The executives found a solution in technology to cover their own deficiencies. A technological solution was decided upon in lieu of the wisdom and solutions that should have come from the minds of the CEO and the overworked executives.

I smirked to myself at the superficiality of the commercial, but a thought crossed my mind: Maybe executives really are convinced by the commercial. Why else would such a hefty sum be spent on advertising the product?

I sensed a shadow of a person who was probably watching the commercial as intently as I was. With a touch of gray hair, the man standing behind me looked like he was in his mid-40s. He was tall, too—probably 6'2". He was wearing khakis and a sports jacket, brown leather loafers, wiry glasses, and a baseball cap. He had a computer bag on his left shoulder, a smartphone in his right hand, and a half-empty water bottle in his left hand. His face was slightly tanned, indicating that he flew in from a warm and sunny place.

As I caught a glimpse of his face, I couldn't help but feel like I knew the guy from somewhere—but where? I couldn't guess for the life of me.

"How are you? I'm Bill. I was a student of yours."

The question was addressed to me.

I turned around.

My former student was evidently pleased to see me. The former student I couldn't remember.

"Do you remember me? I was a student in one of your MBA strategy classes."

"Sure, I remember you," I lied. "How are you? Are you working somewhere?"

Bill happened to be a product executive in one of the most well-known public firms on the East Coast. His appearance gave that much away even if he hadn't told me. No wonder he was so interested in the commercial, I thought to myself. The newest victim of business travels, he sat down next to me and we started a conversation.

The conversation started off as much of a cliché. The same things you'd expect from any conversation held at an airport between two people who haven't met in years: comments about the weather, and not-so-pleasant words for airlines and service providers after the delayed and cancelled flights that left thousands stranded at the airport.

I asked Bill how life had changed for him since we last met in my class nearly two decades ago and what he was doing lately.

"I have been involved in strategy development, mission and vision definition, and organizational planning," Bill replied almost immediately, as if he was waiting for me to ask.

"It's so frustrating," Bill continued, "recognizing that these things have nothing to do with reality. They're nothing more than case studies from MBA textbooks that my job requires me to work on."

And in an instant, it all came back to me. That was Bill, all right. The one type of student that you are bound to find in every class—the one student who questions anything and everything.

"So, what brings you here?" I inquired hoping that he was returning from a mini-vacation and would tell me all about his trip instead. I had already had a very long day with overbooked and delayed flights. Hearing an executive complain about the corporate world was the last thing I needed.

Unfortunately, I had only fueled the fire.

"I'm coming back home from this stupid company offsite that is held every year at the company retreat. Every year they give us the same message that we have to pick back up and put something in place that makes more sense than what was there before, and be the change agent in our department," Bill snapped back, raging.

"Our five-day offsite at the company retreat tried to explain to us—the leadership team—how to improve operations using a small team dynamics approach. We got together with our peers to share best practices, discuss what does and does not work, and devise creative solutions to deliver value to the customer more efficiently.

"Our team-building exercise in the past did not grow into new collaboration and innovation," Bill continued. "I think it's not going to happen this year as well. The funny part is that our CEO addressed us with the typical: 'We need an inquisitive mind-set; people who are trying to be innovative. Our goal is not to slow you down or hinder you. Assess where your strengths are, which areas your weaknesses lie in, and in what areas you really need to grow. Do not take lightly what you are doing on a day-to-day basis.'"

The main purpose of this exercise, as Bill told me, was to increase the profitability of the organization. In most cases, the imagined linkage between strategy and operations, strategy and profitability, and strategy and continuous process improvement was broken as soon as strategy was approved and in the process of being implemented. Very soon, the strategy would become inefficient and obsolete, showing a large disconnect with the dynamic, highly volatile, and highly competitive outside environment.

"They divided us into small groups to tackle some of our company's top challenges in communications, collaboration, and innovation. One group even tried to innovate operational processes. They almost innovated the company out of money!" Bill was very vocal about his hatred towards the tactics that his company was following—vocal just as I remembered him.

"This morning we presented our proposed recommendations. They said, 'Thank you,' and encouraged us to spread the word about the week's impact on company profitability and customer-centric focus.

"Sounds good, right?

"What I'm annoyed the most about is that someone from our leadership team said to the CEO, 'We are inspired and empowered by you for encouraging us to lead at our level, and to pick up the ball and charge forward with the enthusiasm that our generation brings.'"

The predicament that Bill was going through was evident. The workers wanted to stay pragmatic. They could reference, but it would be impossible to apply a natural systems approach to the organizations as is. It was understandably difficult for the organization to be seen as a living system. This was not only because the management concept of command and control was rejected but also because the organization was put in a situation of uncertainty where they couldn't assess what would come next.

Bill stopped for a second to catch his breath. This gave me an opportunity to ask him a question.

"You are so frustrated with your leadership," I said. "What do you think causes all of these problems?"

Bill looked at me perplexed. He couldn't believe the words that came out of the mouth of one of his MBA professors.

"How can you not understand, Joseph? They all graduated from business school with management disabilities!"

I wasn't quite sure what Bill meant by this.

"What kind of disabilities?" I questioned in return.

"I can't believe I have to spell it out for you, Joseph." My student was disappointed. "All of the people in managerial and leadership roles in my company have a common set of learning disabilities that they never worked on—strategic disability, decision-making disability, sense-making disability, logic disability, and disability of the lessons learned. "Speaking of lessons," Bill continued, "the term 'lessons learned' is something that my boss is really not a fan of. He likes to call it 'best practices' instead."

What my student said got me thinking long and hard. Sure, he was probably exaggerating the situation far more than it should've been. However, there wasn't one thing that he said that I'd disagree with.

And what are best practices anyway?
Which ones are the best and who gets to decide?

The realization that followed shook me. It's true that most of us are getting tired of the endless attempts to identify change management methodology that would be applicable to the organization—if any. In most cases, when we start talking about change, change management, and potential or current resistance from employees, it's already too late. The issue usually only gets noticed by management after it has gone from bad to worse from the perspective of the executives.

Countless articles and books are written in search of the "silver bullet" or some sort of methodology called change management that will solve organizational and managerial problems. Unfortunately, none of the techniques and tactics that authors swear upon actually work.

Companies and businesses spend a lot of money day in and day out as they try to survive and secure a profitable and viable future for their organizations. However, the problem more often than not is that the realization kicked in a little too late, the solution wasn't planned thoroughly enough—if it was planned at all—or, in some cases, change management wasn't needed at all. With time, all of this just became a people issue, which it is not.

The term "resistance" found its way into corporate language and is blamed for a lot of failed projects, initiatives, and unsuccessful executives who could not make practical and sane decisions. In fact, employees are often even blamed for their resistance to new initiatives or not being accepting and supportive of a brand-new executive vision.

The fact of the matter remains, however, that we are surrounded by uncertainties, and it seems very unrealistic to speak of or try to implement a strategy, the results of which will continue to manifest themselves 50 years in the future. This is only possible hypothetically and is much like seeing the future looking in a crystal ball and trying to assess what the best course of action will be for results that are to be seen years—if not decades—in the future.

"Do you feel like your company is agile?" I inquired of my new friend.

Bill wasn't happy upon hearing my question.

"Not at all," he replied before launching into a lengthy explanation of what is wrong with his company, industry, and customers in general.

"Agility! What is agility?" he exclaimed in a tone as loud and full of anger as an airport setting would allow. "We do not even know what the word means in our corporate environment. Every time, the conversations start off pretty simply—'lean' if I may—before the words drift and the topics of conversation change to transformation and what it means to a company or organization. We are transforming, they say. Hah! Transforming to what?"

Transformation is a word that is indeed tossed around in the corporate world far more than necessary. I could understand where the frustration and anger in Bill was coming from. The sad part is that the corporate sector—as a whole—likes this word a lot and has adapted to it. Owing to the common use of the term, over time, it has started to have a feel of accomplishment associated with it.

In the corporate sector today, it's all "transform this, transform that," and the most impractical expectation of them all: The transformation has to come into effect immediately! Nobody has time to think about anything anymore. And as accustomed to the word as we have become, it sounds even better when it comes with the label of "lean" attached to it. "Lean" sounds more meaningful and important, and it makes one feel as if management is up to date on everything, particularly on the subject of processes and process improvement. Lean brings importance to the cause.

Whatever we do, it's all about achieving the outcomes and not the activities themselves. In many projects, there is a tendency to measure the value of the solution being delivered rather than the business results.

"We change our strategy every six months during our useless offsite executive meetings. We go back home and expect that maybe something will be different. Unsurprisingly, it all stays the same. It's like the circus left town, but the clowns are still around. What is organizational agility anyway?" Bill continued.

Bill tries making a point by telling me a story—a habit he hasn't let go of since his days in my MBA classes.

"We give a name to everything. It is convenient for human transactions; it is easier to establish relationships and describe things. If we do not use names, things become complicated and difficult. All movements are impossible without attributing names to them in this world. There's a catch though. As soon as we give a name to something, we reduce the limitlessness of the thing in question and make it a limited entity. Try to understand this a little: When we name an object, we limit it within a certain boundary. Do you see what I mean?"

I nodded. I did understand what he meant, but he looked like he wasn't done making his point.

"Good," he said in reply to my nod. "I always connected agility to the Westminster dog show. It's like sort of a special qualification or set of requirements to select the best breed."

I chuckled. My student still had it in him. His statement reminded me of the time when we used to debate about anything and everything during our classes. A good sport, he was. Even when he was left speechless, he was always seen racking his brain to break free from the impasse.

"Yes, if you do an online search for the word *agility* and click on images, most of the pictures you will see are of dogs taking the agility track," I said matter-of-factly. I took out my phone from my pocket and continued: "What dogs are doing on the agility track is defined pretty well on Wikipedia, too. Look, it says that '[a]gility or nimbleness is the ability to change the body's position efficiently, and requires the integration of isolated movement skills using a combination of balance, coordination, speed, reflexes, strength, and endurance.'[1] Organizations get bombarded constantly by internal and external factors that influence strategy execution."

I took a small pause as I let Bill take in the long definition.

"And to me," I continued, "it means knowing."

Bill looked at me even more intently than he was watching the commercial earlier, and I could tell that he wanted me to continue. And so I did.

"At the organizational level, strategic decision making constantly gets influenced—and sometimes overpowered—by such external factors as market changes, also known as market volatility; unpredictable changes or uncertainty; constant reconsideration of key decision factors, which you can call complexity; and elusiveness of current situational and potential outcomes, which means that there is always a sense of ambiguity to decisions at the organizational level.

"These challenges, however, are not external to the organization. It's about time we face reality: In our corporate lives, we feel more secure when we agree and follow previously implemented methodologies and frameworks, even when we have difficulty connecting to the accepted perspectives of organizational performance, company strategy, and objectives. Internal issues often prevent us from objectively evaluating external challenges and form a barrier to objective decision making in strategy execution.

"The painful truth is that we understand that there is a problem, but close our eyes and disregard the obvious. In order to survive these challenging problems, we have to have the ability to predict, plan, and define how to respond to environmental dynamics and complexity."

It is a well-known reality that many executives are kept up at night worrying about their company's ability to execute clearly defined strategies. According to PricewaterhouseCoopers, only 56% of strategic initiatives have been successful, and a meager 9% of surveyed companies are rated excellent at execution.[2] It is not time to address the agility of organizations because if an organization, company, or business lacks agility, even the best strategies will fail during execution and it will cost you extensively.

Agility is not new, but when we read the definitions available in countless articles, books, and papers, it becomes abundantly clear that agility is not just about quick reactions to events and situations. In fact, it is about the responsiveness and timeliness of an action, and how to be proactive and ready for the unexpected.

"So, what are the key factors critical to an agile organization?" Bill asked, evidently concerned.

I was proud of my student. "Not surprisingly," I replied, "the PMI's Global Executive Council, comprised of executives from leading businesses and federal agencies, met in Prague and asked the same question as you just did.[3]

"The entire meeting was focused on organizational agility. The situation they addressed was that most management frameworks and philosophies have failed to evolve despite rampant changes in external market conditions, government policies, technology, and customer expectations. Flexibility, collaboration, and communication, while ensuring alignment to strategy and customer focus that leads to better decisions and increased organizational agility, were among the key factors identified by the Council, which could help identify whether an organization can truly be agile.

"So, organizational agility is not just about speed. It is about how we respond to challenges and the situations determining when it is the appropriate time to act."

My student looked at me closely as I spoke. As keen to learn as ever before, I sensed some worry in his eyes, which made him look like one of the executives from the commercial that we both bonded over. "Moving towards an agile organization seems like a daunting task," my student said, "but do we have a choice?

"We, the industry, have only one problem to solve and a handful of questions to answer: How strong is the competition? How loyal are your customers? How easy would it be for them to switch? We have to find a way of doing business and continuing to stay in business and devise a plan to ensure that the business processes—including those of suppliers and service providers—are always able to meet critical needs, depending on the situation and external factors. These solutions, contrary to popular belief, are not as simple as a specific product or technology or service or a project with a beginning and an end."

My student was making some very valid points, and I couldn't help but nod in approval.

"They are telling us that you have to know. But nobody answers the real questions here anymore. What does it mean to know? We have to change our very method of knowing. Knowledge is not a power anymore—knowing is! So, tell me Joseph, is knowing the same thing as agility?"

Bill posed the question very sternly, without the slightest hint of sarcasm to it. The question to me, however, was very vague.

"What do you mean by knowing, Bill?" I asked my question to be able to better respond to his question.

"First of all, strategy and operations should have elastic processes in order to execute flexible strategy. In order to do that you have to have four essential capabilities.

"Firstly, it is important that you know what to do. What I mean by this is that you should know how to respond to regular and irregular disruptions and disturbances by adjusting normal functioning. This is the ability to address the actual.

"Secondly, you should know what to look for. This means that it is important to know how to monitor that which is or could become a threat in the near term. The monitoring must cover both that which happens in the environment and that which happens in the organization itself or its own performance. This is the ability to address the critical.

"Thirdly, you should know what to expect. This means that you should know how to anticipate developments and threats further into the future, such as potential disruptions, pressures, and their consequences. This is all to address the potential.

"Lastly, it is important to know what happened. In other words, it is important to learn from experience—particularly, to learn the right lessons from the right experiences. This is the ability to address the factual."

"So, what's the problem that you were talking about?" I questioned Bill, whose eyes were now gleaming as he spoke passionately about the subject.

He answered my question with a story:

> It is said that one day there was great confusion in a famous dramatic company in Russia. The main actor, who was to act the role of a stammerer, fell ill. The show was about to begin and the management did not know what to do. But then someone suggested that the son of a rich man in the village had a stammer that was incurable. The boy was brought and after a little briefing was prepared to go on the stage. But then a miracle took place: The boy could not stammer, try as he would! What happened? Psychologists say that if a person becomes fully conscious of a thing, that thing is lost.[4]

In return, I reminded my former student about the story of Rumpelstiltskin.

> Rumpelstiltskin was a dwarf who helped the miller's daughter weave flax into gold in return for a promise that she would give him her firstborn son. Once her son was born, she refused to keep the bargain. Rumpelstiltskin told her that if she could learn his name by midnight of

the third day, she could keep the child. At midnight on the third day she told him his name and Rumpelstiltskin disappeared. Identifying your problem is the first step toward solving it![5]

Bill smiled and got back to the painful subject.

"Some important questions to ask are by how much and by when do we want to improve performance?" he said. "By urging a series of flexible, measurable processes that account for time, speed-to-decision, time-to-action, course correction and not just bottom-line or unit-driven metrics, and by balancing goals with results, strategy, and operations, the data from an analytics effort will tell whether your program is achieving either the rate-of-change or progress that was expected—and results will follow. Whether they are profitable, knowledge-based, or better operations, people need to know which of a company's goals or objectives they are supporting if they decide to make a change and improve a process," he added.

It is fair to say that all of us who have—at least once in our career—been involved in strategy development, mission and vision definition, and organizational planning have become increasingly frustrated, recognizing that these have nothing to do with reality, but are just case studies from MBA textbooks.

Bill started to ask me more questions—very specific questions about agility and an agile organization: "How is agility any different from change in an organization?" he asked.

And this is where I found that his concepts are still flawed.

"Agility is not just the ability to change. It is a cultivated capability that enables an organization to respond in a timely, effective, and sustainable way when changing circumstances require it. Management literature increasingly refers to this ability as a 'dynamic capability'—the potential to sense opportunities and threats, solve problems, and change the firm's resource base. This allows outperformers to maintain or enhance their relative advantages in ways that their competitors fail to see or do not fully implement. Agility is also strategically relevant. Although agile organizations often change, they do not pursue change for change's sake. They pursue it for the sake of competitive advantage." I replied as calmly as I could to ensure that Bill understood what I had to say and my take on agility completely.

"So, what is the difference between being agile and staying resilient?" he asked me.

"I strongly believe that for a business, resilience means being able first to absorb the impact of, and then effectively react to, severely disruptive change. In some cases, when businesses cannot or should not revive a business model that has failed, they must be able to reinvent themselves and find an entirely new model or ways of operating that preserve their core identity in the face of change."

I could tell by his face that he would retain this for a long time. Bill, however, had more questions, which followed. As I remembered, Bill would dive deeper and deeper into any subject that interested him by asking all sorts of questions.

I didn't mind it one bit.

"Why do we have to be agile? Why can't we stay traditional in our approach to deal with uncertainty? How much agility do we need? How can we measure agility? How can we learn agility? How can we apply and implement agility?"

Just as my new friend bombarded me with further questions, an announcement informed us that our flights were boarding, and I was sad that I did not have a chance to give him even partial answers based on my understanding of the subject.

I was hoping to continue our conversation and hear his opinion and the problems that he, as an executive, was experiencing on a daily basis. We exchanged business cards, with a promise to call each other to continue our conversation. Going to his gate, Bill said, "I still remember you quoting someone famous: 'We are all in the gutter, but some of us are looking at the stars.'[6] You gave us a few examples from history that I still remember. Thank you." And with that, he left.

The famous person that my student spoke of was Oscar Wilde.

This was much more than a typical brief interaction of two travelers. I was thinking about the conversation that we had all the way back to Boston—thinking about Bill, his place in this company, and his company's future, and wondering what is going to happen to them. Honestly, I did not have a very good feeling about their future.

I told myself that in order to answer Bill's questions, I have to start a search on agility: What does agility really mean on the enterprise level?

This book is the result of this search and a summary of my discussions with Bill.

References

1. Retrieved from https://en.wikipedia.org/wiki/Agility
2. PwC. Strategy and Execution Survey 2014. Retrieved from https://www.strategyand.pwc.com/media/file/Strategyand_Infographic-Strategy-execution-survey.pdf?utm_campaign=LGC-5NOV15-EM-Commercial-BTGFactAuditInfographic&utm_medium=email&utm_source=Eloqua
3. Federal Times. (2015, November 3). Organizational Agility Creates a Path to Customer Centricity. Retrieved from https://www.federaltimes.com/opinions/2015/11/03/organizational-agility-creates-a-path-to-customer-centricity/

4. Rajneesh, Bhagwan Shree. (1979). *The Way of Tao, Part 2.* Delhi (India): Motilal Banarsidass.

5. Raynus, Joseph. (1998). *Software Process Improvement with CMM.* Boston (MA): Artech House.

6. Wilde, Oscar. Retrieved from http://philosiblog.com/2012/04/25/we-are-all-in-the-gutter-but-some-of-us-are-looking-at-the-stars/

Chapter 2

Searching for Answers in History

Let's Start Searching . . .

[T]hought Alice and she went on, "Would you tell me, please, which way I ought to go from here?" "That depends a good deal on where you want to get to," said the Cat. "I don't much care where —" said Alice. "Then it doesn't matter where you go," said the Cat. "— so long as I get somewhere," Alice added as an explanation. "Oh, you're sure to do that," said the Cat, "if you only walk long enough."

— Lewis Carroll, *Alice in Wonderland,* 1865, p. 51[1]

The next afternoon, I started walking to my class as usual. I have a full class, with 35 students. This class is about strategy—one of my favorite subjects to teach. I was on a mission as I walked into the class with some very important questions in mind:

"Do you know about Admiral Nelson and why he has an important place in history?"

Silence took over the room.

"What do you know about the Battle of Trafalgar?"

Silence again.

Countless examples can be found in history of strategy, strategy development, and innovation that one can learn from. Since this was one of the classes of my strategy course, I was planning on teaching my students what strategy is and is not through timeless examples from history. But I knew that not everyone has a liking towards history and is as keen on learning from the mistakes and lessons of the past as I was. For this reason, I decided to first go over and analyze some strategy announcements from well-reputed companies and the approaches and tactics that they resort to, from company mergers to acquisitions, what it means to be a low-cost provider, and how a company can be said to provide the best customer service.

So, what did these strategies have in common? The fact of the matter is that these are not strategies *per se*. These approaches represent goals, tactics, and objectives but cannot be classified as strategies. These goals, tactics, and objectives are not strategies by themselves, but they can sure be called components of larger strategies that a company or business might be using.

The problem here is that the term "strategy" has become a buzz word and is tossed around these days much more often than it should be. As a result, it is being used interchangeably with words such as objectives in an attempt by people to show off their business acumen. Unfortunately, however, the meaning of the word is lost due to its overuse.

With all of that, you might be wondering what exactly is strategy. If that is indeed the case, then you've come to the right place. Strategy originally comes from the Greek word "strategos" or the art of the general. From this, we can understand that the word strategy originates and has roots in the art of war itself. The master of strategy, Sun Tzu, is a good enough example from history of how to strategize to your advantage. The main goal of every strategy and strategic planning is to win. The idea behind strategizing is that winning is good and losing is detrimental.

Hannibal's strategy was not that he had to defeat Rome. This was only his goal. His strategy was to bring the hidden strength of his troops against the weaknesses of his army at the point of attack to achieve his goal and cross the Alps when the enemy believed that he and his troops did not have the ability to do so. The role of a general is to have a vision and to understand the environment and surroundings to win every battle and war that they have to lead. A great general can hence evaluate the whole picture and knows how to put every piece together in order to win.

It was probably too early in the morning—or too early on in the class, perhaps—to start talking about history. Instead, I began by trying to explain strategy to my students in class that morning, with examples that they would be able to relate to.

"The role of a modern-day executive is in many ways similar to that of a general leading an army going to war. They have to have the vision to develop a set of complex tactics and plan the activities and strategize efficiently in a way that victory will be guaranteed.

"A clear strategy provides answers to four key questions:

1. Where do we compete?
2. What unique value do we deliver to the marketplace (or the question of differentiation)?
3. What resources and capabilities do we utilize in order to deliver that value?
4. How do we sustain our capability to provide this unique value?"

My students listened intently as I told them the importance of strategy and how the role of an executive in the world today is not much different from what was expected from generals and leaders of the past. Evidently enough, however, they had questions in their minds that were unanswered. The puzzled and quizzical looks on their faces gave that much away.

I realized that teaching them with examples that they can understand and relate to would be the best approach to take in order to guarantee that the information that I share with them is retained by them for the rest of their lives.

"A great market example in the world today for strategy is furniture giant IKEA®. The company sells inexpensive furniture and has devised a strategy that its competitors find difficult to imitate. This is because these competitors would have to completely change the way in which they design and ship their furniture. What IKEA does not do, however, is compete in the high-end furniture business."

Relief took over most of my students as they could finally understand where I was going with strategy and how it could be applied to real businesses and companies around them.

Internationally renowned academic and author on business and management Henry Mintzberg has a concept of strategies intended, emergent, and realized. According to his observation, strategy is more about what you actually do rather than what you intend to do.[2] Timing is another factor that accounts for the success or failure of the strategy that is to be implemented. If you do not have the right timing for strategy execution, it is bound to be a failure. This is another reason why focusing on the four questions is essential for proper strategies.

I asked my students for companies and businesses that they thought were succeeding at strategizing effectively. For a third time, silence took over the classroom to the extent that I could hear the ticking of the clock. We were only 15 minutes into the class, but it was too much for the students to take in.

But I wasn't disappointed.

The concept of strategy is a difficult one, and the term being tossed around countless times has not helped its case. I knew that it would take time for my students to understand what was going on, which is why I thought of explaining the concept to them with another—more simple—example.

"Walmart®, too, is another good example in the world around us. The retail giant is not only focusing its energies on customer service and improving the quality of the goods being provided, but it is also letting customers shop on their terms, which is something its competitors have not considered so far. With a vision statement such as the following: 'To be the best retailer in the hearts and minds of consumers and employees,'[3] it is no surprise that the retailer is going the extra mile to make its mark in the world."

Already a household name, Walmart's example was enough to help my students understand the basics of what I meant by strategy.

The examples above are proof that we have to continuously monitor the changing landscape of a business, identify problems, and address challenges with actionable strategy.

I noticed that one of the top students of my class was listening to these examples with great concentration—one of the only students who were taking notes.

"These are all modern examples, and, from what I understand, these strategies were devised after studying consumers and market trends. I find it hard to believe that strategies as well thought out as the ones implemented by IKEA and Walmart were possible in the past," he said almost as soon as I paused my lecture to take a breath.

I was hoping someone would ask me a question like this, as history is one of the first things that I mentioned as soon as I walked into the class. History shows that countless civilizations have seen their rise and fall due to a number of factors. The most prominent of these factors, however, was the fact that the leaders or rulers of these civilizations were pressured and unable to cope with the challenges that they faced on a daily basis. When the challenges became too overwhelming, this was when the civilizations started declining at an unprecedented rate—a rate that couldn't be countered.

The inability to make wise decisions and propose practical solutions was the number one cause of the demise of countless civilizations throughout history. The astonishing part is that these civilizations were not limited to a certain time period or era. In fact, civilizations in different parts of the world and in different time periods all saw their destruction simply because their leaders did not learn from the mistakes of their predecessors, ultimately falling victim to the same subtle and easily avoidable mistakes that their ancestors fell prey to.

But the correlation would be too great a challenge for my students to grasp, especially in a class this early in the morning. I took a seat and started thinking of how to answer the question that my student had asked, primarily because this was the focus of my lecture today. I could see in his eyes that my student was proud of the fact that he asked a question that left his professor speechless—or so he thought. I stood back up and explained the correlation between history and modern times to him with examples and studies of a well-known historian. Who else could be more credible?

"In his 12-volume history book, *A Study of History*,[4] renowned British historian Arnold J. Toynbee talked about a historical philosophy which he proposed. The decline of civilization and cyclic development were analyzed as the basis of this philosophy. Toynbee deeply studied the rise and fall of 26 different civilizations over several different eras of human history and reached the conclusion that civilizations would only progress when leaders were able to respond to challenges in a viable and practical way, and that the lack of creative responses were the reason for the decline for most— if not all—of these civilizations. In other words, according to Toynbee, the progress and decline of a civilization was highly interlinked with the attitude that a leader has towards the challenges that are being faced by the civilization or community.

> *It is a paradoxical but profoundly true and important principle of life that the most likely way to reach a goal is to be aiming not at the goal itself but at some more ambitious goal beyond it.*
>
> — Arnold Toynbee, *A Study of History*

"According to the conclusion that Toynbee reached, it is possible for a civilization or community to continue to be in existence given that the leaders of the civilization in question are able to creatively respond to the challenges that the civilization is facing.[5]

"Identifying each of these civilizations as separate entities, Toynbee demonstrated through his philosophy the responses and challenges of each era and how the civilizations that he was considering reacted to the situations that they were facing.[6]

"Another idea that Toynbee believed in was that the creative minorities of any civilization play a major role in bringing it out of shackles and helps bring solutions that can completely restructure and rewire the way that these societies and civilizations function and exist."[7]

Perplexed, my student looked at me closely as he fidgeted with a pencil in his hands. Not only had all of the pride left his eyes, but they now looked like he was more confused than ever—perhaps even a bit shocked. It apparently never occurred to him that such parallels could be drawn between history and modern times.

It was clear that he had many questions running through his head all at once and couldn't find the words to form them—especially in front of the entire class. I walked toward his seat to answer his questions personally. The page before him was all empty save for a small self-formed equation in the middle: "corporation = civilization." It would be enough if he took that much home from this part of the lecture. The parallel that was made would keep him pondering for quite a while, and this is one of the concepts that I knew for a fact he would not be able to forget anytime soon. My work here was done.

I walked back to the front of the class and continued with my lecture:

"Toynbee was also of the opinion that humans are capable of predicting the consequences of their stand-alone actions and seeing how said actions will impact the future of humanity and the world at large. With the power of anticipating how an action will affect the situation for countless other people and the world as a whole, humans know which behaviors or actions can spark and ignite consequences of the worst type, and hence, humans are capable of changing their behavior to ensure that nothing goes wrong.[8]

"As much as challenges need to be responded to in a timely manner, without compromising the creativity and feasibility of the solution, strategic planning is difficult for quite a few reasons. The needs, requirements, and specifications are practically endless. Responding to situations and challenges is not only a necessity, but there is also a lot of pressure to make the right decisions at the right time. Similarly, the development of an effective and practical strategy itself is complicated. This is primarily because all of the divisions of the strategy and the components that make up the strategy are interconnected and work together for viable solutions that are optimal.

"Prioritization of challenges is another factor that is related to strategic planning. To devise an effective and efficient strategy, the future must be predicted—and there is always a risk involved in doing so. The risk increases exponentially, if the environment of the business or industry is turbulent. The ideas and thoughts that people have about certain situations can vary a great deal, and it is extremely likely that the executive devising the strategy will not be on the same page as the customers or consumers.

"The strategies, plans, and work assignments of the business or company all go hand in hand to fulfill the business mission. As the foundation of the business itself, the business mission is in many ways the basic starting point for designing the managerial roles and even for designing the management structure. The business of a company has to be one of the most simple and obvious things possible.

"To explain the business of a company, however, is one of the most difficult things to do. This is where strategists come into the picture. The 'What is our business?' question is something that needs to be answered by strategists. In fact, it is one of the foremost responsibilities of a strategist to ensure that the question is given the right amount of attention and that the answer which is given is comprehensive and elaborate enough for the objectives of the business to be set and the course of the business to be plotted in an effective manner.

"Going back to the concept that Toynbee proposed with regard to challenges and responses, the corporate life cycle can also be seen through the same lens as was used to observe the evolution and progress that civilizations have made, on a wide scale. It is not an inevitable cycle that Toynbee suggested was the cause for the rise and fall of civilizations.[9] In fact, there are substantial factors that people of a civilization can take into consideration in order to predict how the environment and culture will change.

"The same holds true for companies, businesses, and the corporate sector. Like mentioned earlier, civilizations go into decline when the response that comes within is unable to match the external challenges. As a result, leaders no longer resort to creative responses which results in the downfall of the civilization.

"As Toynbee saw it, civilizations, too, were nothing more than complex networks of social relationships. In order to succeed with strategic and efficient planning, it is important to look at business environments and corporate scenarios in the same way as civilizations to guarantee survival and success.[10]

"Reaching stability and achieving a prolonged (or permanent) state of balance may be difficult and complex for many reasons, but it is still something achievable. The upward S-curve needs to be taken into consideration to fully understand how this can be done.

"In a corporation, there are several components that work together to achieve this state of permanent balance and stability. These components are denoted by the trajectory, which shows the performance of the corporation as a whole and how well goals are being achieved.

"The S-curve is a great indicator for several different types of applications and areas of project management, including the targets, time, and cost. S-curves can be used to measure and evaluate the progress being made in many ways. An "Actual" S-curve gives the real progress that has been made on a project up to a certain date or during a specific time period, whereas the "Target" S-curve often shows the ideal scenario and how the project should have been progressing according to the schedule that has been defined for the project.[11]

"More often than not, it is seen that there is a peak in the progress that the corporation or business in question is making, which is almost always followed by a decline. This downfall, however, is avoidable. In most cases, the reverse or downward S-curve is due to the fact that these corporations end up making clumsy decisions after they reach stability or maturity, either in the hopes that poor decisions will not affect the progress that they are making or in the illusion that nothing can make their corporation or business unstable again. "

"Are there any specific civilizations or countries that you can mention?" another one of the students seated in the front row asked.

"Some of the most notable examples come from the Chinese in this regard," I continued. My research on civilizations and history had taught me a lot about different cultures, traditions, civilizations, and the way they reacted to change and strategized their way out of problems and challenges that they were facing, and I was more than happy to share this information with my students, especially since they were actually showing interest in the parallels and lessons from history.

"Chinese philosophers saw the reality of the universe, which they referred to as the Tao, as a process that continuously involves change and flow. How can you relate this to the corporate world?" I cross-questioned my students.

Almost immediately, the first student who heard my question replied: "Isn't change and continual flow a requirement to continue to deliver value to customers as well?"

"Exactly!" I couldn't have been happier. Not only was the silence that had become prevalent during the first half of the class beginning to break, but the effects of "corporation = civilization" were manifesting themselves earlier than I expected.

"The Chinese idea about diplomacy and war is very different from the Western approach. Whether we look at the United States or ancient Greece, the use of force to get one's way and gain victory has always been the primary focus. As a result, all of the tactics and strategies that are devised for war using the Western approach are limited to the confines of the battlefield itself."

I could tell that most of my students enjoyed the parallels that I started to make because I noticed that a large majority of them had started taking notes. Understandably, using real-life examples and comparisons was far more effective than simply talking on and on about corporate culture and how stability and agility work hand in hand in the progress of a business or organization.

"The Western way of war required soldiers or force to fight against their counterparts, all while displaying strength, skill, courage, and maintaining fair play throughout the battle or war. At the same time, sneak attacks, decoys, and integrating noncombatant factors into the war are looked down upon by Westerners. In fact, the hatred for decoy and distractions that are not in line with the "force on force" way of war being followed by Westerners is evident from a quote from none other than the renowned Alexander the Great.

"It was suggested to the King that he should spearhead a sneak attack on the Persians during the nighttime. Furious, Alexander the Great made a statement that will forever be written down in history as proof of the concomitant repugnance of Westerners toward ways of war that they deemed to be deceitful:

> The policy which you are suggesting is one of bandits and thieves, the only purpose of which is deception. I cannot allow my glory always to be diminished by Darius' absence, or by narrow terrain, or by tricks of night. I am resolved to attack openly and by daylight. I choose to regret my good fortune rather than be ashamed of my victory.[12]

"The Chinese, however, have an entirely different point of view. Strong emphasis is placed on strategic and analytical planning. What Westerners call deceitful is known as being resourceful by the Chinese. In fact, the Chinese love strategies and stratagem to the extent that they often even go as far as referring to China as the birthplace of these skills. This isn't even that difficult to believe considering that most of the world's ancient military documents and writings come from China, along with the first elaborate military classic—the infamous book, *The Art of War*, by Sun Tzu.[13]

"The above-mentioned writings and documents may deal with several different topics and talk about different aspects of war; however, the one thing that all of them have in common is the fact that they have extensive discussions about strategies and how stratagem is the key to success and victory. *The Art of War*, too, is not only extremely comprehensive, but it is safe to say that this book is the greatest representation of the Chinese approach toward diplomacy and war. In this renowned book, Sun Tzu sheds light upon several different areas of war and the conduct that the Chinese believe is appropriate for warfare.

"Of all of the thoughts that are discussed in *The Art of War*, three that are shared by Sun Tzu are of particular interest. In addition to an overall explanation of the art of war itself, strategies and stratagem are discussed at length in the book, along with a dialectic view of the approach that should be used in battle and war."

My students were done taking notes and began looking at me intently once again for more information. They were finally interested in the topic and appreciated it being taught using a completely different approach. It isn't often that strategy and agility at the corporate level are talked about by comparing the situations of a business or organization to a civilization—let alone drawing parallels between corporations and the approach that different countries and civilizations have had in regard to war.

"Instead of simply relying on force in the battlefield, like the Western perspective on warfare, the diplomatic, political, and logistical aspects of war and the preparations that need to be made before initiating an attack are defined as the most integral parts of the art of war itself. In *The Art of War*, Sun Tzu also talks about how dealing with the consequences of war effectively and without any complications is an important part of the strategic planning that comes with war. According to Sun Tzu, the art of war is essentially the complete process of diplomacy and fighting, which are a part of the package with every war.[14]

"The Chinese are extremely cautious about the cost incurred when waging war. This is one of the primary reasons why they tend to strategize and plan everything before they act. There is always a significant risk involved in waging wars that goes far beyond facing defeat or losses. A war always has the potential of becoming a disaster for the entire state. An old Chinese saying, '[W]hen you kill 10,000 soldiers, you are likely to lose 3,000 lives as well,' explains the detrimental aspect of war perfectly.[15]

"Sun Tzu, too, was of the opinion that a resourceful ruler is likely to have a completely different approach toward warfare. According to the Chinese general, philosopher, and one of the most well-known military strategists throughout the world, the art of war is fully exploited and analyzed by a good commander.

"If the commander or leader finds that there is no advantage, benefit, or any substantial danger to the country, why should war be waged? It is best if warfare and battles are avoided completely, as they have a tendency to inflict more harm and damage than good. Sun Tzu went on to say that 'those unable to understand the dangers inherent in employing troops are equally unable to understand the advantageous ways of doing so.'"

I went on to explain the perspective of the Chinese regarding war and how they implemented their infamous concepts of analysis, evaluation, and strategic planning using examples from the infamous general Sun Tzu himself. To engage the class a bit more, I asked my students who had heard of Sun Tzu. Unsurprisingly, it was a name known by nearly all of my students. Next, I asked for a raise of hands for the number of students of mine who had read *The Art of War*. This response was admittedly shocking. About 80% of the class had raised their hands, some of whom even confessed that they began to read the book but never got around to finishing it. Regardless, there was one thing in common for all of them. They were all keen on learning how one of the most popular generals in history was able to strategically plan to be victorious and how they could follow in the footsteps of this leader to their advantage.

"So, just for a quick recap, I'm going to ask you some questions. Is everyone ready?"

"Yes!" the now active class unanimously exclaimed.

"All right then. Which one of you remembers what the Western approach was?"

"They didn't like being sneaky and considered force on force to be the best and most practical approach for a battle," one of the shy girls from the back of the class said.

"Very good! And how did the Chinese feel about this approach?" I continued.

"They didn't like it."

"They thought that it wasn't efficient."

"They believe that planning and foreseeing every aspect of war is essential to ensure that the right decisions are made."

"They feel like wars are a waste of resources."

"The Chinese are of the opinion that strategy is the key to success."

Answers came from every direction and this was proof that they loved the course that I had taken for the lecture on that particular day. Strategy, I thought to myself. If only my students understood how every part of this lecture was planned weeks in advance.

"That's correct. I love the diversity of the responses here today. You have all answered the question with a different approach." I appreciated the students who were actively participating in the class.

"Now keep concentrating. It gets even better, I promise," I continued.

The students obliged.

"The preservation of the interest of the state without resorting to force, war, and battle is one of the primary lessons which we learn from the book. To back his point even further, Sun Tzu placed a lot of emphasis on stratagems and strategy in general throughout the book. In fact, some people might even go as far as saying that Sun Tzu treated the entire process of warfare and battle—from the initial stages of preparation to the effective execution and termination without ill consequences—as a challenge of wisdom and a test of making the right decisions before anything else.

"The use of force should always be secondary."

I noticed that all of my students had started scribbling in their notebooks. "The use of force should always be secondary" appeared to be one of their most favorite things that I had said that day. I had even more reason to continue with my lecture than ever before. My students were intently listening, actively participating, and even taking notes now.

"According to your most favorite leader," I joked, to lighten up the mood and ensure that the students continued to listen to the lecture with the same amount of concentration, "there is always something wrong with using force—be it by the winning side of a battle or the losing side."

"A winning side uses force and is reassured that it will be victorious due to its strength, whereas the losing side will try its best to make use of all of the strength and force possible to ensure its survival. For the losing side, the use of force is often seen as desperation or gambling—each of which is detrimental in its own way.

"The concept that Sun Tzu tried to explain is in many ways extremely complicated and complex at the same time. This is particularly because even though there is a lot to war, the most popular opinion among people remains that force is the first thing that should be resorted to—an approach that Sun Tzu not only shunned but also deemed ineffective and something that should not be considered except as a very last option."

I knew that most of my students would have questions in their minds that they were too afraid to ask. Who could question the concepts that were written in a world famous book, by one of the most famous leaders and military generals of all time?

With another raise of hands, I asked my students how many of them knew about the matrix of Sun Tzu? None of them raised their hands—exactly the response which I was expecting. I can swear that I probably even heard a few of them say, "Why would someone so strong and powerful need a matrix?"

For the first time in the entire lecture, I picked up a marker in my hand and headed toward the whiteboard. Even though my students were now pursuing their MBAs, I could tell by the way the class had become quiet that they were afraid of what would follow. And again, I wasn't surprised. If anyone were to hear that one of the greatest generals in human history relied on a matrix for success and victory in all of the wars that they were a part of, the first picture that would come to mind would not be a pretty one.

Contrary to what most of them were thinking, however, the matrix of Sun Tzu was not exactly one of the mathematical matrices that these students had studied countless times in their mathematics classes. To be certain that they were all thinking along the same lines, I started asking them questions.

"So, who wants to volunteer?"

Almost all of the students started looking here and there, acting like they were looking for someone who would like to volunteer to draw the matrix on the board in front of the entire class. Having been a student myself for many years, I knew full well that they were only doing so to avoid being chosen by me to do the honors, lest their eyes meet mine.

"Nice strategy," I said to no one in particular.

The class laughed because they knew that they were all on the same page.

"Very well then. Get ready to start taking notes. You guys will love this."

With the marker in my hand, I drew the positive X and Y axes on the whiteboard as large as I could and put the cap right back on the marker. This was enough to cause confusion in the class.

"What?" most of the students said unanimously.

"Isn't this a graph?" one of the girls from the class said and continued chewing gum.

"I told you you'll need to take notes," I replied with a smile.

Everyone took out their notebooks and pens from their bags. Taking the cap off of the marker once again, I drew a large box on the graph.

No one could understand what was going on.

Next, I divided the box into four smaller boxes—two on the top and two on the bottom. All of the students were worried that they would now be studying the most complicated matrix in history—literally—and in a strategy class. In the rightmost box on the top, I wrote "win."

The students were now feeling relieved by the fact that the matrix was not going to be as confusing and intimidating as they had initially expected; however, they were still not completely sure about what was happening.

I wrote "loss" in the bottom left box and the picture started becoming more clear to my students.

"What do you think should go in the other two boxes?" I asked my students.

"Equal chances of winning," they replied.

"Very good. But there's another way in which you can put that," I replied as I wrote "equal chances of losing" in the remaining two diagonals.

"So, what do you think the axes denote?" I asked my students.

There was a variety of answers. Some of them were still of the opinion that winning and losing depended on the amount of force and strength that armies used, whereas others believed that the axes should indicate the innovation in the weaponry of each army that was involved in the war. Most of the students, however, were thinking in the right way. Words like "strategy" and "ability" could be heard from various places in the class.

One of the quieter students who had been taking notes during the entire class, however, waited for everyone else to answer the question in whichever way they could and then said that the axes were probably defining how well one understands the army.

That was exactly the answer I was looking for.

"Very good job, I'm impressed," I replied as I wrote the right terms on each of the axes. The Y axis defined the understanding one had of their own army, whereas the X axis defined the understanding of the opponent. I truly was impressed.

"As a matter of fact," I continued with my lecture, "Sun Tzu, one of the most strategic generals of history, was of the opinion that the intellectual faculty and moral strength of mankind was of great significance—even decisive—in war. He believed that if these two were applied with perfection, there was a probability of success regarding the wars that were being waged.

"The intellectual faculty that Sun Tzu spoke of was based on a number of factors, including a blend of intuition, common sense, judgment, past experience, and the ability to understand intricate matters and complex situations within the context of immediate objectives and goals. In other words, the general believed that to deal with the constantly changing, complex, nonlinear, uncertain situations like those faced by someone who is leading an army in war, it is imperative for the person to have the ability to see beyond images, sense beyond appearances, and hear beyond words.

"Ability to see beyond images, sense beyond appearances, and hear beyond words" most of my students repeated under their breaths as they continued taking notes.

"This is a blending of the cognitive capabilities of observing and perceiving a situation, the cognitive processing that must occur to understand the external world and make maximum use of our intuition and experiences, and the faculty for creating deep knowledge and acting on that knowledge.

"The reason I am telling you all of this is because the notion regarding strategy and intellect that Sun Tzu had regarding war can be applied to the organizational level with great ease as well as with the use of experiences and insights that individuals would like to bring to the attention of the organization through collaboration and dialogue within teams, communities, and groups within or related to the organization in question.

"Such changes will not only affect the quality of understanding of the organization significantly but also create an impact on the responsiveness of the actions that are taken by the organization."

The pieces of the puzzle were finally fitting. My students were more interested than ever before. They not only loved the approach that was being used, but I could tell by their faces that they loved every bit of what they learned that day and were ready to hear more.

"The scope of complex situations can also be greatly expanded if they can be handled through knowing because of the greater resources brought to bear—all of this significantly supported by interoperability and ubiquity. Organizational knowing is one of the many aspects of the intelligence of an organization and is deeply related to the capacity of an organization as a whole to gather information, innovate and generate knowledge, and act effectively.

"This capacity is one of the basic requirements of an organization to be responsive and act efficiently, optimally, and effectively in the fast-changing and complex world of today.

"Organizational knowing is also linked with organizational learning, common values and languages, knowledge centricity, openness of communication, effective collaboration, and coherent vision—all of which go hand in hand when looking to strategize and create an organization that is agile enough to react to the changes that it is faced with on a daily basis."

It was evident from their faces that my students were very happy to see innovation in their lectures and how many different domains a topic as important as strategy could be taught through. I could tell that they were not only excited but also loved the idea of strategy and how it can be implemented in so many different ways.

On that day—from what I believe is safe to assume was the first time in their lives—my students learned how strategy has no bounds and confines and is certainly timeless. From leaders and celebrated military generals to the organizations and businesses that have become household names, strategy is something that is a necessity of every era, regardless of how technically and technologically equipped one may—or may not—be.

There wasn't much time left before the end of class, but that was the last thing on the minds of my students. In fact, I had not noticed a single student looking at the clock since I started talking about Sun Tzu and his strategies. "They'll all grow up to be great warriors," I laughed to myself. Or was it really possible to compare potential future executives and managers of corporations to warriors? That was a topic for another day.

One thing, however, was certain. Among all of the different topics we had covered and talked about on that day, we had drifted far away from the topic which we started from—the topic I was thinking about since I met Bill at the airport the other day—the question that I was thinking about even as I walked into my class that fine morning.

I decided to test the concentration skills and memory of my students out of the blue.

"So," I continued after a deep sigh, "which one of you remembers what we started the class with?"

Silence once again. But I wasn't disappointed in my students at all. It gave me great pleasure to know for a fact that they had learned a lot more about strategy and agility in those 50 minutes than they had ever before.

"Come on now," I said, smiling. "Don't act like you guys were standing here delivering the lecture for the better part of an hour. Rack your brains; I'm sure you'll be able to remember."

"Probably the Chinese. It seems like that's the only thing we've been talking about all week," one of the girls joked.

I shook my head in denial.

"That historian guy. What was his name again? Tom something?" replied one of the boys.

"See, this is why you're supposed to take notes. His name was Toynbee . . . and no, that's not the right answer either," I replied jovially.

"Right, Toynbee," he replied as he wrote down the name of the British historian in one corner of a page of his notebook—never to open the page again.

I wasn't even surprised to see that none of them was giving me the correct answer. There was indeed a lot covered in that one class. From Sun Tzu to an extensive study on the Chinese civilization and how their approach to war differs from that of the Western world, industry giants like Walmart and IKEA, to S-curves and how they can be used to show the productivity or decline of a business or organization, matrices of one of the greatest military generals in history, to Toynbee and his theories to Admiral—

"Admiral Nelson!" one of the students from the middle of the class rose from his seat shouted louder than he realized. All eyes turned to him. "I'm sorry, was that too loud? You spoke about Admiral Nelson and the Battle of Trafalgar as soon as you entered the class, but when we told you that we didn't know about them, you started talking about something else," he said as he flipped through the pages of his notebook. "What was it again? Oh, there it is. How executives are like generals leading armies."

I didn't realize until that point that my entire lecture was being transcribed by more students than I thought.

"Very good job!" I acknowledged and appreciated the student as he sat back down on his seat. It is always a great feeling to know that your efforts are not going to waste.

"All right class. I promise this is going to be the last topic we discuss for today. I know it has been a long and tiring class but bear with me," I continued.

"You don't have much time left anyway," one of the students from the front row of the class said, as he pointed at the wall clock.

"This shouldn't take too long if you guys take notes," I replied.

"All right then. Let's conclude the last 10 minutes of our class with one of the greatest wars of history—the Battle of Trafalgar. This is one of those battles that will forever be talked about. This battle has great significance in history and has countless lessons to offer. The battle was fought in the year 1805 between the British and the combined forces of the Spanish and the French. This battle is what brought us Admiral Nelson, one of the greatest naval commanders to have ever lived."

"Which side was he on?" asked one of the curious students from the front row.

"We're getting there," I replied. "Now, what's important here is to note the synchronization and management of the British fleet in the Battle of Trafalgar. This battle is a great example of strategic planning, excellent decision making, and knowledge about the area where the battle was being held—much like what we learned previously during the portion of the lecture in which I talked about Sun Tzu's matrix and what he believed was the best approach to wage war. And yes, if you hadn't guessed it yet, Admiral Nelson was a commander of the British Navy."

Just as they had previously shown interest in the matrix and approach of Sun Tzu, my students started taking notes once again. They were obviously very fond of wars and battles.

People often complain that there is not much innovation when it comes to strategies used to conduct wars and battles and that there is barely ever anything new that occurs in these wars. The Battle of Trafalgar, however, is one great exception.

In addition to the trust that all levels of commanders had between each other, Admiral Nelson played his part in making the battle a success by giving clear commands that were understood completely and perfectly implemented by those under his command. In fact, the synchronization of the battle was so exemplary that it began even before the battle officially began, with the firing of the very first shot.

"Admiral Nelson is one of those commanders who will always be remembered," I reiterated. "Not only was he celebrated because of his bravery, but he was also very creative and innovative in his tactics and strategies. In addition to being the commander for the main battle fleet of the British Navy, it was also his job to discover the weak points of the opposing fleet, which comprised the joined forces of the French and the Spanish—and guess what? He did it."

"How old was he during the battle?" asked one of my students. I could tell by her tone and the way in which she asked the question that she was genuinely interested. Students always love to find out how old certain people were when they accomplished something great, to feel better, or perhaps as motivation that they, too, can achieve greatness if they put in the right amount of effort.

"He actually wasn't that old. He fought the battle and led his 27 ships—all at the age of 47."

And it was true. Being able to command and successfully lead into battle 27 ships to destroy 33 ships from your opponent's fleet—and when the opponents were as strong and powerful as the Spanish and French—was truly an accomplishment. Admiral Nelson was rightfully celebrated.

"But that's not even the best part. Who can guess how old he was when he joined the navy?" I questioned my students.

"Forty," said one of the older students of my class.

"No, that's too old. Probably when he was like 28 or something," countered one of the boys.

"When he was a teenager," a girl joked.

"Not even a teenager," I corrected her. Jaws dropped in amazement.

"Yes, he was only 12 when he joined the Royal Navy in 1771. He lost sight in his right eye in 1794 and had his right arm amputated three years later, in 1797. And guess what? He started giving orders again only 30 minutes after he lost his arm. Now that's resilience!"

Needless to say, my class was proud of him and wowed almost in a single voice.

"Wow indeed. But that's enough trivia. Let's get back to what we were talking about."

The students were ready to hear more.

"As you might have guessed, winning the battle wasn't exactly easy—and it's especially difficult when you're fighting against Napoleon's fleets. But Nelson had a plan. Being one of the greatest tacticians and strategists of all time, he sailed all the way to the West Indies from the English waters in search of Napoleon's fleets until he finally found them near the southwestern Spanish coast.

"At the time, it was common for battles involving ships to have 'lines of battle.' The formation usually involved aligning your ships parallel to the fleet of the enemy and sail as fire was exchanged at close proximity. For this reason, it often so happened that two vessels or ships came so close to each other that physical fighting between the crew was possible and, obviously, no one let that opportunity go."

"But didn't the French and Spanish have more ships than Nelson? How many did you say there were—33 against 27?" a student asked.

"That's correct. And here's where the strategic intelligence of Nelson comes into the picture. The opponent's ships not only had more ammunition but were heavier, as well, which gave them the metal-weight advantage. But this didn't stop Admiral Nelson from trying. As I said before, he not only understood the battle space extremely well, but he also knew the weak points of his opponent along with the strengths of the British fleet.

"Even though they had much more ammunition and strength than the English fleet, the sailors and captains of the French and Spanish fleets were not as well trained as those of the English. What's more is that because the ships and vessels of Napoleon's fleets were much heavier, it was difficult to maneuver them with the precision required—and Admiral Nelson knew for a fact that as difficult as it may be and as much planning as it would require, he could use this disadvantage of the French and Spanish fleets to gain victory in what would be written down in history as the Battle of Trafalgar."

"But couldn't the increased ammunition on the Spanish and French fleets make up for their lack of maneuverability?" one of my students questioned out of sheer curiosity.

"You can say that Nelson was lucky," I joked. But that was also true for many reasons, which I would reveal to my students later in the class. "I'm kidding. Even though there was more ammunition on the ships and vessels of Napoleon, the crew onboard the English fleet was more trained in using guns and ammunition, as well. What this meant was that despite the comparatively less ammunition that the English fleet was equipped with, the skilled crew onboard was able to fire more frequently and with more precision than the ships of the adversary."

"But you said that the fleets were aligned parallel to each other to ensure that the enemy could be attacked. Being more powerful and having more ammunition onboard, shouldn't the French and Spanish ships have been successful?" asked the same student once again, this time genuinely concerned. He could not understand how a side with more ammunition, greater strength, and more ships could lose the battle against a fleet that was being commanded by a 47-year-old and that had less ammunition than the enemy.

"I said that alignment *usually* happened. Let's just say Nelson did his homework," I responded.

But the puzzled look on my student's face was enough for me to elaborate.

"Admiral Nelson aligned his ship perpendicular to those of the enemy. Now this is one of those decisions that would have called for a lot of criticism and backlash, had Nelson and his forces lost—but they didn't. And there were a lot of risks involved in this approach, too. This approach was extremely dangerous for Nelson and his men because it involved exposing lightly armed sides of Nelson's ships to the French and Spanish fleets, which had loads of ammunition onboard.

"But I think it's fair to say that that wasn't even the part that Nelson was focusing on. What was probably going through his mind was that once he breaks the impasse, he would be able to use the heavily armed sides of his ships to fight against the Spanish and French. And that's exactly what he did. Once his ships were able to break the 'line' formation that was typical of the time, there would be a different kind of arrangement that Nelson would have to deal with—and that's where Nelson's forces would have the upper hand."

"How so?" a student asked.

"Great question. After the arrangement changed from a line formation to ship to ship, the increased maneuverability, more skilled crew with arms and ammunition, and lighter weight of the ships of the English would come in handy. The English had a higher rate of fire and skilled sailors, which could swerve the ships away from the opponents after the ships of Nelson had initiated the attack.

"The British sailors and captains were already exceptionally well skilled at handling their ships. The idea was to time the moves in a strategic way and sail in the space between the ships of Napoleon to attack with force. What was important here was for the captains of Nelson's army to support each other when dealing with vessels and ships that were not only heavier but also had more ammunition. And they delivered."

"This was over 200 years ago!" one of my students shrieked.

I assumed that she said this because she was surprised at the intelligence and amount of strategic planning that went into a battle so long ago.

"How did they communicate with each other?"

I couldn't have been more wrong.

"This is the best part." I replied. "Can you imagine leading a fleet of 27 ships against Napoleon, being the *weaker* side, having less ammunition, not being able to communicate with your captains, and *still* being able to win the battle? "

The class burst into applause.

"Settle down, everyone. We don't have much time left before the class ends."

I looked at the clock and there were only a little less than 5 minutes left.

"Now, who here has heard of Brydges Rodney? George Brydges Rodney," I questioned.

And the response, once again, was exactly what I had expected. Nobody had heard of him.

"Rodney was a British captain who Nelson should've thanked for his success in the Battle of Trafalgar. After all, Nelson used the tactic in the battle that Rodney introduced over 20 years earlier. He used the 'breaking the line' strategy in 1782 to save the Bahamas from the French.[16]

"To ensure that all of the captains were on the same page and in order to guarantee that no mistakes were made or no avoidable challenges and problems had to be dealt with during the battle itself, Nelson hosted a large conference aboard his flagship, HMS Victory, the night before the battle to be certain that every captain knew the role that he had to play, and knew exactly where their ships would be as part of the first arrangement before the attack was initiated.

"It was extremely necessary to inform everyone of their roles and the formation and arrangement of the ships beforehand because there was practically no room for communication once the battle had actually begun. However, because everyone knew how important it was for them to play their part—and play it right—every captain, sailor, and crew member of Nelson's fleets demonstrated extreme skill and efficiency to the greatest extent possible in order to ensure that they were on the winning side of the battle.

"Effectiveness was also especially necessary because—as I said earlier as well—Nelson was going against the typical and general fleet arrangement of the time, which not only left his ships exposed but also very vulnerable.

"Now here's where Nelson became lucky. Firstly, the wind on that fine day favored his fleet and allowed the ships to attack the Spanish and French fleets without facing any substantial damage. As a result, most of the large ships in Nelson's fleet were able to expose their heavily armed sides to Napoleon's fleet and attack.

"Secondly, since all of the captains already knew the tactics and approach that was being followed, they all worked hand in hand, even though they could not communicate with each other at all. More often than not, when one large British ship was seen struggling with a large counterpart from the enemy's side, other ships from Nelson's fleet would join in the 'ship-to-ship' mini battle and attack the enemy's ship from the other 'exposed' side.

"When multiple ships of Nelson's fleet started attacking a single ship on Napoleon's side simultaneously, the problems for the Spanish and French increased exponentially. Because they had crew members who were not as skillful as those onboard the British ships, it was already difficult for them when they had to deal with the precision and control that Nelson's men demonstrated. Consequently, even though substantial damage was sustained by probably all of the British ships and vessels, and Admiral Nelson was even killed in the battle, the damage and loss that they faced could not—in any way—compare to the losses sustained by Napoleon's side.

"It was the first time a tactic of this kind was planned with such foresight and used to such glorious advantage. Instead of leaving England with a questionable victory, Nelson's strategy ensured that Britain would dominate the oceans of the world for 100 years, and it changed everything the world thought it knew about successful naval tactics.

"Contextual change was best described by Alvin Toffler in 1980 as 'a sea change of such mammoth proportions that old paradigms would no longer suffice.'[17] There have been two major revolutions that changed humanity and caused transformations the likes of which were unprecedented and never seen before.

"With that, however, we cannot deny that there is a third revolution has already come into effect that will revolutionize the course of action that was the norm for nearly every domain, and in multiple ways. It has been thousands of years since the agricultural revolution and a few hundred years since the industrial revolution took the world by storm.

"Each changing the course of human history in its own unique yet unfathomable way, they both had one thing in common: Both the agricultural and industrial revolutions produced ripples of change that had its effects not only on human history but also on our perception of human effort.

"The latest 'Age of Agility,' which is revolutionizing the way we live our lives, too, makes many demands on us. The agility age is bound to transform not only societies but also entire nations, which will shift the approach we take regarding world events and how to deal with or respond to them in a manner that is not only effective but also optimal.

"The most basic challenge for strategic leadership in the digital world of today is to understand the dynamics of change that are now occurring and to develop the clearest possible visualization of the end results of change, with enough lead time to ensure that a competitively advantageous position can be achieved.

"It's too soon to evaluate and make predictions about the changes that will manifest as we progress through the information age. No one knows for sure how technology will affect human lives in the long run; however, it is time that we establish that technology isn't going anywhere anytime soon. The ability to adapt and plan ahead strategically at a time like this is more crucial than ever before—and it all calls for stability.

"Going back to history one last time for today, not only had 20 ships on Napolean's side been captured, scuttled, or damaged to the point of no return, but they also faced one of the most humiliating losses ever—all because of the strategy and agile abilities of one man, by the name of Horatio Nelson." And with that I said, "Class dismissed."

References

1. Carroll, Lewis. *Alice's Adventures in Wonderland* (Chapter 6). Alice-in-Wonderland.net. Retrieved from http://www.alice-in-wonderland.net/resources/chapters-script/alice-in-wonderland-quotes/
2. Mintzberg, Henry and Waters, James A. (1985). Of Strategies, Deliberate and Emergent. *Strategic Management Journal, 6,* 257–272. Retrieved from http://www3.uma.pt/filipejmsousa/ge/Mintzberg%20and%20Waters,%201985.pdf
3. Ferguson, Edward. (2017, March 25). "Walmart's Vision, Mission, Generic & Intensive Strategies." Panmore Institute. Retrieved from panmore.com/walmart-vision-mission-statement-intensive-generic
4. Toynbee, Arnold J. (1987). *A Study of History.* Oxford University Press. Retrieved from thinkexist.com/quotes/arnold_toynbee/2.html
5. Ibid.
6. Ibid.
7. Toynbee, Arnold J. (1992). *Change and Habit: The Challenge of Our Time.* London (UK): Oneworld Publications.
8. Ibid.
9. Ibid.
10. Ibid.
11. Raynus, Joseph. (2011). *Improving Business Process Performance: Gain Agility, Create Value, and Achieve Success.* Boca Raton (FL): CRC Press.
12. Lai, David. (2004, May). "Learning from the Stones: A *Go* Approach to Mastering China's Strategic Concept, *Shi.*" SSI-Strategic Studies Institute—US Army War College. Retrieved from https://www.scribd.com/document/57216345/Learning-from-the-Stones-A-Go-Approach-to-Mastering-China-s-Strategic-Concept-Shi
13. Sun Tzu. (1983). *The Art of War.* Edited by James Clavell. New York: Bantam Doubleday Dell Publishing Group, Inc.
14. Sun Tzu. *The Art of War.* Retrieved from https://suntzusaid.com/
15. Lai, David. (2004, May). "Learning from the Stones: A *Go* Approach to Mastering China's Strategic Concept, *Sh*i." SSI-Strategic Studies Institute—US Army War College. Retrieved from https://www.scribd.com/document/57216345/Learning-from-the-Stones-A-Go-Approach-to-Mastering-China-s-Strategic-Concept-Shi
16. Military Wiki. "George Brydges Rodney, 1st Baron Rodney." Retrieved from http://military.wikia.com/wiki/George_Brydges_Rodney,_1st_Baron_Rodney
17. Toffler, Alvin. (1980). *The Third Wave.* New York: Bantam Books/William Morrow & Co., Inc.

Chapter 3

Searching for the Age of Agility

IT happened. There is no avoiding it, no forgetting.
No running away, or flying, or burying, or hiding.

— Laurie Halse Anderson[1]

A few days after introducing my students to the wonders of Chinese warfare and strategy, I was planning my next lecture, hoping to make it as interesting as the one I delivered to my class the other day. I had set the bar high for all of my future lectures. If they took anything home from that class—which I'm sure they did—my students would have high expectations for the rest of the course. After all, it isn't often that one is taught agility and management in such a unique way.

I searched through numerous books and websites for strategy, agility, and the need to accept and embrace change—both on a personal level and from an organizational point of view—but I realized that I had already spoken far too much about these topics from an historical perspective. Besides, I remembered how the students were able to relate to and grasp the concepts far more quickly when I spoke to them quoting examples from Walmart® and IKEA®.

Naturally, as interested as they were in the concepts and strategies of war and learning how mighty and successful generals and leaders of the past weren't afraid of experimenting and thinking outside box, the fact still remained that it would be much easier for them to understand what it was that I tried to teach them if I used examples and scenarios from the current state of the world.

Besides, talking any more about history than I already did would probably make the information seem redundant enough for my students to be bored and stop listening to what I had to say altogether.

It would be best to be as innovative and creative with my lectures as possible—while keeping the information and examples that I presented as relevant and relatable to my students as possible.

Whether you call it the Digital Age, the Computer Age, or the New Media Age, one thing is for certain: The Information Age has brought with it changes that were not only unprecedented, but their magnitude was such that it could not have been imagined by anyone—not even in the recent past. Not only has there been a complete shift in the way our industries work and function, but the production mechanisms of our industries have also changed.

The Industrial Revolution brought with it industrialization that gave us traditional industries as we know them. Then came the Information Age, which caused a shift in our economy, and the computerization of information became its basis. Industrial production changed to production based on computerization, information, and adequate relevant knowledge. But now, two and a half decades after the introduction of the World Wide Web, the Information Age is at its final stages because of the Internet and mobile screens. And businesses know that they must adapt quickly in order to survive in the Age of Agility, which is now upon us.

One of the world's leading economists, Eric D. Beinhocker, suggests that even though markets display dynamism at their best, the same is not exactly true for businesses. In fact, this American economist is of the opinion that organizations and businesses themselves are not innately capable of evolution or adaptation. He believes that organizations and companies are affected by the transitions and transformations that take place at the market level, and that they die or survive as a result. However, in most cases, they are unable to adapt by themselves.[2]

In his book *The Origin of Wealth: Evolution, Complexity, and the Radical Remaking of Economics,* Eric D. Beinhocker says, "[W]e are accustomed to thinking in evolution in a biological context, but modern evolutionary theory views evolution as something much more general. Evolution is an algorithm; it is an all-purpose formula for innovation, a formula that, through its special brand of trial and error, creates new designs and solves difficult problems. Evolution can perform its tricks not just in the 'substrate' of DNA, but in any system that has the right information-processing and information-storage characteristics."[3]

The age we live in today provides all of those characteristics and more. In the world today, many people feel overwhelmed and burdened by responsibilities and demands from different aspects and domains of daily life. As a result, many people are in constant fear that they will not live up to the responsibilities that they have and what is expected of them. People these days have to deal with meetings, phone calls, emails, and expectations, which it is practically impossible for them to focus proper attention on simultaneously.

On top of it all, there are challenges that need to be addressed immediately—challenges that are not only growing in scope, but also in size. These challenges and characteristics of the environment that we live in today are what was termed by the American Military as **V**olatile, **U**ncertain, **C**omplex, and **A**mbiguous (VUCA). This term was coined by the US Army War College in the early 1990s to refer to the multilateral and multifaceted world of today. Since the end of the Cold War, the world and its environment has become more VUCA than ever before.

The concept of VUCA made its way into the business world in the wake of the global financial crises of 2008 and 2009. Since its introduction in the world of business and management, this concept has been featured countless times and now plays a very important role in the development of skills of leadership for multiple organizations and businesses throughout the world.

This is primarily because leadership in the VUCA world of today is perhaps one of the most difficult tasks and the greatest challenge that people are faced with, not only in today's world but probably throughout the history of mankind. It is up to leaders to be more agile and capable—rather, responsible—for making practical and viable decisions like never before in an environment that is constantly changing.

In the business world, this concept is described in a slightly different way from when it is used to define the state of the world in general. For a business environment to be described as VUCA, it is important for the environment to exhibit certain qualities and demonstrate certain characteristics. The business environment usually is:

Volatile: There is an increase in the speed, volume, scale, and types of challenges that affect all of the businesses and the workforce of the business environment in question.

Uncertain: Due to the volatile nature of the business environment, people are unable to predict the way in which progress will be made in the environment and how future events will be different from the current scenario.

Complex: There is confusion to the extent that all of the businesses are affected by the changes and are unable to put their finger on the causes of the changes or the connections between the causes of change and their outcomes.

Ambiguous: There isn't a precise definition for most of the conditions of the business environment, and multiple meanings exist simultaneously.

Needless to say, nearly all of the business environments of today—if not all of them—exhibit the qualities and characteristics mentioned above. We now live in a world where change is not only unpredictable but also greater than ever before—and more than it was ever believed would be possible. With the unpredictability of the world, the future, too, cannot be predicted. We now have exponentially increasing options, and our perception and the way we think about all of the options that are now before us has undoubtedly—and inevitably—changed.

With the ever-changing world of today, leaders and managers need to up the game with their decision making and hit the ground running as they analyze huge amounts of information that they have access to as a result of the hyperconnected world of today.

One of the biggest problems that these leaders and managers face when making decisions in the digital age of today, however, is that for centuries, it has been believed that there is a degree of certainty and predictability in the world. Being raised within this context, people tend to focus more on the probability of things. What is needed for the progress and success of an organization, company, or business in today's world is a shift in perspective. It is imperative for leaders of today to shift their focus and divert their energies and efforts to what is possible instead of the probability.

But the question here remains: How is one to change the mindset that has been the norm for centuries?

The answer lies in one simple truth. As mentioned before, today's world is unpredictable and in many ways different from the past. This means that it is not a wise idea to use the information and experiences of the past as a basis for our decisions regarding the future. Even though this approach proved to be successful for hundreds—if not thousands—of years, the limits of the approach are manifesting themselves in today's world because the challenges and changes that we face and experience today are like nothing that was ever witnessed in the past.

Even though using past information to identify risks and take the necessary steps to protect oneself and prosper has come in handy for humanity for several hundreds of years, the VUCA environment of the world today demands more innovative solutions that are comprehensive and elaborate instead of being dragged and slightly tweaked and modified versions of the same solutions that have been used for years—all of which had one thing in common: They were based on predictions.

Since we have established that anything is possible in the VUCA environment, we need to understand that focusing only on what is likely to occur based on the trends, experiences, and information of the past is a guaranteed recipe for disaster. Instead, it is crucial for people to think outside the box so that they can successfully consider all of the possibilities and make the right decisions so that they will be prepared for anything that happens.

As simple as the reason for the change that is required may sound, making the said change won't be as easy. In fact, research shows that our brains are not particularly fond of this approach either. This is primarily due to the fact that we, as humans, love to reduce the amount of information that we have to analyze and minimize, and thereby simplify the process of making decisions.

For us to be informed and prepared with regard to all of the possibilities, we will not only have to move away from what has been the norm for years but also change the patterns and habits that we use and follow for the gathering, collection, and retrieval of information, as well as the steps we take to reach conclusions and make decisions based on this information.

Fortunately, a few small steps can be taken to ensure that we are successfully able to deal with the changes that come as a result of the increased levels of complexity in the world and evolve and adapt accordingly.

There are four habits that can help us evolve and improve our ability to deal with higher levels of complexity. These four habits are easy to implement:

– Asking questions of various types
– Taking on different perspectives
– Development of a systemic vision to approach events
– Understanding the holistic view of things and picturing all of the possibilities

The challenge that we are facing is extremely critical—so much so that not only does the survival of our enterprises and organizations depend on it, but the risk also extends to the future of humanity as a whole. It is only through agility and accepting change that we will be able to survive and thrive in a VUCA environment of unpredictability and uncertainty.

But this will only be possible if we accept the VUCA environment as the new normal.

I was browsing through incredible amounts of text from every source possible to make my lecture interesting and engaging when I noticed that my phone had begun to ring. As I headed to the other room to pick it up, the only thing that crossed my mind was a piece of the text that I had read earlier, which talked about mobiles and the internet marking the final stages of the information age.

"What could be next?" I wondered to myself.

Before I could reach my phone to answer it, the ringing had stopped. Instinctively, my sight fell upon the wall clock. It was 10:10 p.m.

"This must be a real emergency," I thought to myself, hoping that it was nothing too serious.

As I picked up the phone in my hand, I realized I had been more immersed in my studies than I had thought.

"Six missed calls, and I only heard the last one of them. That's odd," I said to myself, as the phone started ringing once again.

It was an unknown number, but I decided to pick it up anyway. A prank caller wouldn't be this persistent, especially not at this hour.

"Professor?" a familiar voice was audibly glad to know that someone had picked up the phone.

"Hello, yes?" I replied.

"I'm so glad you picked up. I'm sorry to be calling you this late but—"

"I am sorry. Who am I speaking to? I'm afraid I don't have this number saved. Apologies." I replied as courteously as I could at this late hour.

"Oh, I'm sorry. It's me, Bill. I hope I didn't disturb your sleep."

Ah, yes. Bill. We had exchanged phone numbers just the other day at the airport, but I didn't have the time to save his number on my phone—or at least that's what I said to him. The fact of the matter was that I had completely forgotten to.

"No, no. I was just studying a little to prepare some lectures for class. You see how much effort us professors put into the lectures for you people?" I joked.

"Well, I've been trying to speak to you since over an hour so I guess you weren't studying just a *little*," Bill said.

"Oh, I'm so sorry. I just saw that you had called six times. So, what is it that you wanted to speak to me about? Is everything all right? I hope it's nothing too serious," I replied.

"Not serious at all," he said. "I wanted to speak to you about something important though . . . but if you're busy maybe I could call back at some other time," Bill continued courteously. I could tell from his voice that something was bothering him deep down inside, but I didn't know what it was.

And I certainly wouldn't let my new friend down when he called for help—especially so late at night.

"I'm as free as I'll ever be," I lied.

Bill didn't fall for it either, but he understood that I was ready to hear whatever he had to talk about. He laughed an anxious laugh.

"Joe, I'm thinking of quitting my job," Bill said as straightforwardly as he could.

I knew that he wasn't happy with the way things were going at his company, and he felt like he couldn't fit in, but that was the case with countless other executives his age. I was afraid he was making an impulsive decision after the conversation that we had had the other day. I wanted to hear him out and understand his problem before giving him the green light to take a step forward in that direction. Besides, since he called me at this late hour, it was safe to assume that he wanted advice and someone to hear his problem, more than anything else.

And so I did.

"What's the matter?" I replied.

As vocal as Bill always was about his problems, he didn't hold back on telling me anything and everything that he thought would be important for me to put things into context and perspective. Almost like a continuation of our conversation at the airport the other day, Bill began to tell me about how his company felt almost static and on a mission to control—or govern—employees.

After my conversation with him the other day at the airport, my student had realized how there was a lot that his company could reconsider. He talked at length about how the executives were all more or less on the same page and had similar feelings about the company and the decisions that they were making—but it felt like the executives themselves had no say in anything. A lot of decisions were made at the upper level—without much strategic thinking—and the executives could do nothing more than follow orders, like puppets.

I wasn't surprised. That is the problem that still exists within a lot of the companies, businesses, and organizations of today. Those in leadership and managerial positions are making decisions without doing a proper analysis first and fail to take the bigger picture into consideration. As a result, there is internal chaos and confusion, which results only because of poor decision-making skills and lack of adaptability.

"That is inevitable. It has been proven time and again that if you try controlling people, chaos will ensue," I replied matter-of-factly. As paradoxical as that sounded, it was true.

"When you start dictating to people in an attempt to dominate them, it might seem as if you have control, on the surface, but a deeper analysis will make you realize that this is far from the truth. This is primarily because there is a lack of a common purpose in situations like this. As a result, there is chaos and confusion at all levels of the organization or business. Because there is no common agenda that is being followed or worked toward, everyone is guided by his or her own motives and agendas, which causes disruption."

"I feel like that's exactly what's happening here. Nobody is on the same page," replied a very worried Bill.

I chuckled. "I know, Bill. You're not the only one who feels that way. In fact, if you were to ask your colleagues, you would find that they are of the same opinion. There needs to be a vision or a strategy-based purpose that everyone feels comfortable about and will buy into. Next, it's essential for your organization to have a system of values based on principles that are constantly put into check and reinforced by a holistic information system. The mission statement comes into play here. If all of the stakeholders work together for one mission statement—which everyone agrees to—there is no reason why order will not be established, even in a chaotic situation.

"Once a common goal is set, people and teams become more self-managing. When a common strategic intent, vision, and value system is established, people love to work together, and this goal-oriented approach makes them work together to the extent that they are willing to bond as much as required to reach the pre-defined goal or target. In situations like these, it is common for people to even let go of their egos and work together with their colleagues and managers for a higher and greater purpose."

There was a pause. Bill said nothing. I couldn't even hear him breathe on the phone for a good few seconds. He was probably just very worried, I figured.

"I appreciate your taking the time out for all of this—especially at an hour as late as this—and I'm sorry for all of the trouble. But it's tough to believe. I mean, all of this almost sounds too good to be true. Do you understand what I mean? Do you have any examples for times when this has worked in the real world? Something that I can learn from or relate to?" As always, Bill wasn't convinced. And he wouldn't be until he got his fair share of real-life examples and stories. That had always been the case with him. Luckily, I knew just what would grab his attention.

"I knew you would say this," I laughed. "And don't worry. Helping my students is part of my job. Don't ever feel like you're bothering me," I reassured him.

"As for your question about examples," I continued, "I have just the right example to convince you. Now, this isn't something that was very recent, but I'm sure you've heard or read about it more than once. You remember the divestiture once of a very large and well-known company?"

"Yeah? What about it?" Bill snapped back. He wasn't in the mood for rhetorical questions.

"At the time of the divestiture, they had a lot of problems. They were more focused on their products than they were on their customers. They had rules and bureaucracies that were ruining them. You know what happened when the divestiture happened? They knew that they'd have to deal with informed customers and customers who had knowledge about the bigger picture—customers who knew their options. Something had to be done. Acting efficiently, they were able to manage and develop empowerment within a decade all because they started working toward a common goal."

Bill was not the kind of person who would be impressed easily. "Yeah, but that was so long ago," he replied as quickly as he could. "When was that? The late 1970s? Early 1980s?"

"It came into effect in the year 1984," I replied. "But the same holds true for today. It is a fact that an organization or company will not work efficiently and effectively unless the employees on all levels are on the same page. Once that happens, you'll see wonders. Take the case of another large and well-known company. Much like the one mentioned above, this company had the problems of rules and bureaucracy as well. The environment was politicized and full of rules—so much so that it is safe to assume that the employees felt pressured and frustrated. Now, the divisions of the company have focus on empowerment. That's what true leadership is. One must understand how their decisions are affecting the lives of employees and colleagues and impacting the environment, and make amends whenever and wherever necessary."

There was a pause. Bill never said anything when he was thinking long and hard about something, so I took the opportunity and continued talking.

"My definition of leadership has evolved to this. The creation of a culture around a shared vision and value system based on principles—that's what true leadership is. If those in managerial positions keep on trying to dictate the lives of others and making decisions that can prove to be detrimental in the long run simply because they are afraid of losing control, the only backlash that will follow is that the employees will be more focused on trying to gain back control in their own lives and rebel in an attempt to make their own decisions based on personal notions, ideas, perspectives, and thoughts.

"At a time like this, neither the managers nor the employees are concerned about what is in the best interest of the organization or company. In fact, when a situation like this arises, people do not even consider their own colleagues or other employees. Everyone is just attempting to make their own opinion heard and noticed, regardless of the effects that this might have. Always remember: Nobody wants to give up control."

"How can I make this work out for myself?" Bill questioned, the disappointment he had for his organization was audible in his voice. It was almost like a plea for help. He had no direction and was lost, with nowhere to go. What he failed to understand, however, was that he had pinpointed what was wrong with his organization—something that most people are unable to do, even after they have spent years in the industry.

This is one of the biggest problems for people who are working in the corporate sector. Having spent years in the same industry and field—or, in some extreme cases, spent years upon years in the same company—people not only become desensitized to the problems of the environment that they are in, but they also become complacent and refuse to make any progress.

As unfortunate as it sounds, the same thing happens with organizations when leaders and managers do not realize that there is a greater underlying problem. What happens as a result is that these organizations and companies remain stagnant—almost as if they were stuck in time—simply because they refuse to adapt and embrace change.

"The first thing that you need to understand is that it's not your fault. If those in managerial and leadership positions in your company or organization are unable to understand that their employee is not happy—or that all of the employees feel the same way about the company—then the problem isn't limited to you. And it's important for them to take action and make decisions that can prove to be helpful. Those in leadership and managerial positions often fail to realize that it takes a lot of time and effort to develop relationships with employees that will guarantee that they remain loyal to the company for a long time.

"From what you told me about your offsite meeting, I understand that the company has certain requirements for all of its employees—which I'm certain have never changed in the number of years that you have spent with them. Even though none of you are happy with the pep talk about embracing change and dynamism and obviously might not make the amount of effort that the company expects from you, I believe that it is the structure of the company itself that is not able to adapt.

"I hate to say this but it almost feels as if your company has become static, with no innovation or creativity driving it. I wish I were not the one who had to break this to you but from everything you told me about your company in these two conversations, I feel like your company is digging its own grave."

"I know. I understand all of that but I really want to—"

"I would probably be thinking the same things as you right now, Bill," I said, cutting him off.

And it was true. Be it a company, an organization, a small enterprise, or a large multinational corporation, if it is not agile, it should expect its demise in the very near future. Business environments of today are nothing like they were in the past.

"I want to make this work out. I need to make this work out," Bill continued. "I've already done everything that I could—everything that was in my capacity. I read a lot of management books. I'm trying to follow new trends in management and organizational development. I just wonder why bestselling management books try to convince us to apply the best practices that the other companies incorporate into their departments' systems and processes.

"For the last 25 years, I have witnessed such management movements as management by objectives; BPM, BPR, CMMI, and the balanced scorecard; and Lean and Six Sigma. Why do we persist? What really is a management belief system?"

Bill was losing his patience, and I knew once again that nothing I could say would convince him until and unless it was backed by science, examples, or facts and figures that he could relate to or be able to conceptualize.

"Management is not an exact science that follows the laws of physics, such as gravity," I replied.

"There is a lot that needs to be considered about this domain. Unlike in the past, it is practically impossible now to manage and organize a system or a company based solely on a handful of factors and turn a blind eye to the reality of the situation. The fact of the matter remains that the organizations of today are no longer paying attention to what's going on internally and externally—or not paying *enough* attention, if I may," I responded.

The environment and economy of today need to be viewed holistically. To see the bigger picture, it is imperative for managers and those in leadership positions to be able to see their organizations with fresh eyes and not continue to use the same metrics for success, failure, and predictions that they used in the past. The world of today requires people to strategize and think outside of the box—one thing that most people are failing to do.

Even though all of the institutions of human life are based on linearity, relying solely on the linear approach does not cut it anymore. Going back to the concept defined and described in *The Art of War*, by Sun Tsu, in Chapter 2, it is crucial for those in managerial positions to break down their course of action into tactics and strategy, for both optimality and efficiency. Even though tactics and strategy often go hand in hand and tend to fall in the same superset of planning effectively, both of them are essentially very different.

Where strategy may be concerned with the "usage" aspect of things, devising new and innovative tactics has more to do with individual engagement, which is essential in today's day and age. Unless both of these entities are understood separately, it is practically impossible to comprehend how they differ or even how they are innately related and can be used together for success.

Linearity, as we have known it for the last several decades, has always been associated with Sir Isaac Newton. Linear science has, since its inception and introduction to the common public, evolved and developed until it started being used for describing and controlling the natural course of things.

As expected, it would only be so long before the philosophy that was associated with the science and its powers began to fail. Ultimately, people started realizing that the linear approach for prediction was not only illusory but also vague in many ways.

Linearity was a concept that was best used when limited to systems that were predictable. Unfortunately, however, the environment and systems of today are very different from ever before. In the VUCA environment, it is impossible to only use the linearity approach in decision making. As mentioned earlier, it is impossible to make predictions in an environment that is as haphazard as today's environment.

Another reason why the linear approach doesn't work for the environments of today is because, where a linear approach is being followed, the cause and effects of things are often measurable and demonstrable. In a VUCA environment, however, that is not the case. The VUCA environment of today has so much going on that, in the disrupted confusion of the world of today, pinpointing the causes and effects with accuracy and precision is also impossible due to the fact that there are several different changes and ripples that a single factor can cause today.

With a linear system, having even a small amount of information is sufficient and can help you to make informed decisions that are sane and viable. Practical solutions can be deployed and decision making becomes easy with even minimal information of the past because the linear environments in question and their attributes are systematic and their behaviors are predictable—all of which is untrue for the VUCA environment.

This is where nonlinearity comes into the picture. Literally the opposite of linearity, nonlinearity is a completely different concept in itself. Not only does nonlinearity not conform to or apply to the rules that a linear approach is bound to follow, but the nonlinear approach also covers concepts that are not as systemic and predictable as those that the linear approach covers, including complexity theory and chaos theory.

Nonlinearity is not proportional by any means, and the causes and effects of situations within the system are not demonstrable either. Unlike their linear counterparts, nonlinear systems are not identifiable or recognizable through their parts, or equal to their constituent components in any way.

When talking about a nonlinear system, you cannot even expect the results to repeat themselves. Even if a situation has the exact same factors involved as one in the past, it is impossible to make judgments based on the results of the past because there can be a profound difference between the two situations, regardless of the fact that they were both part of the same system and had the same factors involved. What this means is that there is no way in which you can predict anything about the system with accuracy.

Again, much unlike linear systems, having a little information about the nonlinear system essentially means nothing as it can be of little to no benefit. This has many ramifications. Not only is one perpetually unaware of the workings of a nonlinear system, but this uncertainty and lack of predictability also means that there will always be a risk involved in the planning and control of the system.

As difficult as it may sound and as hard to digest as it may be, the world we live in today is a blend of the linear and the nonlinear. Even though it might be possible to make some predictions based on certain factors and lucky enough to find that they were accurate, the fact of the matter is that most of the scenarios that occur today are much different from those of the past, even though they have uncanny similarities with events that we have all witnessed and learned from in the past.

As with everything in the world, however, nonlinear systems and the nonlinear approach to things also has its fair share of benefits and advantages. Even though instability can ensure and a nonlinear system may result in disconti-nuities and synergies, nonlinear systems also place extra pressure on organiza-tions, companies, businesses—and even people!—to adapt and go the extra mile to devise and deliver elaborate solutions that are not only innovative and creative but are also based on key factors such as dynamism, responsiveness, and flexibility.

To progress, thrive, and succeed in the world today, it is imperative for us to understand how we are all shackled by our own imaginations and the con-fines that have dogmatically been placed upon us. Where linearity may ease the decision-making process for us in many scenarios and make us react to situa-tions according to what we expect or anticipate happening rather than every-thing that is possible, there is also a deep-rooted problem with linearity.

This approach essentially closes our doors and narrows down our viewpoint on systems that are a major part of our social and natural existence. This, in turn, leaves us weak and vulnerable in front of adversaries who are already mak-ing plans and strategizing to get ahead of the game.

Knowing one's constraints and limitations beforehand can not only help minimize the surprise aspect of things but also ensure that one does not remain in shock for a longer period of time than is necessary. This holds true for both organizations and individuals, including leaders and executives of the VUCA world.

With a more holistic view and comprehensive model of the world before us, we will not only be able to adapt in a better and more efficient way, but it is also possible that focusing on nonlinearity will help us develop and implement robust systems that are needed to succeed in today's world. As I tried to explain these very intricate concepts to Bill in as detailed and concise a way as possible, I concluded that he was able to understand most of what I was saying, judging by the lack of responses from his side.

He was thinking long and hard about it all—how his organization and its structure was stuck in time, perhaps never to break free from the shackles that it imposed on itself, all due to a different approach and mindset than what was necessary.

Finally, after I had spoken at length without a word from him, he responded.

"Thank you, Joe," he said, as courteously and politely as he could. But before I could acknowledge his response, he continued. "I don't know if this will be too much trouble, and I know that I've already taken too much of your time, but is it possible for us to meet sometime soon? I think I'd like to talk about this in person. You've been of such great help."

After I hung up the phone, it became obvious to me that this conversation put me on a clear path to agility research.

As close to my heart as the topic of discussion was, I just couldn't say, "No."

References

1. Anderson, Laurie Halse. Quotable Quote. goodreads.com. Retrieved from https://www.goodreads.com/quotes/294471-it-happened-there-is-no-avoiding-it-no-forgetting-no
2. Beinhocker, Eric D. (2007). *The Origin of Wealth: Evolution, Complexity, and the Radical Remaking of Economics.* Harvard Business Review Press.
3. Ibid.

Chapter 4

Searching in Change Management

More than any other time in history, mankind faces a crossroads.
One path leads to despair and utter hopelessness. The other, to total
extinction. Let us pray we have the wisdom to choose correctly.

— Woody Allen
Side Effects, 1980[1]

I thought a lot about my conversation with Bill the other day. His main problem was that his company was trying to implement change without really planning anything. Even though the leaders and managers at his company must have intended well for everyone, the reality was exactly the opposite of what was anticipated. People like Bill were considering their options and thinking about leaving the company. And it is fair to say that he was not the only one who was having these thoughts.

I started doing my research about change and transformation to be able to explain things to Bill in as simple terms as possible when we finally did meet for lunch. I thought of calling Bill to check up on him a few times before we finalized our meeting, but I thought better of it. Knowing him, there was a strong possibility that he would take my concern the wrong way and end up thinking that I was sympathetic toward his lackluster job and the condition of his life. After all, he wasn't in a good place, and anything and everything that I said could be perceived in a way that was exactly the opposite of my intentions.

All of my research ended up showing me a lot of information that I already knew through my studies. Much like a lot of other companies in a number of industries throughout the world, the company that Bill was working at was making the same common, yet easily avoidable, mistakes.

Over the years, transformation and change has become a hot topic; however, the holistic view of things shows us that the overall track record of organizations and companies that have successfully managed to implement change and transform for the better according to the requirements of the environment is relatively poor.

One of the most interesting concepts which I came across during my research was that of very important top officers or VITO. This concept was developed by Anthony Parinello and described in a number of his books, which were published in 2005.[2]

These VITOs are the people who are in control of the entire system. All levels of employees and work fall under the supervision of these VITOs. This was important because unless the approval comes from the VITO for any type of change, it would be practically impossible for the change to be implemented. The problem, however, was that in most cases, even these VITOs failed to make the preparations and plan, as was needed.

Countless CEOs and executives have recently confessed that even though they recognized the need for change and understood the fact that they would otherwise become extinct, efforts that most companies, businesses, and organizations make for organizational change do not yield the results that were expected. This is primarily because, more often than not, businesses end up dealing with the side effects of the organizational efforts that they were making in hopes of revamping the structure of the organization and making it more agile and better suited to the environment.

Even though business environments are full of creativity and innovation at every scale, the same cannot be said about the organizations of today. A claim as great as this seems almost paradoxical, but it is true. Business environments of today are constantly changing. Realization of the fact that our organizations are unable to adapt to that change is not only unfortunate and worrisome, but also problematic.

Organizational change as we know it is based on several smaller ripples of change in multiple domains and across departments. With that said, we do not always have a say in how this change will begin to manifest itself, or which factors will be involved in the entire process of change. However, regardless of how small or great the change is, one thing never fails to happen.

Whether one is ready to accept this fact or not, the incompetence and lack of agility of businesses, companies, and organizations throughout the world is displayed almost immediately after the first ripple of change is seen. This is where change management comes into the picture.

Change management is one of the most popular topics in the corporate sector, and its use has increased exponentially over the years. In fact, the term has so much importance in the corporate world that even those being interviewed for their first jobs are asked how well they think they manage change and the techniques that they use to get the job done. This term, however, is unfortunately being used in vain more often than it should be.

There is a lot more to change management than what is generally perceived. The prevalent use of the term, however, gives us some very important insights and speaks volumes about what goes on in the minds of people in the corporate sector.

With all the talk about change management, it is fair to say that change is almost expected and anticipated, but the same cannot be said about the stability or agility of an organization or company. But there's a catch. Despite the fact that change is anticipated and accepted as being inevitable, people in most business environments—if not all of them—perceive change itself as a problem. This is primarily due to the fact that change—and accommodating to the said change in order to guarantee survival—requires a lot of time and effort. Not only does adapting to change require companies and organizations to change the dynamics of their processes, but it is also imperative for them to do so in a way that ensures that their business models are not adversely affected.

The initiation of change comes with the implication that all of the companies, businesses, and organizations within the environment that is experiencing change need to do something new and innovative to go from point A to point B. This route requires companies and organizations to invest in building a "bridge" of sorts that can help get the task done with ease. Without the vision of the bridge—or without accepting that adapting to the change will do the organization more good than being stuck in time without making any efforts—a company or organization will never be able to reach the state that is required of it.

When talking about change management, in most cases, organizations appear to begin to change in the right way; however, the rate at which progress is made begins to decrease until it reaches the point at which no progress is made at all. And that's where the problem begins. Sure, the onset of change may be welcomed with a lot of chaos that can even prove to be useful and advantageous in many ways; however, since the same amount of effort is not put in later on in the cycle of change management, it is seen that the company or organization that was headed in the right direction eventually turns back to its old culture.

Knowing what causes this return to old culture despite apparently making the right decisions is what's important.

The fact of the matter is that changing an organization and keeping it responsive and adaptive to the changes of the environment is important. But the problems of change management and the reasons why companies and businesses fail to adapt to change is deeply rooted in the processes and techniques that are being used by most of them.

There is a lot more that a company or organization needs to do than just revise its policies and implement new strategies, the results of which cannot be estimated with precision. Everyone in the corporate sector understands that this is not the solution. However, often, executives and managers alike end up ignoring the fact that change management goes beyond these basics. Unless those who are in the corporate sector learn to accept that, we are bound to struggle with strategies regardless of how properly they were devised or how well thought-out they were.

One important question to ask here is why this problem exists when everyone is already aware of how detrimental it can become? A popular opinion about this question is that of Richard Boland and Fred Collopy from the Weatherhead School of Management at Case Western Reserve University (CWRU). These two professors believe that managers and executives are forced into positions where they are given a certain responsibility and are required to make decisions that are important for the success of the company.[3]

Boland and Collopy are of the opinion that the problem space in which these individuals are expected to operate and devise plans and plausible solutions is one in which there are no real metrics to figure out whether or not one approach is better than the other. Despite all of this, however, these managers, executives, and leaders are expected to continue putting in efforts for a solution—a solution that will be limited to the problem space in question.

The solution to this problem, as unbelievable as it may sound, is fairly simple. Instead of keeping solutions limited to a certain space and time, it is essential to represent the problem on a wider scale, which helps devise solutions and think of strategies that are more practical and can be used effectively in the future as well. Another aspect of the solutions that are being proposed today is that they do not have any real targets associated with them.

As mentioned earlier, there is also no real way to determine whether one solution is better than another. This problem could be solved if we used certain goals or set target results for each of our problems. This will not only bring about successful change, but it will also make the ability to deliberately respond to a challenge inside or outside the adapted business process and practices in a timely and cost-effective manner.

To manage change effectively, it is important to understand that the way in which people behave is an act of balance. What this means is that there will always be forces that are trying to make people change their behavior and change the way in which they respond to situations, whereas there will always be others that attempt to limit or resist the change that the former is causing.

Balance isn't an issue of time but rather an issue of choice. It's about living your values by aligning your behavior with what you believe is really important. Let's look at what we are trying to balance. There are three main components in this balancing act: people, culture, and process.

Change as we know it demands a response. This response is generally a decision that needs to be made in reaction to the change. Making the decisions that are necessary for change to occur requires facts, data, and information, which all help in the process.

One of the major challenges, however, is to know what to do with the said information, how to reference and correlate it, and how to make plausible decisions based on them that can prove to be successful. Being limited to problem spaces for proposing solutions, we have become reliant on ready-made decisions because our perception of survival is not multifaceted and is based on a single dimension. This is what causes organizational agility to be reduced and also places limits on the value of the organization.

Businesses invest a huge amount of resources on massive change management programs, with the objective of preventing potential problems in the transformation process and to make the company or organization as agile as possible. In many situations, however, these companies and businesses have no idea how a transformed organization is even supposed to look. Even if these companies, organizations, businesses, and corporations have some sort of a vision for their future, they often do not know how to implement the change that is necessary or have any concept about how they need to approach change management.

One important thing to note about change management is that a major production factor of today is human talent. This means that it is imperative for businesses and organizations to invest in humans instead of being focused on the capital and revenue being generated alone.

While the power of the shareholder is being reinforced by the law, capital is still an integral part of the working of every organization and business. More than anything else, this creates problems for corporate management. Even if change is necessary and cannot be worked around, as soon as prices of shares drop, the vulnerability increases. This leaves CEOs and other people in managerial positions in a problematic situation as the focus is inevitably shifted to shareholders and capital instead of human talent.

In most cases, management of organizational performance and change is viewed by organizations as a linear environment. This, however, is not the best approach when it comes to change management. This is primarily because a major portion of performance goals and objectives that impact the management and all of its processes do not fit the linear model.

Using a linear approach for performance management, therefore, will not be successful and is not one of the wisest decisions to make. As mentioned in the previous chapter, reality is not linear, and there are a lot more aspects and domains to a **V**olatile, **U**ncertain, **C**omplex, and **A**mbiguous (VUCA) business environment than one might consider.

For this reason, it is imperative to ask a few major questions. As businesses and corporations try to become more agile, it is important to ask whether success involves making sure that you do not practice the same processes that were relied upon the year before.

What if the business environment is not stable, and therefore a sequence or known formula that worked yesterday is not a guarantee of success next month or next year? What if responding to a change is, with all of its unpredictability, more closely tied to success than dutifully working your plan toward the big objectives? What if you can't respond to the process and update information fast enough because of the challenges of information management?

Managing change requires balancing between strategy and operations. The most effective way to deal with uncertainty contained in strategy development is to have a balancing process that constantly confronts the unknown and creates a new change. Organizations should establish a connection between problem resolution and expected outcome!

- What's changing or what needs to change in your organization?
- What factors external to your organization are causing you to make these changes (e.g., lost market share, reduced product life, increased competition)?
- What difficulties have you encountered in making changes?
- What are your organization's strengths and weaknesses?

Even though change management is extremely important, and all companies, businesses, and organizations need to understand how change must be responded to, responding over-efficiently to the wrong type of change can be a problem as well. Ancient Chinese philosopher and author, Lao Tzu, summed up change and how it must be responded to in the best way possible.[4]

As I researched and prepared not only for my future lectures in my MBA strategy classes but also for my meeting with Bill, I learned that the renowned philosopher was of the opinion that a large country should be governed like one cooks a small fish—stirring too often will make it come apart.[5]

The same thing can be said about corporations as well, I thought to myself. As with countries, for companies, spending too much time and effort on the wrong changes is also something that should never be done. Doing this will not just affect the company, corporation, or organization in a negative way. People are bound to resist these types of changes and all further changes as well. In addition, it could be dangerous in many ways, causing a number of underlying problems that will probably only be realized once it is too late.

Seeing what Lao Tzu thought about governing countries[6] and how the concept could be applied to corporations immediately reminded me of the lecture that I had delivered just a few days ago in my strategy class. It was particularly interesting to see how unique and creative these governors and leaders were in their thinking and how even something that sounds very bizarre and completely unrelated could be used to make references or draw parallels to the current scenario.

This immediately reminded me of my conversation with Bill. Perhaps the changes that his company was trying to make were unnecessary. Even though the thought crossed my mind more than once, I still couldn't muster the courage to give my former student a call, simply because I was afraid that he would take my concern in the wrong way. Considering how frustrated Bill already was, he would probably even go as far as cancelling our meeting altogether if he felt like something was out of place or if something gave him the idea that I was feeling sorry for him.

As these thoughts crossed my mind, I realized that the conversation the other day had ended so haphazardly that we had not even decided when and where we would meet to discuss the problems that Bill was facing at his job and, ultimately, in his life. I also wanted to discuss the possibility of the wrong type of change being implemented or that change was being implemented or suggested in his company for all of the wrong reasons. However, I still didn't call him to talk about any of this or anything else.

Another great suggestion by Lao Tzu regarding change management and the acceptance of change was that people should not be disturbed without reason or unnecessarily if one wishes to govern a country successfully. He believed that a good government does not make many policies or issue many orders, which is why the people of that country remain at peace. The country is run in such a way that the entire process appears to be very natural to the people, and they do not have problems with whatever happens.[7] This wise piece of advice should also be applied to corporations, businesses, and companies that wish to adapt to change but fail to do so successfully.

Going back to the example of the company that was mentioned earlier on in this book, imposing new rules and regulations isn't the solution that should be resorted to. In fact, imposing rules and policies that employees are not happy with is a recipe for disaster and is bound to cause chaos. Unfortunately, this is another one of the factors that is completely ignored when companies are embarking on their journeys of transformation and trying to get ahead of the game.

Much like me, Bill experienced the realization a little too late. Once, when I was doing my studying and research for an early morning class and finalizing the lecture that I would deliver, my phone started to ring. The calls came at times that were quite unusual. Initially, I got a bit startled, but I eventually had a feeling that it might be Bill. As always, my phone was in the other room while I was busy studying and browsing through countless web pages, gathering as much information as I possibly could from all of the books that I had available to me.

As soon as I reached the phone, I realized that I was right all along. "Hi. I knew it would be you," I said, smiling ear to ear as I picked up the phone. The fact of the matter was that I really wanted to speak to him about a lot of things and was holding back on checking on him for quite a few days now.

"I'm glad you called," I continued. And it wasn't a lie. I was certainly glad that he was doing all right and decided to call me.

"Hey professor," the familiar voice replied, "I'm glad you picked up this time." He sounded particularly cheery.

"Who else could it have been at an hour this odd?" I joked.

"I'm sorry, professor," he replied politely. "You know how it is at work these days. This is the only time when I'm not flooded neck deep in projects, deadlines, and proposals, so I decided to give you a call. How's everything going?" he continued.

"I know, I know. Don't mind me, I was just kidding. All is great at my end. How are things going with you, Bill?" I wanted to ask him how things were going at work, but I decided to be a little more discreet in my questions.

"It's all the same, Joe," his cheery tone suddenly disappeared. "In fact, I don't think it will change anytime soon. I would be extremely lucky if it did. We all would be. As expected, other colleagues are as bored and frustrated as I am. But I'm surprised that some are still completely all right with the way in which things are going. It's unbelievable, really."

Once again, he had started becoming vocal about his problems.

"I thought everyone here would be on the same page, but that's apparently not the case. There are still some people who are ready to put in the effort that the company requires—and more! Can you believe it? It's just absurd if you ask me. Nothing is going as planned. In fact, there really isn't any plan that we can rely on. The company and all of the employees are going in all directions. It's chaotic and crazy!"

From what I understood, Bill must have been extremely excited to be working at his company at one point, but the way in which things had gone haywire, practically overnight, caused him to change his mind. He probably even regretted his decision of applying for the job and accepting the offer letter in the first place.

Unfortunately, however, I knew for a fact that he wasn't the only one who thought that way. Millions of individuals in the corporate sector share the same feelings as Bill. The initial excitement that people throughout the world have of landing their first job or their dream job fades almost as quickly as it kicked in. And it really isn't the fault of the individuals.

No one is certain about what to expect from a certain company, business, organization, or corporation before they join, and they can only have high hopes for landing the job. It is only after accepting the offer and living through the environment of said organizations, corporations, or companies that people actually realize how much is wrong with their dream jobs and working environments.

Once you start working at an organization or company, you begin to understand the mistakes that are being made in the environment. There will always be certain people who are on the same page as you, but others will always feel like the company and whoever is in charge or in managerial or leadership positions is making the right decisions just because they have the authority.

In fact, more often than not, people in managerial roles and leadership positions tend to misuse this very trust and belief that people have in them for making the right decisions and end up exercising their own opinions regardless of whether these decisions will be positive for the company or in the best interest of the people and employees of the company.

I thought of explaining all of this to Bill, but it would be too much to convince him about all of this on the phone. Besides, I could never be certain whether he would understand all of this at an hour so late—and not in person. Once again, I thought better of it and let the thought pass. I knew exactly why he had called me. We would be meeting soon enough as it was. It would probably be best to save all of these discussions for later.

"I know exactly what you mean and understand your frustration. It's completely valid," I reassured him. After all, reassurance and lending an ear to all he had to say was all that I could offer at the time.

"Yeah . . . that reminds me, we're still meeting right?" Bill continued. He finally got to the point of the phone call. I was surprised he actually stalled about it and made small talk for so long.

"Of course we are. In fact, I was thinking of giving you a call about that just a few minutes ago."

Bill started laughing. "Yeah, I'm sorry I was so caught up at work and all that I completely forgot to ask you when you're free. The conversation ended without deciding a time and place the last time I called you. It crossed my mind a few times at work as well, but then I got caught up with something or the other again."

I accepted his apology and told him that I was mostly free except for the classes that I had to take. He asked me for my schedule and we finally reached a conclusion.

A few days after the phone call with Bill, we finally met at a small local restaurant in my neighborhood. The restaurant itself was nothing too fancy but that didn't matter much—we were there to have an important discussion and couldn't care less about the food at that time. Besides, the location was convenient and the food wasn't that bad after all.

We decided to meet at 1 p.m. on a Tuesday. Much to my surprise, the weather that day was exactly as it had been during our first meeting. There had been a thunderstorm the night before, and showers continued for the rest of the day.

When I entered the restaurant a few minutes after 1 p.m., I was glad to see that my friend was already there. Punctual as always, he was seated at one of the tables at the corner of the restaurant and faced the wall. It wasn't too difficult to recognize him when there was only one other occupied table.

"Hello there!" I said as I put my hand on his shoulder. I knew that he was very worried about his situation and how things were going at work, so I tried to spread as much positivity as I could. "Sorry I'm late."

He stole a glance at his watch before he could reply. "Oh no, professor. I'm just glad you made it," he said, feigning a smile—a smile that was unable to hide the panic on his face. "How are you?"

"I'm good, thanks. But we're not here to talk about me today, are we?" I smiled at him warmly.

"Yes, yes. I know. I'm sorry. Just trying to make small talk, I guess," he confessed, smiling himself this time.

"I don't understand what I'm supposed to do professor—"

"Not even after that phone call the other night?" I joked.

He laughed. "No, I mean . . . why do organizations so large make such stupid decisions? I just don't understand!" he continued in a more serious tone.

"I guess that's what I'm here for today," I said smiling.

"I think you didn't completely understand what I was trying to explain to you the other day," I continued. "Let's start with the basics now. Most people in the corporate sector do not understand why change is necessary or required. They believe things are perfectly fine the way they are going. They will solve the next problem that arises with a temporary fix. You remember the advertisement we saw at the airport the other day?"

Bill nodded. "Yes. But that's not the way I think. I feel like there has to be something that can be done. Temporary fixes aren't the solution. They only work for a certain amount of time until another temporary solution is proposed."

I smiled. "I agree. I know that you aren't like the rest of them. But the problem here is that you can't do anything to change an entire organization all by yourself—and when you know for a fact that they are not on the same page as you and do not recognize the need for change.

"Change is pervasive. There is no denying that. Anyone who has the power of developing and proposing effective strategies knows that change is continuous in every type of environment, especially when the environment is as uncertain and intricate as that of our organizations and businesses these days.

"When talking about the environment that is changing, it is true that this term applies to both the internal environment of organizations and the external environment in which they exist. For the sake of simplifying things, let's assume that the external change is called environmental change and the internal change within an organization is called organizational change. With that said, it is important for leaders and managers to understand when the changes in the environment should be responded to with subsequent responsive changes within the organization itself.

"Now, let's say you speak to the managers or leaders in your organization and tell them that the employees on lower levels are not happy with the way in which things are going at the company and suggest certain changes—whether those changes are important is a debate for another time. It is probable that they will laugh in your face and condescendingly ask why you think there is a need for change. This isn't because they are mocking your opinion or questioning your logic. In fact, they will have this unexpected and unprecedented response only because they don't know any better themselves.

"Change is all about survival. The problem that we face in today's environments is that the changes are not temporary. Had that been the case, it wouldn't matter even if the organizational changes were slow. This is because if an organization was unable to keep up with the temporary changes of the environment, it certainly would have struggled for a limited amount of time after which things would go back to normal. Now, with all of the developments in science and technology constantly changing the environment of every industry in the world, it is also imperative for the workforce to develop new skills, which is a requirement for today's organizations.

"Unlike the in the past, when it was still relatively sane for organizations to question whether they should implement change and when it should come into effect, organizations in today's world need to adapt as quickly as possible to ensure that they do not become irrelevant. But the problem here remains that change can be perceived in several different ways, depending on your environment.

"Some may view change as a condition and the resulting process of the said condition, while others may worry about whether the said change needs to be planned or unplanned. Then, there will be others who wonder whether change is strategic or tactical, and another group may question the evolutionary process of change."

Bill looked at me with a puzzled expression on his face. "I'm sorry to interrupt, but what do you mean by these perceptions of change? Isn't change the same for everything and everyone?"

"I knew you would ask me that question." I smiled. "Allow me to explain. Let's start with planned and unplanned change. You do understand that change can be planned beforehand, if the leader or manager of the organization is proactive, right?"

Bill nodded but said nothing. I wanted a verbal response but it didn't come. It was evident that he had started thinking deeply about the topic at hand, once again. Not only was he anxious, but Bill was also more uncertain about his decision than ever before. Since I wanted to hear his thoughts on planned change, I said nothing either. He understood exactly what that meant.

"I agree with you on the fact that change can be planned, and I would like to add that it's completely necessary. In fact, we wouldn't be having this conversation over here right now if that were not the case," Bill said, almost as if he was being forced to respond. I understood that he wasn't interested in talking much that day, and so I started giving him the information he wanted, which was why he had called me to meet him at the little restaurant where we were now seated.

"I'm glad we have the same views about planning change and its necessity," I replied. "The fact of the matter, however, is that whether you plan change or it is unplanned, there is a likelihood of both types of change being good and bad. Unplanned change is often just a reaction to certain factors that were neither anticipated nor could be seen. For that reason, it is almost impossible to figure out what caused unplanned change, and in some cases it might even be difficult to find out how or why the change was initiated in the first place."

Once again, Bill said nothing. This time, however, he was listening to what I had to say much more intently, and the panic and anxiety that were previously visible on his face had started to fade away. Since he didn't respond verbally again, I took the opportunity to continue with what I had to say about planned and unplanned change. After all, the conversation was more about my perspective on these topics than it was about how he would react to what I had to say.

"Planned change, as you might already know, is much different," I continued. "Unlike unplanned change, there is always a lot of thought that goes into planned change. After seeing the way in which the business environment is progressing, managers or those in leadership positions often end up strategizing and planning effectively to ensure that they are making the right decisions for the sake of the company, business, or organization that they are handling.

"Another way to put this is that planned change essentially deals with the relevancy of the organization of the business in question and ensures that it does not lose its spark and that it continues to make a mark when the business environment is full of pressures."

"So, you mean to say that environmental change and planned organizational change go hand in hand?" Bill finally spoke.

"I feel like you are generalizing things a bit too much here," I responded. "What you said may be true to some extent, but that is not always the case. As I said before, you can never really know what caused unplanned change. It is always possible that unplanned change is caused by certain changes in the environment itself, but there is no definitive way to pinpoint whether that is the case."

"All right, I see what you mean," Bill responded.

I really liked his response and decided to continue. "Great. Now coming back to your question about the perceptions of change and how they differ, the difference between planned and unplanned change was just a minor example of the types of change that exist and what causes them. Another great distinction about the types of change is that between those who view change as tactical and those who view change in a completely different light altogether.

"Tactical change is often short lived. This short-lived type of change is often associated with dealing with a single problem and responding to it with a short-term solution. As long as the problem is being dealt with in the moment, those who view change as a tactical weapon are fine with it.

"Strategic change, on the other hand, is much more complex, elaborate, and comprehensive. Strategic change involves analyzing the vision, culture, and direction of the organization or company where change is required and finding solutions from there. As complex as this type of change is, it won't be simple.

"One of the first and foremost requirements of strategic change is that the current reality of both the organization and the environment in which the organization lives must be understood completely. Unless this happens, it is practically impossible for strategic change to be implemented successfully and effectively.

"Once the environment and its native complications, limitations, changes, and pressures are completely understood and evaluated, the agility of the organization or company in which change is being implemented can be forged to ensure that it remains relevant in the face of even the most extreme challenges and changes."

"I think I lost you at agility," Bill said, without hesitation. This is another one of the qualities of Bill that I admired. He was never hesitant or thought twice before asking for help or clarification on something that he did not understand. Since the time when he was in my MBA classes, I was more than happy to clear his confusions. He always asked very clear questions whenever he had any problems with understanding something and never asked questions in vain.

"Let me explain. What I meant by the agility of a company or organization is its ability and capacity to foresee changes in the environment and act in a way that the change is not only adapted to but also responded to effectively to ensure that the organization has an edge above its competitors.

"Maintaining agility is extremely important when it comes to uncertain environments and those that are susceptible and prone to constant changes. Remember how I said strategic change is much more complicated than tactical changes? The maintenance of agility is why I said that.

"Maintaining and improving the agility of a business, company, or organization is a lot more complicated than you might imagine. The process can be seen in three different ways or divided into three subtasks. Regardless of how you wish to view them, however, all three of these ways or subtasks depend on each other.

"First of all, as mentioned earlier, the values, beliefs, and vision of the organization must be elaborately understood to ensure that nothing is missed when you are strategically planning to adapt and respond to the changes of the environment.

"You may also have to question the beliefs or values of your organization to maintain the agility and plan strategically to adapt to the changes of the environment. Having the freedom to question the beliefs and assumptions of your own organization or company does not only mean that you will be able to make decisions that are best for the organization but also guarantee the agility of the organization or company, ensuring that it can respond to changes in a positive manner.

"Secondly, it is essential for the organization or business in question to be self-sufficient in terms of resources. More often than not, a large investment is required to successfully implement strategic change, and it is impossible to maintain the agility of the organization without the required resources.

"The last—and perhaps the most important—aspect of maintaining the agility of an organization involves managing credibility with the strategic constituencies."

I took a long pause and waited for Bill to ask questions but none came. Although he was generally very vocal about his opinions and what he was thinking about, he said nothing for a long time. Although I anticipated a question from his end, what Bill responded with didn't shock me at all.

"This is exactly what the problem is, Joe."

He knew all of this too well.

Bill had experienced the effects of poor strategic management and complacency first hand at his job. These were all of the reasons why he had decided to quit his job in the first place. Not only was the management at his firm adamant about following the same techniques and continuing to work in the same way year after year, but even the methods they chose to encourage and convince employees to adapt to the environment, respond to change effectively and efficiently, and be the pioneers of change within the organization had nothing innovative or creative about them.

In all of his off-site meetings, Bill was tired of hearing the same things over and over again, and it was now that he realized, for the first time ever, that his company not only failed to plan strategically but was also unable to maintain agility.

"I know, Bill. I understood all of this the first time you started telling me about your company and job when we met at the airport the other day, and since then, the only thing I've wanted to do is speak to you about this problem.

As I said before, if I were in your place, I would probably be thinking of and considering the same things as you are at this point."

"I just don't understand how they will ever be able to survive with this attitude. It isn't like things can change overnight. Besides, I'm sure that a lot of my colleagues think the same way as I do. I just don't understand what I'm supposed to do at that place anymore. Even if I do try to be the *pioneer of change*, as they want me to, I doubt it will make any difference. They are all just stubborn and adamant about keeping things going the way they have been for so long," Bill said, as he held his face in his hands.

"I'm not sure about your other colleagues, but there's one thing that I'd like to disagree with you on," I responded.

He looked straight at me. Evidently enough, he wasn't expecting me to respond with negativity or disagreement when he was venting about his problems in life—the reason why we had decided to meet at the restaurant.

"What are you talking about?" he snapped back at me.

"I understand that you are frustrated and angry at the system and how your company has not been able to adapt to the environment in years, but I will disagree with you on the part where you said that they can't change overnight."

Bill was now confused and the emotion, as usual, did not fail to show on his face. He waited for me to continue for awhile before he finally asked, "What do you mean you disagree?"

I responded with one of the most important aspects of change management: The nature of change must be understood to ensure that the right decisions are being made.

"So we've already talked about planned and unplanned change," I reiterated, "but change can also be evolutionary or revolutionary. What this means is that change can either take place within the existing system, or it can come in the form of a dramatic shift to an entirely different system altogether."

The fact of the matter is that organizational change, much like environmental change, can be quick or very slow, depending on the factors that are involved. Depending on whether the change in the organization that is being talked about is evolutionary or revolutionary, the change will manifest itself in the organization in different ways.

Most people, however, are unable to recognize the difference between the two and their consequences, which is why they end up disregarding the fact that there is a substantial difference between evolutionary and revolutionary change.

Evolutionary change, as the name suggests, occurs progressively. Needless to say, evolutionary change is much slower than revolutionary change and is often characterized by smaller sequential or linear changes. What this means is that evolutionary change involves smaller changes that come one after the other. One problem with evolutionary change, however, is that when these changes come into effect, it is common for competitors to be able to guess what is going on since the slow and gradual nature of evolutionary change and small changes following each other are sure telltale signs that something is going on.

When a company, business, or organization is trying to implement evolutionary change, people often have a say in the change. However, regardless of whether people have a say, one benefit of implementing evolutionary change is that people have the time and capacity to adapt to the changes being made because they are all slow and gradual.

Additionally, although leaders and those in managerial positions are in the loop even with evolutionary change, they cannot be called the pioneers of the change. Rather, they are just rooting for the company or organization in question instead, hoping that the change will be for the better.

Revolutionary change, on the other hand, is completely different altogether. Revolutionary change, unlike its evolutionary counterpart, is sudden and often dramatic. When talking about revolutionary change, it would not be incorrect to say that revolutionary change is almost synonymous with a completely thorough and elaborate transformation of the company, business, or organization in which the change is being implemented.

The best part about revolutionary change is that its magnitude can vary. What this means is that revolutionary change could be caused by something that was incredibly small and would probably even be insignificant in any other setting, or it could large and sweeping.

Another factor of revolutionary change is that, unlike evolutionary change, it is not very easy for competitors or those in the industry to predict what is going on because the change is implemented practically overnight. It is, however, possible for revolutionary change to be recognized by employees and those within the company, business, or organization itself if it is properly thought through and worked out.

Communication, too, is extremely important for revolutionary organizational change. Since this type of change often comes as a surprise to people, it is common for them to take a lot of time to adapt to the changes that are being made or implemented. Naturally, the longer it takes for employees and those within the organization to understand and adapt to the changes that are being made and implemented, the longer it will take for them to make sane decisions and act in a way that can be considered responsible and necessary for the change. In other words, without proper communication, it will take much longer for employees to respond and behave in a suitable manner after the revolutionary change process.

Another difference between evolutionary and revolutionary change is that when talking about revolutionary change, the leaders and those in managerial positions in the company, business, or organization where the change is being implemented have a lot of say in the changes that are being made. Since revolutionary change is highly dependent on the decisions and opinions of leaders and those in managerial positions, revolutionary change could take anywhere from a day to a few weeks.

Unlike revolutionary change, however, employees and other people who are not in leadership positions in the company do not have a lot of say in how the change is implemented or how it will come about. When talking about revolutionary change, these decisions are often for those higher up in the hierarchy to make, and there is generally no way to work around them or such changes or improvisations.

I tried explaining all of this to Bill in as simple a way as I could, and after a few cross questions, he understood the point that I was trying to make. Regardless of this, however, he still had one question that he had been hesitant to ask for a long time.

"Which type of change do you think is better for the organizations of today?" he finally asked, with apparent curiosity on his face. He was probably holding back on asking me the question because he probably thought that it was something too straightforward to ask and perhaps he didn't want to look like a fool in front of his former teacher, who had now become a friend and a person he could—and would—often run to for advice.

The answer to this question, however, is not as simple as it may seem.

"The fact is that to determine which of these two types of change—namely, revolutionary change and evolutionary change—are better for a company, business, or organization, it is extremely important to assess the conditions and factors that are involved.

"This not only includes environmental factors and any changes that are being made in the environment but also factors within the organization itself. Given the right factors and under the right circumstances, both evolutionary and revolutionary changes have the potential to be good strategic choices.

"The environmental conditions that need to be considered include the mass, velocity, and complexity of the expected or anticipated change or the change that has already begun to be implemented. The velocity of change can be defined as the rate at which the change is occurring. As mentioned earlier, this can either be slow or fast, depending on the type of change that is chosen as well as many other factors.

"Next comes the mass of the change. The mass of the change can be defined as how widespread the change is. Lastly, since change is never independent and always affects many other things, the complexity of the change could be referred to as a measure of the other changes that occur as a result of the change that is being talked about."

After listening to all of this, even though there was not much that Bill said, it was obvious that he was trying to take in every word I said and was assessing the different types of change that I had mentioned throughout my conversation with the young lad that afternoon. Neither of us spoke for awhile, and after an unsettling silence, Bill finally told me what he had wanted to say since the first time I met him at the airport.

"You know what, Joe?" Bill said, "I can't seem to disagree with a single word that you said, but I think I finally understand what the problem is. I feel trapped when I'm at work, and I can't be expected to feel any other way.

"All of these types of changes that you spoke about, I understand that there is a lot of difference between every single one of them. But I think that, to some extent, thought needs to be put into the changes that are being implemented in any company, business, or organization. What happened at my workplace was that even though there was a transformation, no one had taken the time to think about or plan in advance for the consequences."

This is exactly what I had tried telling him from the first day we met, but I am glad that he figured it out for himself and was able to put things together without having me spell it out for him. As intelligent as he was, it didn't surprise me that he was able reach these conclusions by himself.

Since the day I met him at the airport, I had tried to explain to him that the approach that his company was following was not correct. What his company failed to understand was that change can come from a number of different directions—be it technology, political situations, education, new social norms, or even the law.

However, regardless of whether the origin of said changes can be traced back to a ripple caused by a change in the strategic environment, the planning room of a multinational corporation, or the tirelessly working mind of a young CEO, the fact remains that there will always be certain reactions that are directly linked to the culture of the organization in question.

Unfortunately, however, as much as one may hate to admit it, the reactions that are seen in the wake of the change innately strive toward delaying, derailing, or stalling the change that is being implemented.

Since people commonly fail to realize this aspect of change management, changes that could seamlessly be implemented and incorporated within the setting of the company, business, or organization in question in the minds of the instigators of these changes often end up failing. Luckily for many, taking the right measures proactively can help to mitigate the risk of failure involved in the implementation and widespread acceptance of change.

Before change is implemented, it is extremely important to know the pitfalls of the organization, business, or company in which change is being introduced. Additionally, it is also equally important to know where these pitfalls lie. Even though some of these pitfalls are extremely common, people fail to realize and acknowledge them simply due to the lack of education about the pitfalls themselves.

One of the most common problems that are seen in companies, businesses, and organizations throughout the world when they are trying to implement change is the fact that they try to find and implement a solution for a problem that is nonexistent. What this means is that when you are trying to find and introduce a solution (in the form of a new change in the environment of the company, business, or organization) for a problem that is either nonexistent or isn't defined elaborately enough, there is a high likelihood that the change that is being introduced will fail.

Another reason why change is seen to fail is because large businesses, companies, or organizations are not particularly fond of changing their course. Since people are generally comfortable with working in a certain way and do not like any changes in the way in which they carry out day-to-day tasks and activities at work and otherwise, businesses, companies, and organizations that are trying to implement change end up failing to overcome the status quo, despite a great deal of efforts and energy being expended by the leader or manager in charge of the change.

The fact of the matter is that even when people understand that change is needed and that the current approach that is being followed isn't optimal or ideal in any way, they prefer the circumstances that they are familiar with compared to problems and complications that will manifest themselves in the wake of the change that is being introduced.

Another one of the most common problems in organizations, businesses, and companies throughout the world that are trying to implement change is that people are not ready to accept the change that leaders and managers are trying to introduce unless the change in question serves their personal interests in some way or form.

This means that if people do not see any personal benefit that they can gain from the introduction and implementation of change, chances are that they won't be ready to assist these changes. In fact, in some cases, people might even attempt to derail the changes that the company, business, or organization is trying to implement because they don't see how the change will prove to be advantageous to them.

In other situations, if people are content and satisfied with the current approach and workings of the organization, business, or company that they belong to, they will try to stall change for as long as possible, even if the change would be better for the organization as a whole.

Leaders and managers also fail to realize that change can only be implemented after certain conditions have been met. Since all changes are best implemented at a certain time and place, it is up to the leader or manager responsible for the implementation of the change to choose the right time for the introduction and implementation of the change. It is important to introduce the change slowly and gradually whenever possible, and to try to make the change appear to be something that is necessary and beneficial for the people.

As mentioned earlier, if people find that change is not necessary or that it will disrupt the working of the business, company, or organization, they will resist the change no matter what it takes.

Additionally, if people fear that the change that is being implemented will be overwhelming, you will find most of your employees getting defensive and trying to keep things going in the manner that they have grown accustomed to for as long as possible. This problem can be prevented by scheduling the change sensibly and sharing information with your employees in a way that guarantees that they will be satisfied with the change that you are trying to implement.

In most cases, the best way to go about introducing and implementing change is by making sure that the said change is being introduced incrementally. This means that instead of giant leaps, one should try to make sure that the changes being implemented comprise a number of small steps and goals that can be met without overwhelming the employees and other people involved in the business, company, or organization in question. Incremental changes are not only easier to implement, but they are also more readily accepted by people.

Additionally, since people love seeing results, one should make sure that the change being implemented provides many small payoffs that employees and other individuals in the company, business, or organization can view as incentives. These payoffs will not only ensure that the change is readily accepted, but the possibility of people looking forward to further change is also greatly increased.

Voltaire summed up the resistance of change perfectly in his timeless words, "It is difficult to free fools from chains they revere."[8] This goes to show that regardless of the era or context in which change is being implemented, the fact remains that complications will always arise unless the change is implemented strategically, efficiently, and effectively.

The concept of change and its implementation goes far beyond a vision statement that most people have reduced it to. To successfully introduce and implement change, one must effectively scan the environment, make estimations and calculations of the current situation, and determine the problems that exist with the current course of action.

Additionally, it is also extremely important for you to figure out which direction the business, organization or company needs to move in and look forward to, to know how to leverage the current scenario effectively and decide the complete process for scheduling and implementing the change effectively and in a manner that ensures that it will be accepted instead of resisted.

Leaders must be educated about the different aspects of change and the pitfalls that cause change to fail. Unless leaders are trained by experienced professionals, companies will never be able to reach the level of agility that the VUCA world demands.

One more thing that must be remembered at all times is that the human element is of significant importance when you are trying to transform any business, company, or organization. In other words, change can never be implemented successfully by ignoring the human element. Since all types of change directly impact the employees of a business, company, or organization in one way or the other, it is important to consider the effects of the change on the employees involved in the environment, first and foremost, to ensure that the change isn't faced with resistance in any way that can affect the stability of the environment.

> There is an old story that makes the point well.
>
> At a gathering of rabbis, the wise men were debating a passage of holy law. One rabbi found that he was in disagreement with the rest of a group on a point of implementation. The others put great pressure on him to concede, but he knew that he was right and that God would be on his side. So he called upon the Almighty to help him to prove his case. "Please, God, if I am right, let the streams of Israel flow uphill," the rabbi begged. Immediately, the waters of the land changed direction. Unfortunately, his adversaries were unmoved.
>
> "Please God," the rabbi asked again, "if I am right, may the trees bend to the ground." And they did. But his fellows were unmoved.
>
> "Dear God," the rabbi called out in growing frustration, "may you speak aloud and support me in this painful dispute." The clouds parted and a great voice from heaven boomed: "Rabbis, hear my words—you others are wrong and this man is right. Such is my will and intention."
>
> The lone sage smiled in triumph, but the group remained unimpressed. "Oh, we pay no attention to heavenly voices," they said. "After all, the correct determination on this point was written down long ago."[9]

This story says it all.

References

1. Allen, Woody. (1980). *Side Effects*. New York: Random House.
2. Parinello, Anthony. (2005). *Getting to VITO*. Hoboken (NJ): John Wiley & Sons, Inc.
3. Boland, Richard, Jr. and Collopy, Fred. (2004). *Managing as Designing*. Stanford Business Books.
4. Lao Tzu. (n.d.). *The Tao Te Ching* (Translated by Gia Fu Feng & Jane English). Retrieved from http://www.dankalia.com/more/taoteching.pdf

5. Ibid.
6. Lao Tzu. (1963). *Te-Tao Ching*. New York: Penguin Books.
7. Ibid.
8. Voltaire. (2016, October 28). Quote. Blog by Frank O'Meara. Retrieved from https://blindfaithblindfolly.wordpress.com/2016/10/28/it-is-difficult-to-free-fools-from-the-chains-they-revere/comment-page-1/
9. Raynus, Joseph. (2011). *Improving Business Process Performance: Gain Agility, Create Value, and Achieve Success*. Boca Raton (FL): CRC Press.

Chapter 5

Searching in Strategic Leadership

Business environments of today are nothing like they were in the past, which is one of the reasons why agility has become such a necessity in today's world. One of the major problems in today's corporate environments lies in the fact that most businesses, companies, and organizations are making poor decisions, even when it is evident that the consequences of these decisions will be detrimental. Most companies today, for instance, have started showing interest in acquisitions and mergers, which are visibly bad ideas.

The failure rate for mergers and acquisitions, or M&As, is anywhere from 40% to 80%. That means that most deals fail to achieve the strategic aims for which they were initiated. They make money only for the lawyers who conduct them.[1] A similar study in this domain, carried out three years later (in 2017), showed that 70% of these mergers or acquisitions fail.[2]

A KPMG study[3] indicates that 83% of merger deals did not boost shareholder returns. George Bradt suggests that this is because of mismanagement of risk, price, strategy, cultures, or management capacity.[4]

The statistics mentioned above are disturbing. Considering the aforementioned data, only one out of three mergers or acquisitions succeed. Even though this sounds more like a gamble than a strategy, the fact remains that businesses, companies, and organizations of today are still resorting to this option when things start to go haywire with their own management.

Mergers and acquisitions change a lot more than just the management. When a business, company, or organization opts for a merger or acquisition, change is seen in everything—from the way in which decisions are made to the process that the company uses to plan and strategize. In most cases, when mergers and acquisitions fail, it can not only damage the company at its very core, but it can also affect the human community of the company or organization in an extremely negative way.

The fact of the matter is that most people are fully aware that managerial changes such as acquisitions and mergers dehumanize the environment of the business, company, or organization in question, but they still believe that the change will bring about some good. So why do people make such decisions, even when they understand that these changes have the potential to give birth to consequences that can be extremely dangerous for the business, company, or organization in question?

The answer lies in poor strategic management.

Corporate environments of today are characterized by cohesive and tightly knit communities that are well aware of the working and management of the business, company, or organization that is being managed. However, when leadership and management fails to act according to the requirements of the time, leaders and those in managerial positions are not left with many options except handing management over to other—often larger—companies.

As unfortunate as this sounds, countless businesses, companies, and organizations have seen their demise simply due to the lack of proper strategic management and decision making . . . and Bill's company was one of them.

The conversation at the small restaurant the other day didn't end on a positive note, and even though Bill understood what the problem with his company was and why so many other people felt the same way as he did, he was more confused about his decision than ever before. He was running late for an important meeting which is why we couldn't really reach any conclusions.

Regardless of whether he stuck to his decision to quit his job, he would need a game plan before he made any decisions, and that is what he needed my help for, as professional who has dealt with countless other people going through the same situations, and as a friend.

Even though Bill had clearly mentioned that he wanted to quit his job, and I reassured him by telling him that I would do the same in a situation like that, I personally felt that Bill needed more time to think about what was going on. This is why I wasn't too sad about the conversation ending haphazardly the other day. I was certain that Bill wouldn't make any impulsive decisions and would wait to discuss his options with me.

Since our conversation had to end the other day without reaching any real conclusions, Bill would get to spend a little more time at work and decide once and for all if he wanted to stick by his decision. At the end of our previous meeting, Bill excused himself politely and told me that he had to rush out for another meeting but that he still had more to talk about. Before he left, he asked me if I was free at the same time the following week, and I said, "Yes."

A week later, we met at the small restaurant again. The sky was clear this time, and a lot of people were out and about. As I entered the local restaurant, I noticed that there was barely anyone inside. The waiter and owner, however, were more than happy to see me.

I was surprised to see my old student in the same position as I did the same time a week earlier. He was slouched on the same seat as before, with his head in his hands. I knew exactly what that meant.

I knocked on the table lightly to break the ice a little.

"Hey, professor," Bill said without lifting his face. "I'm glad you're here."

"Of course I would be here. I couldn't leave you to yourself in a situation like this." I was genuinely getting concerned about his condition and everything he was going through.

He finally let go of his face and lifted it up to look at me. I was taken aback as his bloodshot eyes looked me in the eye. It was evident that he hadn't slept well for quite some time. He was more tense than I ever remembered seeing him.

I knew that he was in a bad place and didn't want to ask him any questions that would make things worse. But seeing him like that killed me inside. I waited for him to continue the conversation for about a minute, but he said nothing.

I figured that he wasn't in any condition to say much, so I decided to continue myself.

"How's it going," I asked instinctively and cursed myself immediately for choosing a question like that.

"How do you think it's going?" he replied, with a heavy voice. I shouldn't have expected anything less than sarcasm at this time.

I was mentally prepared for the fact that it wouldn't be easy to talk to him and that he wouldn't be very approachable, but I never imagined that his condition would have been this bad. I tried to think of something to say in response to his sarcastic question but to no avail.

Fortunately, he realized that I was becoming uneasy and decided to continue talking by himself.

"Everything is a mess. I'm so sorry I had to leave in such a hurry the other day," he continued, as courteously as he could.

I was just glad that he was finally talking.

"Not a problem. I'm guessing the week didn't go too well?" I asked.

"You bet," he responded, with a smirk that was anything but happy.

I had hoped that he would have time to think over his decision in the week before our next meeting. Evidently, something had happened at his workplace that made him more positive about his decision than ever before. By the way he looked at me, I knew that he wasn't looking for sympathy. It was reassurance that he wanted.

"So, what happened at work during the week?" I figured this would be the best question to ask him at a time like this to get him to start venting.

I was right.

As soon as Bill started telling me everything about his work week, I completely understood why he looked and sounded the way he did. As he spoke, I noticed that his face had started showing signs of aging. His eyelids were droopy, his skin was sagging, and his dark circles had become more prominent than I remembered them. The way I saw it, he had experienced many sleepless nights. As vocal as Bill was about his problems, one thing was certain: He wasn't the type of person to give in or give up without reason. And that is exactly why I was glad that he had the time to think over his decision, without being influenced by my opinion, for an entire week.

Even though he looked and felt terrible, I knew for a fact that it was extremely important for him to spend some time at his workplace and figure out exactly what was wrong. Had I imposed my opinion on him too much and forced his hand at resigning by telling him that it was the right decision to make, too often, he would probably regret it later on. Since he had the time to think about his decision and weigh his options one last time before he met me, he wouldn't have any doubts about the decision that he was making, regardless of whether he planned to stick with the company that he had worked at for so long.

And it wasn't long before Bill confessed.

After going on a small rant that was typical of every conversation that I had had with him recently, Bill came straight to the point. Even though he hated the position that he was being put in, he was grateful to me for not forcing him into anything. Bill told me that the week had gone terribly—but that much I already knew. What came as a shocker was that, amidst all the chaos and drama that was going on at his workplace, those in managerial positions had tried implementing certain new changes that were not only uncalled for but that were also extremely irrelevant.

The approach that his company was following was never right. Even when he told me about the offsite meeting that his company organized every year, I figured that the employees were not satisfied with the same "tips for success" being repeated every single time without management changing the way in which they dealt with people. The leaders and managers at Bill's company had always wanted all of the employees to be the pioneers of change, to bring about a revolution and to be as innovative and creative as possible, however, none of that was possible without changing the structure of the organization, since the fault lay in its core.

Fortunately, Bill understood that without having me spell it out for him.

I knew that Bill wasn't going through the best time in his life, but I knew that this decision would be best for him in the long term—and I'm sure he did too. To get a better understanding of the situation that Bill was experiencing, and to find out whether we were on the same page, I decided to ask him a few questions. Much as before, however, I knew that he wasn't doing too well and that anything and everything that I said had the potential to be interpreted in a negative light.

Considering the current situation, I wouldn't want to worsen anything for Bill. Besides, based on what he looked like, there was a strong chance that if he misinterpreted anything that I said and thought that I was just sympathizing with him or making fun of his situation, it would be extremely difficult to convince him otherwise.

This was a problem that I certainly didn't want to deal with at the time. But since it was important to know what he was thinking, and how he would proceed with his decision, I still decided to go ahead with asking him the questions that I had in mind. I did, however, try to the best of my ability to minimize the negative vibes that he was getting from everything and tried to frame my questions in a way that he wouldn't have anything to feel badly about.

The most important question that I had in mind was how he reached the conclusions that he was so vocal about. I did, however, realize that this wouldn't be a good question to ask as he hadn't been feeling very positive about his company since the day I had bumped into him at the airport. Instead, I asked him what he thought was wrong with the management. This was a genuine question, and even if he understood that I was simply trying to gain insight from his perspective, he probably wouldn't mind sharing his point of view.

Besides, we had spoken about the mistakes of management several times earlier as well. The only difference this time was that one of his most important decisions was related to the opinion he had about management and the shortsightedness of leaders now—especially that of the managers at his own company.

As expected, he didn't hold back regarding what he felt about his managers at all this time.

"Honestly, Joe, I feel as if they have no idea what they are doing. It seems as if they live in some parallel universe where all of their absurd decisions make perfect sense. It's beyond me how they even think of new rules and regulations and let them pass. I mean, sometimes I feel like they just get things done for the sake of doing something new in the workplace."

As soon as he said that, I knew that he wasn't buying any of it from any of his managers or leaders in the workplace anymore. I did, however, want to let him vent as much as he needed to. As exhausted as he was, it looked as if he had a lot to say, and this meeting gave him the perfect opportunity for that.

Instead of giving my two cents, I just kept nodding. Whether he understood that that was a signal for him to continue or not, I'm not sure.

But he continued talking, regardless.

"You know what? The worst part about the decisions that they make is that they aren't even ready to listen to any criticism or feedback about them. I don't know if this is a problem with every leader and manager, but I feel sorry for those who have to listen to their every decision. The managers and leaders at my company feel like they are the only ones who can make the right decisions and that everybody else is a fool. They need to understand that the human element is almost gone from the workplace."

Even though it probably came as a revelation to Bill when he thought long and hard about his workplace, I wasn't surprised that he said any of the things that he did. In fact, I was waiting for him to realize it all, and say it by himself. Most managers and other people in leadership positions often fail to understand that they are not thinking about things in the same way as employees or other people who are in positions that are lower in the hierarchy of the business, company, or organization in question do.

It is often seen that when managers or other leaders make decisions, these decisions are neither in the best interest of the business, company, or organization that they are representing nor are they a good option for people. Instead, managers and other people in leadership positions tend to misuse their power and implement strategies, rules, and policies that are based on their own personal interest. With that said, most new policies, strategies, or rules that are implemented by managers or leaders are not at all necessary and are only promoted and backed by the people who are higher in the managerial hierarchy due to personal benefits.

At other times, the managers and leaders that Bill spoke negatively about believe that they are making decisions that are indeed good for the people, even when everybody else may disagree. These people believe that their cognitive ability is unmatched and that they only got selected to "lead" or "manage" the rest of the employees at the business, company, or organization and all of their subordinates due to this ability. Fortunately, extensive psychological research has been conducted on people who exhibit these types of traits.

As soon as he took a pause (after speaking endlessly about what he thought was wrong with the managers at his company), I couldn't help but ask Bill if he was aware of the Dunning–Kruger effect.

"I know you aren't done talking yet, and I'm sorry to cut you off like this, but have you ever heard of the Dunning–Kruger effect?" I asked Bill.

"The Dunning—what?" he raised an eyebrow in curiosity. I'm sure that my question seemed to be uncalled for, especially at a time when he was venting about the problems with his workplace and everything that he thought was wrong with the managers and those in leadership positions at his company. He did, however, realize that it wasn't random and might have been important in this context.

"Dunning–Kruger," I replied.

He shook his head no.

"I wish you were still in my class," I responded jokingly. I find this concept extremely interesting and make it a point to share it with all of my students in my current MBA strategy class.

He wasn't taking my jokes very well, so I decided to continue.

"In my opinion, the Dunning–Kruger effect[5] is one of the most important studies in the field of psychology. The term refers to a cognitive bias that people suffer from. Sufferers of this cognitive bias often have low ability; however, they feel like they are above and beyond everyone else that they know or are in charge of. In other words, people who suffer from this cognitive bias have the illusion that their cognitive ability is far greater than what it actually is."

Bill listened to me as intently as he always did, as I told him about one of the most oft-repeated topics in my strategy classes. Unlike earlier, however, this time he responded as soon as I paused to take a breath.

"Wow!" he exclaimed almost immediately. "I can't believe there's actually a word for this."

"Not just a word," I corrected him. "There have been multiple studies on this condition that prove how dangerous the combination of incompetence and overconfidence can be."

"It sounds like this is exactly what all of them suffer from," he said in disdain, referring to the top management in his company.

"The worst part about people who suffer from cognitive biases like the Dunning–Kruger effect is that they won't ever be able to understand what is wrong with them. This is particularly due to a lack of self-awareness. Unless people are truly aware of their level of competence, they can never truly understand how and why they are different from the rest of the people in their surroundings."

Social psychologists David Dunning and Justin Kruger, who coined the term, have something very interesting to say about the people who suffer from this kind of bias. They were of the opinion that this cognitive bias is associated with the illusion of superiority in people of low ability and that "the mis-calibration of the incompetent stems from an error about the self, whereas the miscalibration of the highly competent stems from an error about others."[6] Interestingly enough, the opposite often holds true for people of high ability. They not only tend to underestimate their abilities but also feel as if they are not putting in enough effort and that they are incompetent.[7]

Bill was now more interested than ever before. He not only understood that the root of the problem in his company lay in poor management, but also that these poor managerial decisions probably had a reason as significant as a cognitive bias behind them.

"I think this just might be the problem," he reiterated, with a worried look in his eyes. He was certain that the best professional and personal decision for him to make was to leave this company, which had ruined so many years of his life. However, he knew for a fact that things would not be changing at his company anytime soon and that his colleagues would have to suffer from poor management and unfair decision making until they decided to throw in the towel and leave the company as well.

"Isn't there a way for it to all get better?"

"There is," I replied. "But the success or failure of the solution depends on the person who is responsible for making important decisions for the sake of the company."

"What is that supposed to mean?" my curious student asked.

"There are certain questions that every person involved in strategy needs to ask," I replied.

"What are you talking about?" replied my curious and frustrated former student.

"Leaders and other people in managerial positions need to ask themselves how they can align all levels of the organization, from top to bottom, to ensure that they are working around the same shared goals. It is practically impossible for decision makers and those in leadership or managerial positions to implement—or even think of—strategies that will be beneficial for the company, business, or organization that they are responsible for unless they understand the structure from top to bottom." Apparently, my response didn't convince Bill very much.

"They're the leaders! Aren't they already supposed to know everything about the business, company, or organization that they are making decisions for?"

Bill's rhetorical question wasn't justified, but I knew that he was too worried and frustrated to put things in perspective. Even though I had told him about the Dunning–Kruger bias only a few minutes earlier, he was too preoccupied with what had been going on at his company. Therefore, he didn't realize that while people know all about the structure of the business, company, or organization where they are leaders or managers, they fail to keep the structure in consideration when they make decisions.

I knew that I would have to be extremely patient with Bill, considering his current situation, and spell it all out for him. Once he understood why maintaining the structure of a business, company, or organization is essential, and that all levels need to be taken into consideration when making decisions, we were finally able to focus on the other questions that are important for leaders and managers to ask themselves.

"Another important question that leaders and managers need to ask themselves is how they can link the goals that they have in mind across all of the divisions or business units of the business, company, or organization that they are responsible for. Once this is out of the way, they need to start to focus on how these goals or new strategies can be kept in line with corporate strategy. This is extremely important, yet very commonly ignored when people are trying to implement new policies, strategies, or decisions in any business, company, or organization."

As unfortunate as it may sound, this problem is indeed very common. Even when people are not being selfish and trying to make decisions that are based solely on personal interest, they often tend to ignore some of the divisions of the business, company, or organization where they are implementing new strategies or policies and end up making decisions that are not in the best interest of the business, company, or organization in question.

The next most important thing that must be done when people are trying to develop or implement new strategies or policies, or process change, in any business, company, or organization is to have a clear picture of the approach that must be followed in order to ensure that all of the employees or other people in the business, company, and organization are successfully able to adapt to the changes being implemented without fighting or resisting them.

I could tell Bill all of this because I have worked with countless clients to help them quantify and define performance parameters and relate them to their organizational strategy. The problem that most people faced was that even when they tried to implement strategies and policies that were indeed good for the business, company, or organization where they were leaders or managers, business environments of today are so competitive and prone to change that as soon as one new strategy was implemented, there was a need for another strategy.

Another problem I have experienced with countless clients is that as soon as a method, technique, or way to measure performance is defined, there is a change in the strategy again. This problem has given birth to the same question over and over again. When strategies become obsolete or irrelevant almost as soon as they are approved and implemented, countless people in businesses, companies, and organizations throughout the world wonder how they can continue to be competitive and profitable in business when everything around them keeps on changing—and without any advance warning.

It is evident that the **V**olatile, **U**ncertain, **C**omplex, and **A**mbiguous (VUCA) environment has affected businesses, companies, and organizations throughout the world in several ways. Critical challenges are present in both external business environments and internal organizations.

One may feel as if there is barely enough time for the leaders and managers of a business, company, or organization to strategize and act according to the requirements of the environment. However, this time will only continue to decrease as the world grows more competitive and challenges continue to grow. As the world continues to move faster, the past, present, and future are getting closer and the speed at which one is able to make sane and relevant decisions determines the possibility of survival or extinction in the competitive world of today.

All of this was very difficult for Bill to grasp, not because he wasn't paying attention, but probably because he was too preoccupied with how things would proceed for his colleagues and friends at his workplace. I know for a fact that he had tried as much as he possibly could to come out on top, and that there were several other people at his workplace who were really ready to put in a lot of effort, but nothing really seemed to help.

At one point in the conversation, as much as he wanted to blame everything on poor management and the lack of the human element in his company, he somehow got the feeling that he probably hadn't given it his all.

"I can't help but feel like no matter how fast I ran at my workplace, it just wasn't fast enough. I just couldn't move forward, regardless of how much I tried!" he exclaimed with a shaky voice, as he lifted his head back up from the table.

For the first time all afternoon, I saw tears in Bill's eyes. He was feeling ambivalent. Even though he realized that the managers and leaders at his company were at fault and that they failed to make the right decisions more than once, he started to feel as if it was probably his incompetence that had led to the situation he was facing at work.

Although many people feel the same way as they plan to resign from their workplace, these feelings are very dangerous, especially when you are clearly in the right. People who believe—or are forced to believe—that they are incompetent or hadn't given it their all, end up feeling as if they won't be able to succeed no matter where they go. Since I knew that Bill could easily develop this attitude, I knew for a fact that I had to act fast to save him from eternally thinking ill of himself and cursing himself for "not trying hard enough."

"Why would everybody else at your workplace feel the same way as you about the company if it was only you at fault?" I asked.

It didn't help. He wasn't ready to listen to anything. Bill started to raise his voice and got really agitated.

"I'm sorry," he said with a fake smile. "I don't know about everyone else. I just feel like I probably could have—I probably should have—tried harder than I did at work. Maybe that's what they really wanted. Maybe that's the only reason why they kept asking all of us to work harder and be the pioneers of change in the company. That was all they wanted. If I had tried harder, they would be satisfied with my work and with all of the efforts that I had made. I guess it's too late for all of that now."

Fortunately, after a lot of convincing, he was finally able to snap out of that negative mentality, and he stopped blaming himself for everything that had happened.

As difficult as dealing with the situation was, I wasn't surprised that he was acting the way he did. He had been through a lot at his workplace, especially during this last week. Besides, making a decision as big as leaving, especially when you have spent years in a certain place and have grown accustomed to it, can be extremely difficult.

The mood had become extremely tense, and even though Bill was no longer blaming himself for everything that had happened, I was still very worried about him. Resigning from his workplace would be the best decision for him to make, as all of the stress had taken a toll on his mental health and well-being to the extent that he broke down in front of his former professor. To lighten up the mood a bit, I decided to quote Lewis Carroll's famous masterpiece, *Through the Looking Glass*.

You know what they say," I said to Bill, quoting the Red Queen from this book, "[I]t takes all the running you can do to keep in the same place. If you want to get somewhere else, you must run at least twice as fast as that!"[8]

Bill smiled for the first time that day, and I couldn't have been happier. "I think I'm ready," he said.

I couldn't help but walk over to his side of the table to give him a hug and pat him on the back.

"You can do this!" I reassured him.

"Thanks for everything, professor," was the only thing he could say in return.

As much as I wanted the conversation to end on a good note, there was one little problem: He still had no game plan about how he would finally implement his decision. Since I wanted to be sure that he knew what he was doing later on, I continued talking about how businesses, companies, and organizations are supposed to strategize. I only did this because I wanted Bill to know exactly what he was supposed to look for whenever he started the hunt for a new job.

I did, however, try to link all of the information about strategic planning on an organizational level to the extremely important decisions that he had had to make in his life recently.

"Speed isn't the only thing that is important when you are making decisions," I told him. "I'm sure you realize that by now." I winked.

"You bet I do," Bill laughed.

"I knew you would say that." I smiled. "Even though the speed of decision making is extremely important and critical to survive, you need to know the direction that your strategies and decisions have the potential to take. The ability to move fast and knowing your direction are critical to the definition and execution of any strategy and goal achievement. There is a lot of balance required between organizational flexibility and financial stability."

My student nodded, and I could tell that he was actually interested in everything that I was saying and would retain it at least long enough to successfully be able to find a good job after he resigned from the company where he was working at the time.

"There is also another balance that is required," I continued, seeing that he was ready to hear more about what I had to say.

"Which balance are you talking about now?" he replied, as inquisitively as ever.

"The balance between change and challenge," I replied. "If you can control the change, you can control the outcome." I told him.

Bill was evidently very confused, but he was also very interested in this concept, even though I could tell by the look on his face that he really couldn't understand what I was talking about.

This, however, was one thing that I wouldn't explain to him.

"You'll figure it out," I replied to him.

"I'll try to," he smiled back at me.

"I'll tell you this much though," I replied. "Remember that strategy and the change that you implement should constantly revolve around the challenge presented to you by the outside environment. You respond to a challenge with change, which in turn represents a challenge to your competitor."

"I think I won't be able to forget your lessons for a long time, Joe," my student replied.

I could only hope he meant that.

The problem that nearly all businesses, companies, and organizations face in the world today is that they are unable to align strategy with operations. While thinking of the right strategy that will prove to be beneficial for the business, company, or organization is a lot of trouble in itself, it is also important to know that executing these strategies is a different—multifaceted—problem altogether.

There is a gap in between the day-to-day performance that seeks to achieve measurable goals and the guiding strategic vision. If this gap widens, the business, company, or organization where change or strategy is being implemented can only hope to survive. Even when people try to make the right decisions for their business, company, or organization, instead of having their personal intent as the motive behind all of the decisions that they make, these people try to execute their decisions based on motivating factors of the past instead of focusing on the present reality and the current scenario.

Most people fail to realize that it is imperative to focus on long-term objectives during the execution of strategies, policies, and decisions and while operational activities are being performed. Although management of the execution of operational strategy is one of the most important aspects of supporting the overall strategy and vision of any business, company, or organization, it is often ignored, thereby creating problems that prove to be detrimental for the business, company, or organization in question.

Even though Bill probably didn't realize the importance of knowing all of this at that point in time, I knew just how much it would help him in the corporate sector. Besides, I had already spent years in the field and knew just what he needed to know to find the perfect job in the future and all of the moves that he needed to make to achieve success. To help him out a little and to ensure that he wouldn't get bored of me talking endlessly, I decided to start helping him out with another extremely important topic.

"Have you ever heard about scenario planning?" I asked Bill.

"I'd say, 'Yes,' because scenarios are planned all the time. But since this sounds like one of your rhetorical questions, I think I'll go with 'No,'" Bill smiled.

"You're growing smarter with every second," I laughed.

"I guess it's all because of your company," Bill winked at me.

"I must admit," I laughed back at him.

It had been quite awhile since we had arrived at the restaurant, and the waiters and manager were evidently not very happy about the fact that we hadn't ordered anything. The only other table that was occupied emptied about half an hour ago and nobody else had walked into the restaurant since I arrived there. Even though the restaurant served decent food, and the ambiance wasn't too bad either for a small local food joint, it wasn't doing very well and that made me very sad.

"This was one of my favorite restaurants a long time ago," I told Bill as I remembered all the times I had come there decades ago with my family and friends. "They have barely changed anything around this place. I'm not surprised it ended up being as deserted as this," I said to no one in particular as I looked across the small restaurant.

The restaurant has not changed with the times. They still offer an old-fashioned menu that does not conform to the modern trend toward healthier choices.

Bill really had nothing to say, so he started flipping the pages of the menu that the waiter had brought when I signaled for it a few minutes earlier.

"You know why, Bill?" I continued.

"Huh?" He was searching through the menu for his favorites too intently to follow. "What do I know, professor?"

"You know why this place barely has any customers now?" I asked him more elaborately this time.

All Bill did in return was shrug and shake his head in denial.

"They weren't agile enough to keep up with their competitors, either," I responded. "We're sitting in a restaurant in the middle of a street with all of the latest fast-food chains. Lavish interiors, appealing exteriors, elaborate menus— they have it all! Compare all of that to this little place right here and it doesn't even feel like we're in the same city, let alone the same street!"

Even though Bill did get to thinking about this for awhile, he wasn't particularly interested at that moment. I didn't want the rest of my talk about scenario planning to go unheard, so I decided it would be best if we continued over a snack or two.

"Now let's order something, shall we? I'm starving!" I continued without waiting for a response.

I don't have words to explain how glad he was to hear that. He was sleep deprived and had had a breakdown not too long ago. Food sounded like a good option to both of us.

We both ordered appetizers and our personal drinks of choice. Gulping it all down in a matter of seconds, we ended up ordering main courses as well.

Since our waiter told us it would take a while for our orders to arrive, we decided to continue with the conversation we were having before I got distracted by how the restaurant was almost stuck in the past.

"Weren't you saying something about planning a while ago, professor? What was it again? Scenario planning?" Bill asked with his second drink in his hand.

"That's right," I said with a smile on my face. "I knew you wouldn't be able to pay much attention without having a meal first."

"I'm sorry," Bill smiled back shyly. "It's been a long week. Cut me some slack."

We both laughed.

"Very well then; let's make the most of the time we have before you get distracted by our main courses," I joked as he twirled the glass of his drink in his hand.

He nodded with a smile on his face.

"All right, scenario planning," I said.

"Scenario planning," he repeated indicating that he was finally ready to listen to what I had to say.

"The tool scenario planning was developed by the military in WWII and used by Royal Dutch Shell, in the 1970s.[9] The tool was applied by Royal Dutch Shell to integrate uncertainties and changes in the external environment and bring things into context and perspective. What this basically means is that the tool acted like something that linked the changes in the business environment to the strategy of the business, company, or organization where it was being used."

"Is it still being used?" Bill asked inquisitively as he continued to twirl his drink.

"You bet it is!" I replied. "In fact, experts call it one of the 10 best tools being used in the world today for management."

"Something from the 50s is still being used and considered 'one of the best' today?" Bill asked in surprise. "I find that just a tad hard to believe."

He finally put his glass down.

"Haven't you heard of Sun Tzu's strategies?" I replied rhetorically.

He nodded because he knew exactly what I meant and didn't say anything in return.

"Just as Sun Tzu's strategies are something that are still revered and used globally, I don't see any problem in using tools from the past, such as the one I was just talking about," I continued.

"You really love talking about that guy, don't you?" he grinned.

"Sure do!" I replied cheerily.

"I honestly feel that tools like this will always be relevant, just as they are right now. Regardless of the business, company, or organization that you are a part of, everywhere you look you'll find volatility, uncertainty, complexity, and ambiguity in the corporate world of today. And I guess it's safe to say that this will only get worse," I continued.

"That's what the VUCA environment is all about, right?" Bill asked.

"That's correct," I replied. "In the context of business environments, a scenario is nothing more or less than an interactive, dynamic, and complex story that is told from the perspective of the future. Now, it is imperative for every business, company, and organization to develop useful scenarios, and that's exactly where scenario planning comes into the picture.

"To develop scenarios that will prove to be useful for you, you need to know the industry that you are a part of, inside and out, and have a rich understanding of the macroenvironmental factors and global conditions that have the potential to affect your scenarios. These factors and conditions not only need to be understood, but it is equally important for businesses, companies, and organizations to monitor and analyze them in order to create advantageous scenarios."

Bill had a look of curiosity on his face, and that's exactly what I expected. Since I knew that what I still had to say would clear up all of the doubts and questions that he had in his mind, I didn't ask him what was confusing him.

"There are six steps involved in formulating the *perfect* scenario plan," I said. His facial expression began to return to normal almost immediately.

"The first thing that you need to do is understand—rather, decide upon— the problem, era, and scope that the scenario that you will be formulating is expected to explore. Unless you decide upon the problem and time frame that you are trying to formulate a scenario for, chances are that you won't be able to do it the right way."

"Fair enough," my student started nodding again.

"Good. Next, you have to figure out conditions and drivers that will influence the scenario that you are formulating. If there is anything that can make an influence on your scenario, you need to have it figured out and need to keep it in mind.

"The third thing that you need to do is accept that there is always a substantial difference between uncertain factors or conditions and uncertainties and that they should not be dealt with in the same way. When you are formulating a new scenario, you will often be able to predict how trends will be able to affect the market and—ultimately—affect your scenario as well. "

By the look on his face, he was not only taking in all of the information that I provided without any problems, but he was also particularly interested in how a tool that was introduced in the 1950s could be so comprehensive.

I decided to continue talking, considering how attentive he was at that moment. "The fourth step is to have an understanding of what the future could look like. When you have an understanding of the future, you will not only be able to formulate the right type of alternative scenarios, but you will also have a baseline in mind for the type of scenario that you must formulate to ensure that it is able to keep up with changes in the environment.

"Effective and efficient completion of Step 4 requires a lot of time and effort on your part. There are a number of considerations that you will have to keep in mind when you are working on understanding the future and creating alternative scenarios. You will have to work together with analysis tools and keep different types of scenarios in mind to formulate a scenario that will be perfect in your case."

At that point, it was almost as if Bill was registering every single word I said in his brain through mental notes because his face lacked any and all emotion, and all he wore was a look of someone who was concentrating very hard.

I wanted to invoke a response from him, so I decided to stop talking for a moment. As expected, that was exactly what was needed to get the job done.

"Step 5?" he said inquisitively.

"We're getting there," I replied, with a smile on my face.

The waiter had finally arrived with our food, and I knew that talking while we were being served wouldn't be one of the best things to do. Besides, there would be so much noise and distraction that he wouldn't be able to understand half of the things that I was talking about.

A pleasant aroma filled the air almost as soon as the waiter placed the steaming dishes on our table. When he was done, he asked us if we had wanted any drinks. While I refused and settled for water, Bill was apparently in a different kind of mood. He ordered the same drink, for the third time that afternoon, and even though I wanted to make him stop, I let it be because he had had a very rough and long week.

The drink was brought almost immediately, and Bill began twirling his glass in his hand again.

"So, what were we talking about again?" I asked him, just to find out whether he was still paying attention.

"The fifth step of scenario planning, professor," he said.

I was glad that he hadn't gotten distracted by the food on our table.

"Once you have made an analysis of the future to the best of your ability and are able to formulate alternative scenarios that will prove to be beneficial for your business, company, or organization, you will have to figure out the impact that the scenario will have. For this, it is extremely important that you assess the influences of your scenario, determine how your scenario will make an impact on the environment, and determine the effects that the scenario that you have formulated will have. Only then will you be able to find out when the scenario that you have created is unfolding."

"Last one?" Bill asked. There wasn't any haste in his tone nor was he hoping for me to get done with my talk soon.

"That's correct," I nodded and smiled at him.

"Since the purpose of planning scenarios was to create and formulate useful scenarios for a business, company, or organization, the sixth and final step of scenario planning is extremely important. To implement the sixth step effectively and efficiently, you must ask yourself how you can reach your 'desired' future with the scenarios that you have planned. For this reason, you will not only have to assess whether the scenarios that you have planned have strategic implications that are in line with your desired goal or future, but you will also have to identify strategic actions and performance measures.

"As with all of the rest of the steps, there are a number of considerations that are important for this step as well. To figure out whether your scenarios will help you reach the goal or future that will be beneficial for the business, company, or organization in question, you need to keep the feedback and advice of stakeholders in mind for the blueprint that you have created for the future and the scenarios that you have planned.

"Next, it is important for you to keep in mind all potential actions, investments, and policies. This step will help you to realign your vision if need be, and will also help you plan to monitor progress.

"Another extremely important output that this step will give you is that you will determine the performance measures that are required to assess the progress of your business, company, or organization."

Bill listened as intently as ever until he finally realized that I was done talking and telling him about the six steps of scenario planning that were introduced over half a century ago. Even though he did know and realize that scenario planning was very important for every business, company, and organization regardless of the industry that it was based in, I could tell that Bill was still not sure how many benefits this tool offered.

After a small pause, during which he fiddled with the fork in his hand, Bill finally asked me the question I knew that he had had in mind since I stopped talking.

"I understand that it's important and all," he said to ensure that I didn't feel like everything that I had said fell on deaf ears, "but what are the advantages of scenario planning?"

As always, I was glad that he was asking questions, regardless of how vague or unimportant he thought they were. Bill had always been the type of person to ask questions whenever he couldn't understand something, and I was glad that this habit of his hadn't died, even after he had been through rough times at his workplace and elsewhere.

"I'm glad you asked, Bill," I said to him to acknowledge and appreciate his questioning. It always made me happy that he would ask questions instead of acting as if he understood everything.

"I was as surprised as you were when I first heard that a tool such as scenario planning, introduced in the 1950s, could still be in use and considered to be one of the best tools available to get the job done. But after I found out about the benefits that the tool has, all of my questions were put to rest," I continued. "Remember what I told you about the VUCA environment, Bill?"

All Bill did was nod in return.

"I believe that one of the major reasons why scenario planning is still so important and popular among businesses, companies, and organizations in the world today is because the VUCA business environments have made way for a lot of ambiguity and uncertainty. Thanks to ingenious tools such as scenario planning, ambiguity, and uncertainty in the workplace and business environments can be accommodated very easily, and they won't have the negative impact that they would have if the tool not been used.

"Uncertainties and ambiguities have been too costly in the past, and the businesses, companies, and organizations in today's world can't afford to deal with more problems that can easily be avoided."

Even though Bill was listening as intently as he always did, he didn't look too convinced. That just wasn't a good enough reason for him, and he became vocal about it almost instantaneously.

"I'm sure there are plenty of other tools available in the market that can accommodate uncertainties and ambiguities better than something that was introduced over half a century ago," Bill said, almost as soon as I stopped talking.

"There are," I replied. "But there are plenty of other reasons why scenario planning is still being used."

"Oh." Bill was embarrassed that he had spoken too soon, but I didn't mind as long as I could teach him a lesson or two on the importance of scenario planning and avoiding costly mistakes in VUCA environments.

"Just to add to the point I made earlier," I continued, "the uncertainty in the business environments of today is much higher than any leader or manager can cope with. Since managers and leaders of today are unable to adjust to or predict uncertainties, it is best to make use of tools like this, which can help minimize the negative impact that uncertainties will make."

"That makes more sense." Bill was starting to be convinced.

"Moving on, I think it would be fair to call scenario planning a tool that helps leaders and managers think and make decisions more strategically. I hate to say this, but without the help of tools such as scenario planning, it would be impossible for leaders and managers in the businesses, companies, and organizations of today to make decisions that are practical and sane. Strategic thinking these days is too bureaucratic, and making good decisions is impossible with the quality of strategic thinking or planning that I see in the world today."

"I'm sorry professor but I don't think I understand what you mean by that," my student replied as humbly as he possibly could. He was evidently not too happy that he hadn't let me finish what I had to say earlier.

"No need to apologize," I said with a smile on my face. "It feels like every industry has already experienced or is on the verge of experiencing some changes that will require all businesses, companies, and organizations within them to change the way in which they function and operate. This will obviously require a lot of strategic planning and thinking, which is practically impossible these days without the right tools.

"Without scenario planning, businesses, companies, and organizations of today will not be able to generate or perceive opportunities when it really matters. What this means is that even when the time is right, businesses, companies, and organizations will not be able to hit the ground running simply because of incompetence and poor decision-making skills if they don't use all of the right tools.

"With the help of scenario planning, businesses, companies, and organizations of today can prepare for a lot of things beforehand. The best part about scenario planning is that this tool can be used to predict and evaluate a wide range of possible outcomes and scenarios long before they are even in their nascent stages, unlike most other tools that only accommodate and allow a single forecast at a time."

I took a small pause and signaled the waiter to clear our table. When he arrived, he asked us if we wanted anything else. Bill had started flipping the pages of the menu again but couldn't make up his mind. I ordered some more water for myself and, this time, for Bill as well. He had already had enough drinks for the day.

"Thanks, professor," he said with a smile on his face. "I really did have more to drink than I should have in one day."

"Always here for you," I replied returning his smile.

"I understand what you mean by predicting multiple scenarios since that's what all six steps involved in scenario planning were essentially all about," Bill continued with the discussion that we were having before the waiter had come to our table. "But I'm not quite sure how this is supposed to help businesses."

"Let me explain," I replied. "When you are using a tool that allows you to see things in a different light and allows you to see a multifaceted view of something as important and crucial as the future of your business, company, or organization, you will naturally be able to make decisions that are more beneficial for both you and all of the employees or your colleagues in the business, company, or organization that you have the responsibility of making decisions for."

Bill started nodding. I could tell by the look on his face that he was finally convinced of the benefits of the tool.

"And there's still more!" I continued.

Bill raised one eyebrow inquisitively as I took a sip of my water.

"Since you can predict a number of scenarios and see how they will create an impact on the future of your business, company, or organization, it will be possible for you to test out the decisions that you are planning to implement and see whether they will be best for your business, company, or organization."

Bill was impressed that a tool that was introduced and created so many years ago would be this comprehensive and could help businesses, companies, and organizations so many years later in such a large number of ways. "The tool can also be used by stakeholders and other people who have a say in the operations of the business, company, or organization to determine which policies and strategies should be chosen among others and which ones should be avoided.

"With the help of this tool, these people can also identify factors that will be critical to the future of the business, company, or organization where scenario planning is being implemented and to assess which changes will be best for the business, company, or organization in question.

"It really is a very comprehensive tool, and I applaud the people who could think of such a thing so many years ago," I continued. "Scenario planning is easily one of the best tools available in the market since it helps solve so many problems all at the same time."

"I must agree, I'm pretty impressed too. And who knows better than you how difficult it can be to impress me," Bill joked.

"Tell me about it," I joked back.

"But really," I continued. "This tool is so great that it allows leaders and mangers to think at the systematic level and strategize and plan effectively, efficiently, and optimally to ensure that there are no problems when decisions, policies, and strategies are actually being implemented. Since they have so much time to think over what must be done, managers and leaders will be confident in the decisions that they make.

"This essentially does two things. It makes the business, company, or organization more resilient in the face of challenges and problems that may arise, and it also makes them more adaptive to changes in the environment, which would make organization agile."

"If only someone had told the leaders at my company about scenario planning when they should have," Bill replied with a tint of disdain in his eyes.

I knew exactly what he meant. The number one reason why his company was in such a terrible position and was facing so many different problems was because the leaders and managers at his company were unable to plan effectively and efficiently in advance.

Changes in the business environment were bound to cause disruption, and regardless of whether the leaders and managers at Bill's company acknowledged that, they should have made better preparations for the sake of the company.

All of this is, however, easier said than done.

The challenges that businesses, companies, and organizations face in the world today have reached unprecedented levels. This is exactly why the need for leadership teams to play their part is now more real than ever before. It is the responsibility of these teams to encourage and promote transformative thinking, which helps the people involved in the business, company, or organization in question to see things in a different light.

The importance of agility and innovating or transforming at a speedy rate, too, cannot be undermined. In fact, these factors have become so important that it would be safe to call them the metrics that determine the possibility of survival or extinction of the business, company, or organization that is being discussed.

Unfortunately, most of the businesses, companies, and organizations in the world today are not adaptive or resilient enough to deal with all of the changes, challenges, and pressure around them.

How can I say this with so much surety? Let me explain.

The problem fundamentally lies in the way that businesses, companies, and organizations of today are structured and designed. Everywhere you go, you'll see that leaders and managers have set unrealistic goals and targets for their employees. Despite all of that, they will still go on saying that every employee must do their part to help change the business, company, or organization for the better.

In the minds of leaders and managers, this may be one of the best tactics to motivate and encourage those who work under them to push their limits and work harder than ever before. However, that is far from the reality of the situation. Countless employees like Bill are frustrated at their workplaces simply because those in leadership and managerial positions were unable to make the right decisions for their business, company, organization, and employees, which has led to the problems that we see in the corporate sector today.

The fact of the matter is that there is a lot that needs to be done to make our businesses, companies, and organizations more adaptive and resilient, and it's about time that we stopped pretending that the problems that surround us aren't real. We have ignored the problem for far too long—perhaps even to the extent that there is no turning back.

As difficult and tiring as it may sound, it is the duty and responsibility of everyone in a business, company, and organization to play their part in effective transformation. How can that be done, you ask? Allow me to answer.

The first thing that must be done is to create proper leadership teams that instigate transformations that will make the business, company, or organization more adaptive, more resilient, and, ultimately, more successful. Unless leadership teams are created to take on the task, it is practically impossible to expect anyone to be able to successfully initiate change and be the pioneers of transformation since they already have so much on their plate.

These leadership teams will not only be responsible for creating and managing hubs for transformation, but they will also engage actively with all employees and members of the business, company, or organization to effectively and efficiently manage change. The leadership teams will also be responsible for the execution of workshops for innovation and transformation, which will prove to be beneficial for the company.

As mentioned above, for successful transformation and innovation to take place, innovation hubs must also be created. These creativity-fostering spaces need to be created skillfully and mindfully to support the leadership team of every business, company, and organization. If created properly, these innovation hubs have the potential to have a major positive impact on the quality of innovation and the speed at which it is implemented.

Another major advantage of having innovation hubs in every business, company, and organization is that they will create a positive influence on the culture in which they are created and managed. With properly managed innovation hubs, it will be possible for the interactions, collaborations and agility within any business, company, and organization to be leveled up—all of which are equally crucial and essential for the survival and success of the company.

As I shared all of these thoughts with Bill over a table at my favorite restaurant that fine afternoon, he became more convinced with each passing second that his company was not ready and certainly not prepared to accommodate transformation and change.

After sitting at the restaurant for nearly two hours, Bill checked the time on his watch and realized that he was getting late for another important meeting, just as before. This time, however, our meeting didn't end as haphazardly as it had previously.

"I didn't realize it has been so long," he said as he glanced at his watch.

"Me neither," I replied. It honestly didn't feel like more than half an hour had passed since we got there, especially since not a single person had entered through the door since our arrival.

"Hope it was productive," I continued.

"You bet it was, professor," Bill said as he extended his hand for a handshake. "Thank you so much for all of this. I really appreciate it."

"No problem, Bill." I shook his hand with a smile on my face. If anything, I was glad that I could help a student and friend at a difficult time in his life.

"I'm glad to have helped," I continued to ensure that he never holds back on asking for help.

After paying the bill and tipping the waiter generously, Bill finally started getting up from his seat.

"Don't you think you're forgetting something, Bill?" I said.

"Definitely not, Joe," he said, as he stood up to leave. "I'm resigning."

References

1. Heffernan, Margaret. (2014, June 18). "Why Your Merger Failed." Inc. Retrieved from https://www.inc.com/margaret-heffernan/why-your-merger-failed.html
2. Wik, Tracey. (2017, August 2). "Why 70% of Mergers and Acquisitions Fail." Business 2 Community (B2C). Retrieved from https://www.business2community.com/strategy/70-mergers-acquisitions-fail-01888557
3. Heffernan, Margaret. (2012, April 24). "Why Mergers Fail." MoneyWatch/CBS News. Retrieved from https://www.cbsnews.com/news/why-mergers-fail/
4. Bradt, George. (2015, January 27). "83% of Mergers Fail—Leverage a 100-Day Action Plan for Success Instead." Forbes. Retrieved from https://www.forbes.com/sites/george bradt/2015/01/27/83-mergers-fail-leverage-a-100-day-value-acceleration-plan-for-success-instead/#39b599705b86
5. Dunning, David. (2011). Chapter Five – The Dunning–Kruger Effect: On Being Ignorant of One's Own Ignorance. *Advances in Experimental Social Psychology, 44,* 247–296. Retrieved from https://www.sciencedirect.com/science/article/pii/B9780123855220000056
6. Retrieved from https://en.wikipedia.org/wiki/Dunning%E2%80%93Kruger_effect
7. Seidensticker, Bob. (2015, February 23). "The Dunning-Kruger Effect: Are the Stupid Too Stupid to Realize They're Stupid?" Patheos.com. Retrieved from http://www.patheos.com/blogs/crossexamined/2015/02/the-dunning-kruger-effect-are-the-stupid-too-stupid-to-realize-theyre-stupid/

8. Retrieved from https://en.wikipedia.org/wiki/Red_Queen%27s_race
9. Office of Operations. (2017, February 1). "Advancing Transportation Systems Management and Operations Through Scenario Planning." United States Department of Transportation—Federal Highway Administration. Retrieved from https://ops.fhwa.dot.gov/publications/fhwahop16016/ch2.htm

Chapter 6

Searching for Agile Organizations

Since most of the problems that arise in businesses, companies, and organizations today are caused by issues of management and leadership, it is important to take a look at what exactly management means in the context of business environments in the **V**olatile, **U**ncertain, **C**omplex, and **A**mbiguous (VUCA) world of today.

First things first, we must understand what the term means and where it comes from. The word manager itself comes from two Italian and French words, *maneggio* and *manège*, respectively. These words were used for the training, controlling, and handling of horses. Since the term "manager" was not meant to be used in the context that we currently see it being used in, the approach involved in management has always been very static. This needs to change.

The advent of the Information Age has brought about several changes and transformations, and it is only fair, therefore, that we introduce substantial changes in the ways in which the businesses, companies, and organizations of today are being managed.

Fortunately, several people in the businesses, companies, and organizations of today have started to develop the tools that are essential, not only for their success but also for their survival. A large number of people are investing a lot of hope in these tools for this very reason. These tools can help with decision making and leveraging anything and everything that is available for the growth of the business, company, or organization in which they are being used. They are becoming increasingly popular among people in our businesses, companies, and organization because people see them as something that will help them to deal with and adapt to all of the changes that the VUCA environment has brought about and will continue to bring in the foreseeable future.

Unless those in leadership and managerial positions in the businesses, companies, and organizations of today start making intelligent decisions, it is practically impossible for any of them to succeed or keep up with the changes in the environment.

> *But how can these decisions be made when nothing about management seems to be changing despite multiple management theories?*

The answer lies in leveraging technology with intellect.

Since tools are already being developed for decision making and the implementation of strategies and policies in a way that will be beneficial not only for the business, company, or organization in question but also for all of the people involved, it is important to promote the use of technology that is essential for survival in the world of today.

Another thing that must be remembered is that the size of a business, company, or organization has nothing to do with success. In other words, it is not important for a business, company, or organization to be very large or have a certain number of employees to be deemed successful or for its chances of survival to increase in the complex business environment of today. And people have fortunately understood that.

Since people have finally come to terms with the fact that large size doesn't necessitate success, businesses, companies, and organizations of the future will be seen to be much smaller and focused than the chaotic environments that we see today. Fortunately, this can prove to be beneficial in many ways.

Dealing with large businesses, companies, and organizations in a fast-paced and constantly changing world will be extremely difficult. If the businesses, companies, and organizations of the future diminish in size and become more focused on specific objectives or goals unlike what we see today, chances are that strategic leaders and managers will be able to make better decisions and implement policies or strategies that will prove to be more beneficial for everyone at large.

All of this, however, will be impossible without the help of the right technologies and if intelligence is not leveraged.

In today's world, what must be focused on most is how intelligence and learning can be used to make better decisions in every business, company, and organization. Although this is an essential part of how our businesses, companies, and organizations can become smarter, more adaptive, and more resilient to the changes in the environment, it is equally important to focus on how these characteristics and traits will be seen in our leaders and managers as well.

The fact of the matter is that regardless of how much we deny it, change in our businesses, companies, and organizations requires our leaders and managers to be equally as resilient and ready to adapt to new environments. As mentioned earlier, businesses, companies, and organizations of the future will not focus much on size and will start investing their time and energies in productivity in domains that have nothing to do with their size. With that said, it is important to invest in human capital instead of focusing primarily on assets and how they can be leveraged.

Knowledge, intelligence, and intellect must be transferred efficiently and effectively into the success of our businesses, companies, and organizations. The competition for resources and human capital is strong, and unless a method is found to develop and leverage knowledge, chances are that it will all be lost in the moment and people will not know how to manage change optimally, even when all of the right tools will be available.

The responsibility of effective change management and strategizing effectively and efficiently lies on the shoulders of leaders and managers of the businesses, companies, and organizations of today, which is why it is important to invest in them. Since technology will be leveraged whether we like it or not, to adapt to change and survive in competitive environments, leaders and managers everywhere must have enough technical knowledge and expertise to help them make good decisions using the new systems that will inevitably be implemented and used throughout the corporate sector. If leaders and managers do not have knowledge and expertise with executive information systems, chances are that all of the investment that is made in leveraging technology will go to waste.

The next most important thing to keep in mind when it comes to leaders and managers is that they must have the required communication skills for the position. If a leader lacks interpersonal skills or is unable to effectively communicate with employees and colleagues, all other investments will go to waste. Lack of interpersonal and communication skills is already a problem that we see too often in countless leaders and managers in the businesses, companies, and organizations of today. When someone in a leadership or managerial position is not able to effectively communicate with employees, colleagues, and other people in the environment, chances are that they won't be able to consider the preferences and opinions of other people and will end up making poor decisions.

Another great and very dangerous possibility is that these leaders who lack interpersonal skills will not be ready to listen to feedback from other people, regardless of whether they have made the right decisions, and people in the business, company, or organization will either end up becoming complacent or secretly start looking for opportunities elsewhere—in places where their opinions are important and where their decisions or feedback is valued.

The third skill or ability that is crucial for leaders and managers of today is that they must have the conceptual skills that are required to make the right decisions. Needless to say, VUCA environments are prone to a lot of scenarios and situations that are extremely complex. If a person who has been hired as a manager or to fill another leadership position lacks conceptual skills that are required for the position, it is impossible for them to be able to make the right decisions, especially in complex scenarios and situations that are confusing or involve a lot of processing.

While the tasks that need to be done by leaders and managers vary, depending on the industry that the business, company, or organization is based in, and also on their structures, someone who is not fit for the position and ready to take on all of the challenges involved shouldn't be made a leader.

I knew that all of this would be extremely beneficial for Bill to know when he was looking for a new job. Even though he had made it very clear in the past, I wanted to be completely certain about the fact that he was no longer blaming himself for whatever had happened at his previous workplace.

There were essentially quite a number of problems with the company at which he was working—the company that he had decided he would resign from. They lacked the technology, they lacked the planning element that is required when implementing change, and they lacked the qualities that are expected of leaders when they are trying to be the pioneers of change. And, in addition to all of that, they had the fundamental problem of not understanding that they were indeed at fault—that people besides themselves can also be right every once in a while.

As mentioned earlier, I was very glad that Bill was able to figure all of this out for himself and without me reiterating it too many times, but there was still a lot that he needed to know before he ended up making the wrong decisions and joined a workplace that had the same kind of problems disguised in other forms.

It is practically impossible for any business, company, or organization to progress and prosper if they don't open the doors of communication. It is one thing to not know that little or no communication is a surefire recipe for disaster. It is a completely different problem altogether if employees and other people that are a part of the business, company, or organization in question try their best to explain this fact to leaders and managers, but these said leaders not only fail to realize that this is a problem but also disregard the opinions of their employees and subordinates altogether.

I wanted to have another meeting with Bill before he finally quit his company and started searching for other jobs. Since I wasn't sure how he was doing and predicted that anxiety might have gotten the better of him, I decided to make the call sound as purposeless as possible. Knowing him in this way, he would open up about any and all problems that he might be facing much more easily than if I asked him how he was doing straightforwardly or if I told him that I wanted to meet him before he started looking for jobs just to be on the safe side and to make sure that he wouldn't make any stupid or impulsive decisions out of fear of not being able to find a company or job that suits him.

Since he had already told me about his schedule and the time when he would most likely be free, I decided to give him a call on a Friday night. I remembered that he had told me that he prefers staying indoors on Fridays after work. "It's the official end of the work week," he had said during one of our conversations. "I prefer to unwind and relax before I get into my plans for the weekend so that I'm not exhausted."

Even though he had told me that he stays awake pretty late on Friday nights, I decided not to call him too late at night. That way, we would have more time to talk and he could even have time to take care of a few things or fit a movie or two into his schedule before he called it a day.

I waited for Friday all week. I hadn't heard from him in nearly three weeks now—not a single message or phone call. The last time that we did talk was at that restaurant, where his last words had been, "I'm resigning." That leaves a lot to one's imagination.

When Friday (finally) did come, I couldn't wait to speak to him. A part of me was getting very nervous about the decisions that he must have made in these three weeks. *What must he feel like? What must he have done?* Questions started running through my mind the entire day. I was genuinely even starting to feel concerned for him.

I got back home on Friday at about 5:00 p.m. from my lectures, but that was too early. I knew he would probably still be at work so I took a little nap. I woke up around an hour later and remembered that I had to get some work done so I stepped out of the house for a while. "It will even help me kill some time," I thought to myself.

When I got back home, I was very happy to find that I had a voicemail from him.

"Hey, professor, it's been a while. I've been trying to call you for hours now. I'm guessing you aren't at home, and I couldn't reach you on your cell phone, either. Give me a call when you're back please. I need to talk to you. Bill."

I wasn't able to determine much about how he was feeling by the tone of his voice on the voicemail. Besides, he said that he wanted to talk to me about a couple of things, and so did I, so I decided it would be best to give him a call immediately. I wasn't sure what to expect from the call.

"Hi professor!" replied a very cheery voice from the other end. "Where were you? I've been calling on your home phone and your cell phone since almost 6 p.m. Is everything all right?"

Only then did I realize that I forgot to take my phone off of silent mode after I was done with my lecture. I quickly grabbed my phone from my pocket only to find seven missed calls and a few text messages. It was now 6:42 p.m.—nearly two hours since I had come back home from the lecture that I had delivered to my MBA strategy class.

"I'm so sorry, Bill. I just saw my phone," I replied as apologetically as I could and continued to tell him what had happened. "I was waiting for so long for your call. How are you?"

"Wow! And here I was thinking that you were trying to ignore me."

We both laughed.

"Things are going great, Joe. Thanks for asking."

I was glad.

"Don't you think you're forgetting something?" he continued almost immediately.

"I haven't forgotten at all," I told him. "How have things been progressing?"

"Everything went well, Joe. I told them that I'm resigning this Monday. I'm currently serving my notice period."

"No questions?" I asked inquisitively.

"Of course there were," he replied. "They asked me where I was going, why I wanted to leave, the problems that I felt that the company had, and suggestions for improvement. Needless to say, I told them everything that was wrong with them. And I was surprised that they revealed that other people had said more or less the exact same things when they were resigning from the company as well. We've had a total of six resignations this quarter. Can you believe that?"

"I was expecting the numbers to be higher. I'm disappointed, to say the least," I joked.

Bill laughed heartily on the phone.

"So, what are your plans now?" I asked out of sheer curiosity.

"Not much, Joe. My job search has begun and that's exactly what I wanted to speak to you about. Even though I feel great about resigning and know that this was the best thing that I could do, I don't quite know how I should get started on looking for a new job now. Besides, I have a little over three weeks of notice left, after which I'll essentially be jobless, if I may phrase it that way. "

Even though Bill didn't sound too worried about not being able to find a job yet, I knew that it must be bothering him. I knew the type of person he had always been. He liked planning things beforehand. His resignation was perhaps one of the biggest and most important decisions that he had made in his life, and he wasn't well prepared for the consequences.

Fortunately, however, after years of teaching countless students that were now well reputed and established in the corporate sector, I had more than my fair share of resources that I could use to help him land a good job.

But that wouldn't teach him essential life lessons.

"You're probably just looking in the wrong places," I said to reassure him. "A smart young man like you shouldn't have much trouble landing his dream job."

"I guess you're right, Joe," he replied. "I don't know what I'm supposed to do, but I'm just extremely happy that I resigned from this place."

I knew what he was going through. I remember seeing his bloodshot eyes the other day and how his skin has started showing prominent signs of stress and aging. The job had taken its toll on him, and staying in the same company any longer would only make things even worse for him. I knew I had to help.

"When are you free?" I asked him. "I think we should probably meet to discuss your situation."

"That's exactly what I was going to ask you to do, professor. I'm free all weekend. Back to the same old routine again on Monday," he replied.

Even though meeting on the weekend sounded like a great idea, I remembered that I had some very important meetings that couldn't wait. And the young man on the other end of the call was waiting for my advice on a matter as important as resignation and finding a new job. I couldn't leave him waiting.

"Are you free right now?" I asked him.

"Yeah, there's not much that I had planned for today," he replied. "As a matter of fact, I was just thinking of dropping by your area to get some work done. But that can wait. Can we meet right now?" Bill asked as politely as he could.

Since I really didn't have many plans of my own for the rest of the evening, I told him that it would be possible. Besides, I didn't have the heart to deny him.

"Where are we meeting, then?" Bill sounded very excited at this sudden meeting.

"The same place where we always do?" I asked.

"Sounds good. See you in an hour."

"I'll be waiting," I replied.

It was rather chilly for a late September night, and it had been raining since the evening began. This wasn't quite like the usual weather in our city, but we decided to go ahead with the meeting. After all, both Bill and I had a lot that we wanted to talk to each other about.

I knew Bill lived quite far away from the area and that it would take him at least half an hour to reach the restaurant, so I decided to stay at home for awhile after our phone conversation had ended. Exactly 25 minutes later, I grabbed my jacket and headed straight for my favorite little restaurant, thinking that I'd arrive there before him.

I was wrong.

Everyone—from the waiters to the manager—at that restaurant now knew us. In fact, it almost looked as if they were expecting us to be there this time. After greeting everyone who had already seen us at the restaurant several times before and had probably started calling us loyal customers, I headed straight to the same table that Bill always chose.

This time around, however, something was different. He wasn't as sad or depressed as I remembered seeing him earlier. In fact, he welcomed me with a broad smile this time.

"What took you so long, professor? I thought you lived nearby."

"I thought you'd drive more carefully because it was raining," I joked.

"I always drive carefully. I was hoping you'd know that much by now," he replied as politely as he could. "I was heading nearby to get some work done. Guess it took less time than I expected."

I looked at my watch. There were still five minutes left before our planned meeting time.

"I'm still early," I replied, as I sat myself on the seat before him.

"I can't deny that," my student said, laughing heartily.

It felt great to see him like this. His job had taken a toll on his health for far too long, and I was truly happy for him since he did not have to deal with all of the pressure and negativity at his workplace for much longer. There still was one small problem left—the problem that we had come to this little restaurant on a rainy night to resolve. He didn't know how he was supposed to approach finding a new job.

I knew that he never liked feeling vulnerable, even though he never shied away from asking for help. That is exactly why I decided it would be best if I would bring the topic up slowly and gradually instead of asking him how his job search was going without talking to him about anything else first. Luckily for me, he didn't let any awkward silences become a part of the conversation.

"I feel great," Bill continued almost immediately. "I feel like the weight of the entire world was on my shoulders and now I've somehow finally become relieved of it all. I don't remember feeling this good about something in a very, very long time."

"I can see that from your face," I replied. "I haven't seen you this happy in a very long time. I'm so happy for you."

"I know, professor. Thank you so much for all of your help," he said as politely as he could. "That place was draining me of all of my energy. I wasn't in a position to do anything when I came back home from work. It almost felt as if I was stripped of all of my creativity and motivation to do anything in life and as if I couldn't do anything at all. And there they were pushing me to become the 'pioneer of change.'" He grimaced as he said those last few words. He never held back on expressing disgust for his company at any opportunity that he got.

There was a small pause because I really didn't understand what I should say to him. Again, he continued talking without even noticing that I hadn't responded. I was glad.

"I know that I should probably start being worried that I don't really have a job at this point, but I guess the feeling of joy is too overwhelming," he continued.

I knew that this was exactly how he felt even before he said anything but, as I mentioned earlier, I didn't want him to feel as if I only wanted to talk to him at the small restaurant on that rainy night because I felt sorry for him.

"Do you have any plans?" I genuinely wanted to know what was going through his mind. I trusted in him to the extent that I believed that a young and talented man like himself shouldn't have any trouble landing any job—any *good* job—but I also knew that his emotions and all of that stress had got the better of him and that he probably hadn't sorted out much about what would happen after he finally did resign. I wanted to make him realize that he needs a plan—and he needs one fast. Fortunately, my question evoked all of the right emotions and responses.

"I haven't thought of any of this yet, professor."

It was evident from his face that this was the first time that he had really started thinking about what he will be doing after he was done serving the notice period at his company.

"I mean, I obviously will need a job. I have bills to pay. I have things that I need to do," he started staring at the wall behind me.

"You'll be able to find one in no time. All you need to do is start looking in the right place," I replied to reassure him.

"Wow!" he exclaimed almost immediately with a small smile on his face—a small guilty smile that showed how disappointed he was with himself. "I can't believe that there was so much that I had to sort out before I thought about resigning. What will I do?"

Bill wasn't exactly angry or frustrated at that point. He was just genuinely worried about what the future holds for him and what he would do if he wasn't able to find a new job in time. I had seen countless other people go through the same situation. It was always the same. They resigned impulsively, they didn't know what they wanted to do next, and they ended up having anxiety attacks on a daily basis.

Even though I knew for a fact that this was probably the case with Bill as well, I could not accept that he would end up with the same fate as all the rest of these people. He was far more experienced and mature than almost all of the students that I had taught in my long career as a professor. And as the friend that he trusted with all of his decisions recently, I just knew that I had to help him out.

"You'll do just fine," I reassured him.

The look on his face made it clear that he wasn't ready to accept anything that I had to say. Any reassurance on my end barely made any difference at that point.

"I honestly can't fathom that I let this happen to me," he replied. "This isn't like me. I can't get over the feeling that I have made an impulsive decision and that I won't be able to fix things for myself anymore."

He was in a bad place all over again. I had to act, and I had to act fast.

"Where have you been applying?" I asked him, to get a clue of his game plan.

"I haven't really applied to many places," he replied. "I already told you I have no idea where I'm even supposed to start."

I couldn't take his look of desperation anymore. Even though I already told him a lot about how he should get started with his job search, I didn't mind reiterations. And I was sure that he wouldn't mind either.

"Allow me," I answered. "The first thing that you should know is that there are several different types of organizational environments. They can be categorized into competitive organizations as well as organizations that are focused on customers. In addition to both of these major types, there are those in the technological, regulatory, economic, and sociocultural sectors."

"How do all of these differ from each other?" Bill asked.

"I'll let you know."

Fortunately for the owner, there were a lot of people coming into his little restaurant on that night. Although most of these people were coming in for a quick coffee to keep warm in the chilly, rainy night, there were also others who came to enjoy full meals. Others walked in just for a few moments and grabbed a quick snack or two before they left.

Despite all of this unusual commotion, however, the waiters were still quick to come to our table when I signaled them. After all, we were probably the most regular customers that the restaurant had had in a very long time.

I asked Bill if he would like something to eat. Apparently, he hadn't had dinner after he had come back home that night—just like myself. Both of us were too occupied in taking care of other work, which meant that both of us were pretty hungry as well.

After browsing through the pages of the menu for a while and flipping the pages a tad more than we should have, we finally decided what we wanted to eat. Bill ordered fish, and I ordered some pasta for myself. Both of us also asked the waiter to bring us our favorite drinks to wash the meal down. The waiter took our orders and headed straight toward the kitchen.

"Now, where were we?" I asked Bill as soon as we were done fiddling with the menus in our hands. "Sorry, I got distracted."

"You were telling me about the different types of organizational environments," Bill replied almost immediately.

"I just asked that to see if you were really paying attention," I smiled. "I'm sure that you already figured out that organizational environments are multifaceted. The competitive aspect of organizations deals with the tactics and strategies that are implemented at businesses, companies, and organizations to come out on top in their industry.

"Next, there's the sales aspect, which is primarily focused on gaining customers and providing better services than your competitors. This is something that is common to all businesses, companies, and organizations, regardless of the industry that they are based in. Do you know how this applies to the company that you were working in?"

Bill had a disappointed look on his face before he finally started talking.

"You've already got the 411 on what I am going to say. Our sales figures reeked. Competitors were putting the hurt on us in a serious way, and it was siphoning money out of everyone's pockets. Nobody was happy there. The only way out of this mess was to trash the losers in the product line and pump the winners.

"I kept telling everyone that we are history unless we grease our marketing skills and persuade the public that using our products will produce euphoric moments. I kept telling everyone that it is imperative for us to brainstorm effectively in order to come up with a spectacular, life-changing strategy. If we do not, we all may soon be asking, 'You want fries with that?'"

I knew how hard he had tried to make things work at his workplace but to no avail. But one thing I was happy about was the fact that he was no longer blaming himself for anything that had happened over there.

"That's everything I was trying to explain to you," I reassured Bill. "Your workplace was the last thing but agile. They didn't know how to strategize. They didn't know how to deal with pressure. All they really had was a static approach to dealing with everything—and that's not how it works in the real world."

"I know, professor," Bill replied, with evident sadness. "But what's unfortunate is that I've been in that place for so long that that's all I really know. I haven't experienced any other workplace in such a long time that I have nothing to compare my current company to. I wouldn't be able to figure out what a truly agile organization is even if it came and slapped me in the face. I just want to find a job without all of the stress that I've experienced at my current workplace—a decent job where I can actually grow, without all of the problems that I've had to face."

I knew what he meant. The anxiety of not having a job had finally started kicking in. He needed a solution, and he needed one fast. The problems at Bill's current workplace were just about as multifaceted as the types of organizational environments themselves, which is why telling him about the rest of the types of environments at organizations was extremely important.

I, therefore, decided that it would be best if I continued telling him how organizational environments differ from each other before I told him about some characteristics and qualities of agile organizations and some surefire signs of finding a workplace that wouldn't drain him of all of his time, energy, and creativity.

Before I got the chance to start talking, the waiter approached our table with appetizers, even though we hadn't ordered any. The puzzled look on our faces gave him the clue that we needed an explanation.

"This is on us. Bon appétit!" responded the tall and lanky waiter with a jovial smile on his face. It was the same waiter who always served us. He was probably about three or four years younger than Bill and wore glasses just like his.

"You really didn't have to," I said as politely as I could. We hadn't been coming to the same restaurant over and over again for freebies. It was just conveniently located and served great food. "Accept it as a token of appreciation from us. The manager sent it," replied the tall waiter with a slight bow before he left to take care of other orders.

"The place where I work could learn a thing or two about appreciation," Bill said as he picked up a piece of garlic bread from the basket before us.

"Everyone could," I corrected him. "It really means a lot to know that they appreciate us coming here even though the restaurant has so many visitors tonight."

The rain outside had stopped, but people continued pouring into the restaurant. Both of us looked outside and noticed that there were so many people inside already that any more people that came would have to wait for a table. Both of us wondered what had caused this sudden change but were genuinely glad that the restaurant was getting its well-deserved business that day.

"There is a technological aspect involved in the environments of organizations of today," I continued to tell him. "In fact, it is practically impossible for any business, company, or organization to function effectively and make profits or carry out processes efficiently if they compromise on the technological aspect.

"This technological aspect of the environments of businesses, companies, and organizations of today pertains to developing optimal new methods and techniques for production. It could also include innovation regarding products and materials or focus on trends in science and research that could effectively streamline processes or make them better. From everything you've told me so far, this is perhaps one of the greatest problems that your company was facing."

Bill said nothing and just silently nodded. I took that as a signal to continue talking because he wasn't in the mood for giving any input. He picked up another piece of garlic bread from the table as I continued talking.

"The regulatory and economic sectors of any business, company, or organization have to do with the policies and rules that can make or break the system. All levels of political development pertaining to the government, too, are associated with the regulatory sector and are of great importance for any business, company, or organization, regardless of the industry that it belongs to.

"Factors such as the rate of inflation, interest, and unemployment rates, as well as other aspects of the economy such as the growth rate, are also highly important for all companies, businesses, and organizations and affect their environments in quite a number of ways."

"Sorry to interrupt you, professor," Bill said out of the blue, "but weren't you saying something about sociocultural organizational environments as well?"

Bill looked at me inquisitively as I picked up the last of the appetizers from the basket that was placed on the table between us. It had been quite awhile since we had placed our orders, and now that we were done with our appetizers, I signaled the tall waiter to bring us our food. All the polite man did in return was respond with a nod and a smile.

"I certainly was," I replied. "And there's a reason why I saved it for the end."

"And may I ask what that reason was?" Bill asked.

"I think this is what will hit home the most for you," I responded.

Bill was eager to hear what I had to say, and I didn't keep him waiting for long.

"The sociocultural aspect of the environment of any place has to do with the employees of the business, company, or organization in question. The social values of the general population are of key importance when sociocultural sectors of organizational environments are being discussed. Demographic trends and a strong work ethic, as well, are of utmost importance when talking about the sociocultural aspect or sector.

"The right sociocultural environment within any business, company, or organization is essentially what keeps employees motivated and feeling their best at all times. If people feel as if they are being respected, valued, and appreciated, they will not only feel more comfortable at the workplace, but they will also naturally become more productive and willing to put in a lot more effort than usual. It's just common sense."

"Ha!" Bill exclaimed with a sarcastic smile on his face. "Apparently, not common enough."

Being as negative as he was at a time like that wasn't exactly the best thing for him. However, I knew for a fact that hearing a lecture on the importance of positivity was certainly the last thing that he wanted, so I decided to save that for another day. What he needed at that point was reassurance, and that's what I tried to give him.

"You know you'll do just fine, right?" I asked rhetorically.

"I sure hope so, Joe."

The companies, businesses, and organizations of today are open systems that need to engage with their environments not only to progress and succeed in the market but also to ensure that they aren't forced to extinction. It is only through engaging actively with the environment that businesses, companies, and organizations will be able to adapt and perform processes effectively and efficiently.

Interacting with the environment can also help these businesses, companies, and organizations gain the ability to deal with limitations and constraints that they might be faced with within the environment. These capabilities can be gained through a number of different ways—each one of which is essential and important for entirely different reasons.

Businesses, companies, and organizations in some industries prefer gaining essential capabilities through acquiring or combining with others in the same industry and with the same goals. On the other hand, there are also a large number of those businesses, companies, and organizations that focus on gaining essential capabilities by hiring new talent with the right set of skills or by gaining insight and data that is easily reflected in the outputs of the business, company, or organization and helps them reach their desired goals.

The best part about gaining ability from the environment is that it is possible for businesses, companies, and organizations in every industry to reach a number of different goals regardless of whether they are in the financial domain or in the operational domain.

I was discussing the possibility of Bill finding an agile workplace and was starting to explain to him how organizations of today are open systems when our waiter finally arrived with our meals and our drinks. He apologized for taking so long, before he placed our food and drinks on the table. We were both quite hungry. However, we knew that our orders took much longer than expected because there were a lot of people present at the restaurant at that time. And we couldn't complain for two additional reasons. Firstly, we got appetizers on the house. Secondly, the presentation of both of our meals was absolutely perfect. The seafood was cooked to perfection, and the pasta had just the amount of sauce that I wanted. Our waiter continued to apologize, even after he was done serving us, and asked us if we wanted anything else, but we politely refused.

The food was as delicious as it always was, and we both devoured it within no time. Not a single word was spoken by either of us while we ate. Fortunately, the silence wasn't uncomfortable at all. Besides, there was a lot of noise in the restaurant at that time of the day, which was different from how we remembered it. Bill also gulped down his drink almost immediately, and he signaled the waiter for a refill right after he was done.

Even though Bill looked much more relaxed and relieved after hearing everything that I had told him about open systems and how organizations now are different from how they used to be, it was evident that there were still a number of questions in his mind and that he needed answers fast. Who knows, he might even have been thinking that all of the information that I had provided him with was irrelevant because he still didn't know where and how he was supposed to proceed—or start—with the search for his new job.

Bill started twirling his drink in his hand like he always did when he was feeling very anxious. I knew him too well not to understand the reason behind his drinking. I was about to start talking to him again about what he should do or how he should go about his job search, but I thought better of it. I even thought of asking him what was going through his mind, but he started talking before I even found the words to start questioning him.

"That was some great food," he said twirling his glass in his hand as the waiter cleared our table. He didn't look up from his glass even as he said this.

I knew that the only reason why he had made that comment was to break the silence, and I can say that he succeeded at it.

"Sure was," I replied.

The waiter, who was clearing the table, heard our conversation, and before he left he told us that he was glad that we liked the meal.

It was only when he started to leave our table that we became aware of a lot that was different this time around at the restaurant. We had been so engrossed in our conversation that we didn't even notice that the interior of the little restaurant had changed.

A medium-sized LED TV had been installed, and a football game was on. That's where most of the crowd was. Men, women and teenagers of all ages gathered around the TV, which was probably the first thing that most people noticed as soon as they walked in through the door—at least people who weren't busy dealing with a midlife crisis.

There was also another major difference in the restaurant that Bill and I had been completely oblivious to ever since we had entered the little restaurant, which had quickly become a favorite for both of us—the same restaurant that was showing us "loyal" customers appreciation with freebies now. Instead of the traditional pen-and-notebook approach that waiters at the restaurant had been using up until the last time we had visited, all of the waiters at the restaurant now came equipped with tablets that they were using to take orders.

Both Bill and I had unintentionally started looking around the restaurant at the same time. The look on his face made it clear that he was just about as surprised and impressed as I was.

"Did you just notice, too?" I asked him, as he looked around the little room to see what all the commotion was about.

"When did this happen?" was all he could say in return.

"I'm not sure myself. But I guess it was after we came here last time—or at least I hope it was and we didn't forget to notice last time as well," I said, with a smile that Bill very politely returned.

"This couldn't have happened at a better time though," I continued.

"What do you mean by that?" Bill asked. The quizzical look on his face showed how confused he really was.

"All of the conversations that we have had over here were always focused around the importance of agility and keeping up with the environment. During all of our previous meetings, nothing at this little restaurant right here was changing. The interior was as old as I had always remembered it, there was barely any entertainment (save for songs that were played in the 80s), and nothing about the ambiance made the restaurant feel like it was in the 21st century."

"And look at it now!" Bill exclaimed, just realizing the point that I was trying to make.

"Look around you. All of these visitors, just because they changed a few things about how they work," I replied.

He finally realized that it was true. There were more visitors and diners at the restaurant than either of us had ever remembered, and we were glad about that.

"They're teaching me a new lesson about appreciation and agility every minute tonight," Bill said, without the slightest hint of sarcasm. I could tell by the look on his face that he was genuinely impressed at the difference that a few changes had made to the business and profits of the restaurant—changes that were obviously well planned.

"Everyone should learn from them," I reiterated. "They delayed revamping the entire place for far longer than they should have, but I'm glad that they finally got around to doing it. 'Better late than never,' as they always say."

"You tell me the truth, Joe," Bill said, almost immediately after I was done making my statement, and he started looking around the restaurant once again to see how great a difference a few changes could make. "I'm actually quite impressed that they were able to pull this off so well. I mean it's only been a few weeks since we came here last. We used to be the only ones here. Look how well they're doing now."

"I can't say I'm not," I replied. "But it was bound to happen. This is why it's so important for every business, company, and organization in the country and the entire world to keep up with the changes within the environment and implement them for success. A little effort truly does go a long way."

Bill simply nodded as he continued twirling the glass in his hand. There was barely anything left inside the glass besides two quickly melting cubes of ice. He noticed this by the amount of noise his twirling glass was making and signaled the waiter for a refill. The tall man was quick to oblige. He brought Bill another drink and asked me if I wanted anything. As usual, I simply said that a bottle of water would do.

"Is there any definitive guide that explains what does and doesn't qualify as an agile business, company, or organization? I mean, I see the difference that some well-planned changes and agility can make. But how am I supposed to explain this to someone else? Don't you think it'll be a tad difficult for someone to just take my word for it if I tell them that the restaurant that I keep going to with my professor made so and so changes and their business practically increased tenfold right before my eyes?"

I smiled at Bill. I could tell what was going on in his head. All this while, he had been thinking about how his company could have implemented changes and strategized effectively to improve the quality of their own processes as well as the satisfaction of their employees and customers. One thing, however, that he was probably ignoring all this while was the fact that it is impossible to create an agile organization or company if someone is alien to the concept itself.

Since there was nothing that Bill could do to make his company agile and make them strategize or bring about changes at this point, I decided not to bring the topic of his company up either unless he decided that he wanted to talk to me about it. Instead, I thought it would be best for me to just answer his question and tell him how you can distinguish an agile business, company, or organization from one that isn't.

"There definitely are ways in which you can tell whether a company, business, or organization is agile," I replied. By the looks of it, this wasn't the answer he was expecting.

"Wow, I didn't know that that was actually possible," Bill replied, in evident surprise.

"You learn something new every day!" I replied with a smile on my face to reassure him that it was all right to not know things.

"Can't deny that one bit—not today at least," Bill joked. It was nice to see that he wasn't quite as worried as he had been earlier during our meeting.

"There are actually quite a few ways in which you can tell agile businesses, companies, and organizations apart from their non-agile counterparts," I continued. "One of the major characteristics that can help you determine if businesses, companies, and organizations are agile is if they have consistent delivery and a great work–life balance."

Even though I hadn't intended to provoke a response from Bill, he instantly became infuriated.

"Ha! Work–life balance!" he exclaimed as soon as I had said the words. "Is that a myth? A legend? A fictional concept from some strange alien land? I wonder if that's a requirement for workplaces because my company obviously didn't get the memo."

"I know how you feel, Bill," I said instinctively because I couldn't find any better words than that to console Bill, who had suddenly become almost as irritated as he was earlier. "You couldn't have helped them if they didn't understand the importance of keeping employees happy."

"Happy is an overstatement, Joe," Bill replied. "I bet most of my colleagues will agree that we didn't even feel sane in that place. There's just one unrealistic expectation and target after the other."

Even though I understood what he meant, I knew for a fact that anything I said would be taken in a negative way by him and that it would be best if I didn't talk about his workplace much. All I did was nod and reassure him that there wasn't much that he could do. Fortunately, that worked better than I had planned.

Bill went on a small rant about how the sales figures at his company were worse than they had been in a long time and kept telling me about how anything any of the employees did at his office wasn't ever enough. I told him I had seen several such businesses, companies, and organizations over the years and that his company was only heading toward destruction. Hearing this, he was relieved that he had resigned at the right time, and he was finally starting to be convinced that there were far better opportunities that awaited him.

Once his rant was over, he started asking me for the rest of the characteristics and qualities of a good agile business, company, or organization so that he would be able to look for the right place in which to find a job in the future.

"Don't worry, I'll try not to take the rest of them to heart," he assured me.

"I'm certainly glad to hear that," I replied.

"Instead of relating them to my current workplace, I'll try to use them to my advantage and find a sane environment to work in next," Bill continued.

"I can only hope that all of my advice will be of help to you, Bill." I meant it. Bill deserved much better than this.

I appreciated how Bill was willing to listen to what I had to say and was ready to put the problems that he was going through aside to give my advice importance. After seeing how my statement about the importance of a work–life balance had made him furious, I decided to pick my words carefully to ensure that he could understand the point I was trying to make completely and not get offended or start relating the advice I was giving to him to his current workplace.

However, since Bill had gone on a rant about how the place where he was currently working did not respect the need and importance of balance between one's professional and personal lives, I did not get the chance to complete what I had to say about how imperative it is for any agile business, company, or organization to deliver consistently. Now that Bill had told me that he would listen to everything I had to say with an open and clear mind instead of drawing parallels to his workplace, I decided to continue telling him about the characteristics and qualities of agile businesses, companies, and organizations with that very point.

"As I said earlier, agile businesses, companies, and organizations have the quality of consistently delivering. What this means is that their goal is to reduce the time taken for the completion of their cycles."

What I had to say next was a sensitive statement that might evoke ill feelings in Bill regarding his workplace, but it was important for him to know the difference between a workplace that is toxic and a business, company, or organization that is truly working toward agility and trying to make things better for both employees and customers. Since Bill didn't respond in any way to the statement that I had made regarding consistent delivery, I decided to go ahead and take a chance and say the last point I wanted to make regarding work–life balance and consistent delivery.

"Now I know this may be hard to swallow," I continued, "but another characteristic or quality of agile businesses, companies, and organizations is that they empower employees and teams that are performing well to ensure that they are satisfied with the workplace and that they don't feel stressed out. I know that you and several others like you at your own workplace and others feel asphyxiated because of all of the unrealistic expectations and stress, but that's not how it's supposed to work at all."

I could tell that Bill had a lot to say, but he held back for the first time ever just because he wanted to stay true to his word. Since I wanted him to release his frustration before I continued, I didn't say a word either. Bill finally got the hint after awhile and started talking.

"I know that's not how it's supposed to work," Bill said, as he finally put the glass down from his hand. "I've read countless blogs and articles about toxic workplaces and environments, and I know that there's not any part of the criteria that my job doesn't meet. But you need to understand that this is the only thing I've known for a very long time. Essentially, this is the only idea that I have of a corporate environment. When you talk about work–life balance and things of that sort, they all just sound like these really farfetched ideas that really don't exist at all."

"I'm glad that you aren't settling for that place even though you don't know where you're supposed to go or how you're supposed to search for a new job," I told Bill. That's all I could really do. "I hope you'll be able to navigate through workplaces better and be able to find a good job once I am done telling you about the rest of the qualities and characteristics of great agile businesses, companies, and organizations."

Bill just nodded in approval, and I took that as a sign that I should probably continue telling him the rest of the qualities that he was supposed to look for.

"Another important quality or characteristic of agile businesses, companies, and organizations has to do with the way in which managers or leaders deal with other employees. I know that the managers and leaders at your workplace didn't get the memo again, but instead of thinking that they know better than anyone else, it is extremely important for managers and leaders to support their teams and all of the employees in their decisions and understand that other people, too, can come up with ideas that will prove to be beneficial for the business, company, or organization that they are responsible for leading."

"All they did was smile superciliously," Bill responded.

"That's where they went wrong."

Since leaders and managers are responsible for dealing not only with their own team members but also with other employees, it is imperative for them to treat people right and ensure that they feel appreciated and that their opinion is acknowledged, regardless of the industry that forms the basis for the business, company, or organization where they are appointed as managers.

In addition, it is also extremely important for these managers and leaders to know and understand which people will be best for the business, company, or organization and how a unique set of skills can prove to be beneficial for multifaceted success. If leaders and managers don't understand how they are supposed to collaborate with the people on their team and ensure that they are happy working with them, it will be practically impossible for them to leverage their skills and talents for the benefit of the business, company, or organization at which they work.

Agile businesses, companies, and organizations are essentially all about collaboration. It is imperative for businesses, companies, and organizations in every industry to hire the right people for the right job to ensure that intellect spreads throughout and that people are able to learn from each other. None of this will be possible if collaboration is not fostered and promoted by the managers and leaders of today.

Additionally, it is crucial for businesses, companies, and organizations to hire and invite people to share ideas that can help guide the corporate vision. In the VUCA environments of today, people can no longer afford to live by a rigid, unchanging vision if they wish to progress and succeed in the marketplace.

* * * * *

As I mentioned all of this to Bill, I could tell that he still had a lot of questions in his mind—that much I could tell by his expression, as he looked at me blankly. But I figured that he might not be completely understanding what I was trying to tell him if he kept silent and didn't ask any questions. I, therefore, decided that it would be best to ask him whether he understood what I had meant. As expected, he replied that he did get the point that I was trying to make but that he was still uncertain how exactly all of this could be implemented.

"How does this even work? I'm sorry if this question sounds too naïve to you, but I don't think I've experienced any of this collaboration that you are talking about up-close. Do managers ever even listen to people?"

"Not often," I replied. "But they're supposed to. Allow me to elaborate."

Bill was finally showing more interest in what I had to say, and the blank expression that he wore for so long was finally starting to disappear.

The tall waiter finally came back to our table and brought me my water. "I'm sorry it's taking so long today," he said. "Is there anything else that I can help you with?"

Bill said that he was in the mood for dessert, and I agreed. A cool, rainy day like this needed to end with something sweet. Bill asked the waiter for the best recommendations, and the waiter replied that their lemon meringue pie was a favorite. Both Bill and I decided that we would ask the waiter to bring us dessert when we were about to leave, and all the tall, lanky waiter did in return was respond with a smile.

"We'll be looking forward to it," I said to the waiter.

"You won't be disappointed," the waiter replied, before he left.

As soon as the waiter headed toward the table next to ours to ask the diners if they wanted anything, Bill started looking at me as intently as ever as he waited for a response.

"What do you know about the top-down approach, Bill?" I asked. He was a bit taken aback by a question being responded to with another question.

"I think I have just about the right amount of information that I should have regarding the top-down approach used in organizations," he responded, evidently finding my question irrelevant.

"Now, the thing with most companies, businesses, and organizations today is that they try to use a single approach—namely, top-down or bottom-up— with some elements of matrix organizational structure and think that they can get the job done. Unfortunately, that could have been a possibility in the past, but relying on a single approach isn't the best thing to do, especially when there are so many changes that come up every now and then in business environments of today.

"Now, it is best if all managers and leaders everywhere use both the top-down and bottom-up approaches to ensure that valuable information is shared throughout the hierarchy. Explicit and tacit knowledge needs to be shared in businesses, companies, and organizations to the highest extent possible to ensure that rhythm and flexibility is not compromised due to inadequate information or the complete absence of important information and knowledge. When leaders collaborate with their subordinates and knowledge workers, the cycle of the transfer of information is completed in such a way that there is no room for problems to occur."

Completely oblivious to the potential that collaboration had, Bill was very impressed with the possibilities. Even though I could tell that it was difficult for him to fathom the fact that leaders and managers in some places *do* collaborate with their subordinates and other employees, I knew that he was wondering if he had the luck to successfully be able to find such a place.

Since I knew that Bill was having trouble coming to grips with the fact that real, agile businesses, companies, and organizations can be so different from his idea of perfection in the corporate world, I decided that it would be best for me to spell everything out for him.

Businesses, companies, and organizations can choose from a number of styles of management, depending on various factors. The management style that should be chosen by a business, company, or organization is often influenced by the industry that it is based in. Not every industry works in the same way, which is why it is important to choose a style of management that is in line with the goals and environment of the industry.

Additionally, the hierarchy of the business, company, or organization also plays a major role in the management style that will work best for it.

Bill hadn't said a word in quite awhile, and neither had I. I figured that talking about the differences between the types of businesses, companies, and organizations through a different lens might be able to do the trick, and so I gave it a shot.

"Now that I've told you about the different types of organizational environments and the characteristics and qualities of agile businesses, companies, and organizations," I said, "I think it's best if I told you how organizations differ from each other."

"What's that supposed to mean?" Bill asked curiously, and I realized that I hadn't been very clear in my statement.

"Let me rephrase that a bit," I replied. "I think I should tell you about the different management styles that businesses, companies, and organizations opt for these days so that it may help you look for a better job when you finally do start searching. Since you'll know exactly what to expect, nothing will come as a shocker and you won't be really taken aback if you find that your new workplace does things a little differently from what you're used to."

"Let's hear it," Bill said. He was very impressed with the idea.

"Well," I told him, "when you're looking for a new job, you need to know everything about how the business, company, or organization that you are willing to join works. If you don't know what to expect, the situation at your new workplace has the potential to escalate into what you're currently facing at your workplace. The risk is too great to take."

"I don't think a risk like that is something I can take again this soon in my life," Bill replied.

I smiled in return because I knew how much the thought of ending up at a place that was similar to his current company was bothering him. That was the most dreadful thing that could happen to him.

"There are three major types of organizations that you should know of before your search for a new job begins," I told my interested former student.

"What are they? How do they differ?" Bill asked curiously.

"There's a lot that's different in them," I replied. "You'll find out the difference between them when I start describing them to you."

"I'm as ready as I'll ever be," he replied.

"Well, I think it's important for us to start with businesses, companies, and organizations that rely on the command-and-control approach. If there's anything that I could relate your workplace to, it would be command and control companies."

"Why is that? Is it what I think it is?" Bill asked inquisitively.

"I think we're on the same page here," I replied. "But I'll still draw all of the characteristics and qualities of these types of organizations out for you so that you can know how you can detect any workplaces that will be similar to your current company so that you can steer clear of them and never be stuck in a place like that again."

"I think I need to hear this," Bill replied.

"You most definitely do," I nodded.

Tables around us were starting to empty. Most of the diners who were present in the little restaurant at that time had gathered around the TV. There were a few moments left for the football game to end, and the cheering grew louder with each passing second. Drinks were served, snacks were eaten, and bets were made. And I could tell that the festive mood at the restaurant wasn't being appreciated much by Bill.

There were only two other people at the restaurant who were still seated at a table—an elderly couple that probably came to that little restaurant often. It was evident from the looks on their faces that they, too, didn't know how the restaurant had changed. I'm sure they weren't expecting so many young people to be present there. They just wanted to spend a cold, rainy night eating good food and enjoying each other's company. They, too, were disturbed by all the racket—it showed on their faces. But the older man and woman still continued to smile warmly at each other for as long as they remained at the restaurant.

I signaled the waiter, and he understood exactly what I wanted.

"I think we should continue talking outside," I told Bill, as the waiter brought us our lemon meringue pie.

Both Bill and I thanked him and asked him to bring us the bill.

Fortunately, the dessert lived up to the claims of the waiter. The lemon custard was just as smooth as we had wanted, and the fluffy topping melted in our mouths just as we had hoped. We were both extremely glad that the restaurant hadn't compromised on its quality of food despite all of the changes that had been implemented and all of the diners that had made their way to this small little restaurant in the middle of a street, despite several upscale options.

The waiter brought the bill, and we thanked him. I was reaching for my wallet in my pocket, but Bill quickly paid the waiter.

"It's the least I can do, professor. You've done enough for me already, coming over to talk whenever I need you," Bill replied politely.

I thanked him.

"Let's go outside now, shall we?

I nodded in return.

Even though it had stopped raining, it was still colder outside than I had remembered. Since we had both brought our jackets, we decided to continue our little chit chat as we strolled on the sidewalk.

"So, I'm sure you might already have guessed this, but your company probably qualifies as the command-and-control type more than anything else," I told Bill. "There are a couple of characteristics that demonstrate this. Businesses, companies, or organizations that use the command and control approach generally don't promote much engagement. As a result, you can expect that any changes will be resisted, and the leaders of such a place will rarely ever be able to implement any changes, strategies, or policies successfully."

"Too close to home," Bill replied with a small sarcastic laugh.

"Managers at businesses, companies, and organizations like this feel they are leaders, which is why they should be the only ones who are responsible for making all of the rules and decisions. There's barely any concept of appreciation in places like these, but if you make a mistake you should be well prepared to pay the price."

"I've been through it all, Joe," Bill said. And he wasn't too happy about it.

"I know, Bill. I'm just telling you all of this so that you know what to look out for in the future and steer clear of places such as these, the first chance you get."

Bill nodded.

"Another extremely dangerous quality found in places like this is that the leaders and managers feel that the best thing you could be doing at your workplace is to follow their instructions, word for word, and to pay these leaders and managers all of the respect that you can. If you notice that this is happening at any place, I'd say it would be best for you to leave immediately."

"Things like this make me so glad that I'm currently serving my notice period," Bill said, as we continued walking on the wet pavement, avoiding the cold puddles that had formed from two hours of nonstop rain earlier that night.

"I'm happy for you, Bill."

"I know professor. I can't thank you enough for all of this," he replied.

"The next classification that you should probably know about is ambidextrous businesses, companies, and organizations. Ambidextrous places are all about strategic innovation and management that is efficient and effective. Businesses, companies, and organizations that follow the ambidextrous style of management are primarily focused on breaking down business units into several smaller and distinct units with their own structure, culture, and processes to ensure that each one of them is getting the attention it deserves.

"The good part about businesses, companies, and organizations that support ambidextrous management is that they have their own teams designated for innovation but are still connected to the rest of the business units to ensure maximum productivity and the highest quality of services."

"How can they succeed if all they focus on is innovation and building new things?" Bill asked.

"That's a great question, Bill. I was just about to come to that point," I replied. "As a matter of fact, these businesses, companies, and organizations don't focus solely on innovation. They know how to strike the perfect balance between innovation and understanding what they must do to ensure that the ongoing processes and structure of the business, company, or organization is still being used as well. That's why they're called ambidextrous."

"Wow, that's impressive."

"Sure is, Bill," I replied. "I'm personally fond of this style of management myself as well because there's just so much that you can do. Just because you are focusing on creativity and efficient innovation doesn't mean that you should give up on the current system entirely. Besides, you already know how difficult it can be to adapt to a new system overnight. I believe that it is best to innovate your business processes and adjust your organizational policies within existing company infrastructure to ensure that the change doesn't come as a shocker and isn't resisted."

"That does make a lot of sense. This stuff is pretty interesting," Bill replied.

"You know what else is interesting? Most people try to explain this style of management by drawing parallels to Roman mythology," I replied.

"And how is that?" Bill asked.

"Remember the Roman god Janus?" I questioned Bill in return.

"I haven't really met him, so no," my witty student replied.

I had a good laugh.

"Well, to be honest professor, I haven't really read much about Roman history and religion, so I can't say that I know him. But I can still say that I'm happy that you got over your obsession with Sun Tzu," Bill laughed as we walked.

We barely noticed that we had walked over three blocks from the little restaurant during our conversation.

"He's not relevant right now," I smiled. "As for Janus, they say that he had two pairs of eyes. One pair was used to see what's going on behind him, while he used the other to see what lies ahead."

"And how does this relate to the corporate world, may I ask?" Bill was more confused than ever. He obviously didn't understand the parallels that I was trying to draw.

"Well," I said, "people say that ambidextrous managers could learn a thing or two from Janus. They need to have a clear picture of what's going on and how much potential the business, company, or organization that they are a part of has."

"Good stuff," Bill replied.

"Balance is the key when talking about ambidextrous businesses, companies, or organizations," I told Bill. "You can't even imagine how difficult it is to learn how to leverage existing capabilities and work on improving them all while exploring new grounds. There's so much that needs to be taken care of. It's no surprise that only a handful of companies, businesses, and organizations successfully manage to pull off ambidextrous management. Striking the right balance is not something that everyone will be able to do. It demands a lot of hard work and effort on the part of the leaders and managers that are a part of the decision-making team."

One of the major problems with the ambidextrous style of management is that not everyone has the ability to pull it off. The reason for this, as mentioned above, is that it is difficult for people to place the same amount of importance and focus on innovation as they do on their current system. If you don't know how to strike the right balance, it is fair to say that the ambidextrous style of management isn't for you.

One of the biggest failures that we see in the modern world comes in the example of Finnish telecommunications giant, Nokia, Inc. The mobile phone manufacturing giant saw its fair share of success—and more—back in its time. The Finnish company for information technology and communications was the first thing that came to mind when anyone said the words mobile communication. It was, indeed, a sad moment for loyal users when they found out that the handset division of the company was being sold off to Microsoft®, proving how the business failed to grow. As unfortunate as the news was, it cannot be said that it was entirely unexpected.

Before being crushed by its well-known competitors—Apple® and Android™ —the Finnish communications giant was the market leader for quite a few years before its downfall began.

The company rose to unprecedented heights in the industry, which is why being telecom-centric can't even be called one of the reasons for its downfall. The main problem with Nokia, Inc., and the business model it followed was that it couldn't deliver what the customers wanted.

Everything went haywire for Nokia when the first Android phone came into the market. As stated above, Nokia couldn't recognize what users were looking for, which is why their customers started looking elsewhere and succeeded in finding devices that met their requirements.

The company may have made its first smartphone in the mid-90s, along with a successful prototype of a phone that came complete with a touch screen on which you could access the internet, at the end of the last century. But this was not enough for it to remain the king of the industry forever.

Kodak® is another great example of a company that used to be a well-known name back in its time. The company was the leader of the market for analog photography, but since the leaders there didn't know how to adapt to change and were unable to leverage their technology to make their way onto the leader-board for digital photography, the popularity of the company fell until people completely stopped acknowledging the fact that Kodak was once the king of the domain.

It was getting very late, and I thought that Bill probably wanted to go home after a long hard day at work since I was pretty tired myself. I, therefore, decided to cut the conversation short and start telling him about the third major type of organization. Besides, it had started drizzling again, and our cars were parked at the little restaurant over five blocks away from where we were at that time. Both of us were in no mood for getting drenched in the cold rain, especially at such a late hour.

Before I started talking, however, I decided to ask him what he knew about the last type of company, business, and organization present in the world today.

He said that he didn't know much about the holacratic structure.

The holacratic system adopted by businesses, companies, and organiza-tions is a management technique that is decentralized. The best part about this system is that decision making is divided into several self-organizing and managing teams instead of letting the upper management deal with the mak-ing and implementation of all of the strategies, policies, and decisions that are crucial for the success of the business, company, or organization that is being managed.

I started explaining how holacracy does not promote authoritarian struc-tures within any business, company, or organization and I could tell by the look on Bill's face that he was very interested in what this system had to offer. He couldn't wait to hear more.

Much like everyone else though, I was almost positive that Bill, too, had cer-tain misconceptions in his mind regarding the holacratic system and how it is used for the management of businesses, companies, and organizations through-out the world.

One of the most common misconceptions that people have regarding holacracy is that it essentially opposes the idea of hierarchy, which is deemed extremely important for the successful working of any business, company, or organization. One of the major reasons why there are so many misconceptions associated with the holacratic style of management is that the system is relatively new—introduced in 2007.[1] This means that holacratic systems have only been around for about a decade now.

The system was created by an entrepreneur named Brian Robertson in a company that he formed that was called Ternary Software. When the system was introduced in 2007, the creator of the holacratic style of management made it very clear that although holacracy focuses a lot on valuing the decision of every individual who is a part of the business, company, or organization in which the style of management is being implemented, it is crucial for people to understand that democratic and consensual decision making does not necessarily mean that the hierarchical aspect of businesses, companies, and organizations will be ignored when the holacratic system of management is being adopted.

In fact, some people even go so far as to say that hierarchy exists and is even more prominent in businesses, companies, and organizations that use the holacratic system than it is in their non-holacratic counterparts.

To explain things to Bill in a manner that was as simple as possible, I started using examples that would help him understand things without any problems.

"Let's just say that there are a few circles that are present in the holacratic system—hierarchical circles. While each of these circles has its share of procedures and rules that help run it, it is important to understand that the overall hierarchy of the business, company, or organization is not ignored when the democratic procedures of each circle are being followed. What this essentially means is that the higher circle that is present in the holacratic system of management is responsible for telling its lower circles what they should do and what is expected of them."

Even though I could tell that Bill understood most of what I had to say, I still knew for a fact that there were a lot of questions that were going through his mind—questions that he was too afraid to ask. He probably either felt like his questions were too irrelevant or that he shouldn't be asking questions that were as simple and basic as he thought they were. However, the fact of the matter is that the holacratic system of management is one that can be extremely difficult to understand, especially if one doesn't have the slightest clue about what it is or how it works.

As always, I reminded Bill that it was completely normal for him to not understand things and reassured him by reminding him that we all learn new things every day. He told me not to worry and that he would ask me questions in case he had any trouble understanding what I had to tell him.

"Now there are a couple of things that I need to tell you about these higher circles that I was talking about earlier," I told Bill. "As I said, hierarchy is extremely important in holacratic systems of management as well, which means that circles that are higher up in the hierarchy have the right to modify the circles that are lower in the hierarchy. What this means is that if there is a circle that isn't performing responsibly or isn't doing the tasks that it was expected to do, a circle that is directly above it or any other circle that is higher up in the hierarchy can change, abolish, or re-staff this lower, underperforming circle whenever need be."

I could tell by the look on his face that Bill had had trouble understanding the part where authoritarian environments were not supported by holacratic systems of management, but hierarchy was still given more than its due importance in businesses, companies, and organizations in which the system is implemented. With my example, however, Bill finally started understanding what I meant by all of that. But there was still a lot more that I had to tell him.

The primary purpose of every circle in a business, company, or organization in which the holacratic system of management is being implemented is to meet the expectations that have been defined for it by the circles that are present higher in the hierarchy. Since I knew that Bill would have trouble understanding what exactly I meant by fulfilling a purpose or meeting expectations, I decided to elaborate on that part just a bit.

"Now the purpose of every circle or the expectations that this circle is required to meet may vary depending on the nature and industry of the business, company, or organization in which it is being implemented. This means that the purposes of circles can vary from making customers as happy as possible to making the maximum amount of money within a certain period of time to increasing sales by a certain percentage.

One of the major collections of information that help businesses, companies, and organizations throughout the world understand the basics of the holacratic system of management and the rules that define the system is known as the Holacracy Constitution.[2] Brian Robertson, the creator of the system, has made it clear that he hopes that the purpose chosen for the circle must be noble.[3] However, there is no mention of this in the Holacracy Constitution. With this, it can be concluded that there are no hard-and-fast rules that must be adhered to at all times when the circles that are higher in the hierarchy of any business, company, or organization are defining the purpose for any circle that is lower in the hierarchy.

I understood that it was getting late, and both of us should have probably headed home. However, Bill genuinely looked interested in this new system of management, and there was a lot that I still had to tell him. Even though I tried cutting things short as much as possible, the fact of the matter was that it was crucial for Bill to not only know the basics but also to understand the common misconceptions that were associated with the holacratic style of management to ensure that he didn't end up with any misunderstandings about the system or make any mistakes in finding the right workplace for his next job.

I apologized to Bill for taking so much of his time, but all he did in return was politely remind me that he was the one who had asked me to meet him to help him search for a new job and teach him everything that he needed to know to prepare him for this endeavor. Fortunately, Bill wasn't getting bored.

"Besides, it's not *that* late," he said, with a warm smile on his face.

I smiled back at him before I continued talking.

"Now what you need to understand is that the holacratic system of management is basically a mechanism based on hierarchy that essentially connects the circles that are present in the business, company, or organization after the implementation of this system of management. Even though these circles have been given certain purposes, and there are things that are expected of them, that doesn't mean that the circles higher in the hierarchy have the right to impose all of their decisions on the circles that are lower in the hierarchy. In fact, this couldn't be further from reality.

"Although the purposes and goals of each circle are defined by those that are higher in the hierarchy, the fortunate fact of the matter remains that each circle is run by its own democratic system. Additionally, there are a number of elaborate procedures and rules that help define how processes and activities within the circle will be carried out. There are also a large number of procedures that are set for other kinds of problems that may arise within the circle, and dealing with them is made easy."

As mentioned earlier, however, democracy doesn't mean that the circle can modify its purpose. For that, it is essential for a circle to always look higher up in the hierarchy because all purposes and goals are set by those that are vertically above it. But that certainly doesn't mean that a circle will be left alone.

As the goal of a circle is defined by one that is vertically above it in the hierarchy of the business, company, or organization in which the holacratic system of management is being implemented, circles that are higher up also provide lower circles with all of the guidance and information that they might require to successfully implement the processes that need to be carried out in order to reach the goal of fulfilling the purpose that has been defined and assigned to them.

The vertical hierarchy of any business, company, or organization in which the holacratic system of management is being used must be respected at all times because explicit hierarchical democracy and thinking is essentially the foundation of the concept of holacracy.

I could tell by his face that Bill loved this system of management that he was learning about as we walked along the sidewalk on this cold and rainy night. The look on his face told me that he wanted to hear more. By the looks of it, this concept was completely new to him, and he was growing more and more interested in what I had to say to him.

Since there was a lot more that I had to tell Bill before we called it a day, we decided to find a vacant bench in a park or on the sidewalk before we continued talking about the holacratic system of management. Fortunately, doing so wasn't difficult at all, and we ended up finding an empty spot in no time.

It was one of those bus stop benches that have a shade over them. We were truly lucky to find a spot that wasn't wet from the hours of rain that had passed. We decided to grab a cup of coffee each from a nearby café that looked like it was about to close its doors and call it a day, and we sat on the empty bench.

"I'd never imagined that there would come a day when I'm out with my professor talking about jobs and life at a bus stop on a rainy night," Bill looked at me. "Thanks, professor. I really appreciate everything that you've done for me."

"You can thank me when you land your dream job," I replied, smiling at Bill.

"And that I shall," Bill replied before he started sipping his coffee.

I took that as an opportunity to continue telling him about the holacratic system of management.

"Remember how I told you that people often use Janus to describe the system?" I asked.

My student nodded.

"We'll there's more to it. The reason why people often draw parallels between Janus and the holacratic system of management is because circles in the businesses, companies, and organizations in which this system is being implemented not only have to keep the vertical hierarchy in mind at all times and seek guidance and information from circles that are higher up in the hierarchy, but it is also imperative for them to focus on personal growth and development through democratic decision making and carrying out processes that are in line with the rules that have been set."

I continued to tell Bill about how the circles of any business, company, or organization that uses the holacratic system of management need to focus on a lot of things for smooth and successful processing and efficient internal operations. In addition to the set rules and policies that must be abided by the circles, it is also imperative for them to have the right mechanism for feedback and strategies that are flexible enough to help them adapt to the environment.

"In order to understand the holacratic system of management," I told Bill, "it is also imperative for you to understand that the rules that the circles within the business, company, or organization have to abide by must not be too strict because this could qualify as oppression.

"On the other hand, if the rules that must be followed are not strict enough or are more loose and flexible than they should be, there is always the possibility that the circles within the business, company, or organization in which the holacratic system of management is being implemented will start to feel as if they don't have to follow any orders from the circles that are higher up in the hierarchy, which could ultimately lead to anarchy—something that is extremely frowned upon in the holacratic system of management."

Bill was finally starting to understand the complications and complexities that are a part of the holacratic system of management. I had already told him that there were a number of misconceptions associated with this "new" system of management that he was learning about on this rainy night at a bus stop, and I could tell by the look on his face that he was wondering more and more about these misconceptions and everything that the system had to offer. Even though he loved the idea of it, I guessed that he was having problems grasping the concept in its entirety.

After I had finished my sentence, I picked up my coffee from where I had placed it between us on the bench. "This is some great coffee," I said. Bill nodded in agreement as he lowered his cup down and placed it exactly where mine had been just a few moments ago.

"This is some pretty complicated stuff," he finally said. "There's so much to it."

My guess was right after all.

"What do you not understand?" I asked Bill, guessing that he was just being shy and holding back from asking the questions that he had in mind.

"Nothing in particular," he responded. "There are just so many things that need to be taken care of in this system of management. I'm honestly not surprised that most businesses, companies, and organizations aren't able to pull it off."

Neither was I. The system truly is complex, and there are quite a few things that need to be taken into consideration at all times when this system is being implemented. I was genuinely impressed and proud that my student was able to grasp as much of what I had to tell him as he did.

"No wonder people have all of those misconceptions," Bill replied, after a small pause.

I laughed. "Speaking of misconceptions," I replied, "we still have a lot of them to talk about."

"I'm all ears," Bill replied, with a smile on his face.

"Another extremely common misconception that people have regarding the holacratic system of management is that this system does not support managers or any positions of leadership.

"Whether someone with the title of 'manager' is present at the business, company, or organization in which the holacratic system of management is being implemented depends on the structure of the place itself. However, it is important to know that the creator of this system of management is not entirely opposed to the idea of having managers or leaders within the business, company, or organization that is trying to adopt this 'new' style or system of management.

"Brian Robertson, the creator of the holacratic system of management, made all of this very clear in his book *Holacracy*.[4] Since the first company for which the system was adopted was his very own Ternary Software, he tried to explain the system and its rules to the ordinary people by further expanding on this idea. Through the first article that Robertson wrote about the holacratic system of management, he informed people that his company supports roles for project management.[5]

"Interestingly, he also stated that the person with this role at Ternary Software will not only be responsible for creating and maintaining release plans for projects but also for facilitating the creation of contracts, sending daily emails to the team of the project regarding its status, invoicing clients at the end of each month, publishing project metrics at operational meetings, and analyzing each phase of the project in retrospect to see what went wrong and what could have been done better."[6]

One thing that confused a lot of people when this article was written was why the "project management role" wasn't just given to a person who was titled the project manager at the company. Although this was a valid concern for people to have, the reason why things don't work that way in the holacratic system of management is pretty simple.

Since the accountabilities of the project manager's role have the potential of changing depending on the rules and policies that govern the circle in the business, company, or organization in which the holacratic system of management is being implemented, the person who has been given this role may have to be more or less than a manager as we commonly define the word.

In simpler terms, since the rules, policies, goals, and objectives of every circle have the potential to change with time, calling someone a manager may not be the best idea since the role may require a lot less or more from the person in question depending on the situation. Saying that there are no managers or leaders in the businesses, companies, and organizations in which the holacratic system of management is implemented is absurd and unreasonable.

One thing, however, that must be noted is that even though there aren't any people that have been given explicit titles, such as project manager, this certainly doesn't mean that there aren't any roles that have been explicitly defined for the businesses, companies, and organizations that are trying to implement the holacratic system of management. As a matter of fact, there are other "core" roles, including Facilitator, Rep Link, and Lead Link that have not only been mentioned in the Holacracy Constitution, but have also been elaborated on extensively in this large, formal collection of information that is used and referred to commonly by countless people at businesses, companies, and organizations that are interested in adopting the holacratic system of management.

Bill didn't ask any questions while I defined the differences between normal roles and the roles of holacratic systems to him. Since we had already spoken extensively about the misconceptions that people had regarding the system, and he finally understood the real picture, I decided that it was time for me to tell him how this system actually works.

Before I started talking to him about that, however, I realized that it was important for me to find out whether he was even paying attention. I asked a few cross-questions, and since he responded to all of them correctly, I decided that it was the right time to proceed.

"So," I asked Bill, "how do you think holacracy works?"

Bill was taken aback by this question, to say the least. To him, the question was probably not only uncalled for, but also irrelevant.

"We have been talking about it for at least the last 20 minutes now, Joe," Bill said, with a confused look on his face.

I had a good laugh at his response.

"I know, Bill. But how do you think it *really* works?"

"This sounds like another one of your trick questions, so I guess I'll pass on it," Bill replied, more confused than ever.

"Well played," I responded, with a smile on my face.

"I think I actually want to hear the answer to that now," Bill replied, looking at me with his coffee in his hand once again.

It was now almost midnight, and the streets were nearly empty. Since our cars were parked several blocks away from the bus stop where we were seated, I thought that it would be best if we headed back to our cars. Fortunately, it had also stopped raining once again. I shared the thought with Bill, and he agreed completely.

"But that doesn't mean that you can leave without responding," Bill said before we finally got off the bench and headed back to our cars.

"Don't worry, it's a long walk back," I replied, smiling at Bill who looked more confident in starting the search for his new job than ever before.

"As for the working of holacracy," I continued, "the system is based on a number of elements that are focused on for efficiency and optimality."

"Fair enough," Bill replied. "And what are they?"

"I'm getting there," I replied.

"Well, the first thing that is focused on when it comes to adopting and implementing a holacratic system of management is the Holacracy Constitution. I'm sure you already know enough about that."

"I'm going to look it up first thing in the morning," Bill replied.

"Good boy," I replied as I patted him on his back. "The next most important thing when it comes to holacratic systems is the structure of the business, company, or organization in which this system needs to be implemented. The structure in holacratic environments is always evolving, which is why constant meetings for reinforcement are extremely necessary. There are also a number of trainings that you could attend if you're interested in learning more about the organizational structure of holacracy."

"Something as complex as this definitely requires training sessions," Bill added.

"That's very true," I responded, as we headed back toward our cars.

The night was growing colder, and even though the area of town that we were in was essentially safe, we decided to speed up. We both had had a few pending tasks that also needed to be taken care of at our respective homes. Besides, neither of us wanted to catch a cold and spend the rest of the weekend recovering or sleeping, so we both decided that we should increase our pace.

I continued telling Bill about how meetings to discuss governance within the entire business, company, or organization in which holacracy was being implemented were also extremely necessary. I told Bill that focusing on governance of the structure of the organization was important because it helps create clarity about what is expected from each of the roles within the business, company, or organization in which the holacratic system of management is being adopted and implemented.

Even though governance of the structure of the business, company, or organization in which holacracy is implemented sounds like a pretty simple concept for now, the fact of the matter is that there's a lot that needs to be taken care of beyond the surface, and this is impossible without a proper understanding of the system and what is expected of different people and circles within the business, company, or organization.

I also told Bill that it was imperative for everyone in a holacratic business, company, or organization to be on the same page as everyone else when it comes to the daily activities, processes, and activities that need to be carried out for success.

Holacratic "tensions" are the next thing that I explained to Bill, at length. In the context of holacratic systems of management, tensions may arise in businesses, companies, and organizations. These tensions are essentially the difference between what it is possible for the business, company, or organization to achieve and what is *actually* being achieved. While they may be referred to as perceived gaps, tensions are essentially problems that can—and should—be resolved for optimality.

One important thing to note when it comes to holacratic environments is that tensions aren't brought up in meetings for the sake of looking for all of the activities that led to these problems coming up in the first place. In fact, these tensions or problems aren't even brought up to find the best possible solution to them. Instead, the only reason for bringing up these tensions in group meetings and discussions is to resolve a single tension pertaining to a specific role at a time.

We were finally only two blocks away from the little restaurant at which our cars were parked when I told Bill about Glass Frog software.[7] This software has essentially been designed to help implement holacracy in businesses, companies, and organizations that are interested in adopting this system of management to improve the quality of the solutions that they provide.

Although most people believe that it is completely possible for businesses, companies, and organizations to implement holacracy without the right type of software, there is just too much that this system of management involves. With all of the processes, activities, operations, meetings, goals, and objectives that need to be tracked, it is practically impossible for any business, company, or organization to pull off this system without making any mistakes. Additionally, with the increasing trend toward distributed environments, and the different circles that make up the holacratic environment, the problem gets escalated tenfold.

Bill and I continued talking about holacracy, the types of environments that are seen in the corporate world of today, organizational environments, and agility as we approached our cars. He continued to ask me questions—none of them irrelevant or baseless—and I told shared with him my own insights and corrected him where he was wrong.

Bill thanked me as he always did, and I could tell that he meant every word he said, so I didn't doubt him for a second.

"You're welcome, Bill," I told him, as he took out the keys to his car from his pocket. "I just hope you have all of the answers that you were looking for now," I said, smiling.

"You've always been of so much help," Bill continued. "I feel so much better and more confident about this job search now. But there's one thing that I think I still need to talk to you about. And I'm not sure if this is a stupid question but just bear with me, please."

"You know you can ask me anything, right Bill?" I could tell by the look on his face that he had to ask something very serious, and I couldn't leave him without the answers that he was looking for this late at night.

"I'm not sure if this makes any sense, professor," he said. "But do you think that it's possible for someone to learn agility or *develop* agile qualities?

As much as I hate to say it, his question left me completely speechless.

I told Bill that I wasn't sure about whether agility is something that could be learned and that I would get back to him on that. Even though Bill felt pretty bad that I didn't know the answer to his question, and he probably thought that I disliked him for asking that question because it made me "look bad" in front of Bill, the fact of the matter was that I was just about as interested in finding out whether agility was something that could be learned as he was.

After a few more formal and informal thank-yous, Bill got behind the wheel of his car.

"I think I know where and how I'm supposed to start looking for a new job, professor," Bill lowered the window of his car and smiled at me.

"I sure hope that's true, Bill," I smiled back. "Best of luck!"

"Thanks, Joe," he replied. "I'll get in touch with you in a couple of days. And don't worry too much about me this time. I'll be fine," he said with a toothy grin.

"Promise?" I asked Bill with a little laugh.

"Cross my heart," he said jokingly before he drove off.

Even though it was great to see that Bill had finally come to terms with the fact that he might not have a job in the next couple of weeks, it was great to see him content with the decision that he had made. Besides, it made me feel extremely glad that I was able to help him out in his search for what was supposed to be his dream job—a workplace at which he not only enjoys the work that he's supposed to do but also a workplace at which his efforts are acknowledged and he is appreciated.

As I dug my own keys out of my pocket and start driving, the only thing that kept on going through my mind was the question Bill had asked me before we called it a day. The question was important to Bill—that much was evident by the look on his face. But it was such a relevant and valid question that it honestly hurt me to not know the answer to it, especially as a professor of strategy who is supposed to be a mentor for his students.

References

1. Robertson, Brian J. (2007). *Holacracy.* New York: Henry Holt and Company.
2. Holacracy®. (2015, June). "Holacracy Constitution." HolacracyOne, LLC. Retrieved from https://www.holacracy.org/constitution
3. Robertson, Brian J. (2007). *Holacracy.* New York: Henry Holt and Company.
4. Ibid.
5. Robertson, Brian J. (2007). "Organization at the Leading Edge: Introducing Holacracy™." Retrieved from http://integralesleben.org/fileadmin/user_upload/images/DIA/Flyer/Organization_at_the_Leading_Edge_2007-06_01.pdf
6. Ibid.
7. Retrieved from https://glassfrog.com/

Chapter 7

Searching for Agile Leadership Qualities

Agility is the ability to adapt and respond to change . . . agile organizations view change as an opportunity, not a threat.

— Jim Highsmith[1]

When I arrived home awhile later, it occurred to me that I should probably do my research and find out the answer to Bill's million-dollar question, but I was too exhausted by that time. Besides, it was past midnight, and I needed to rest so that I could take care of a couple of things over the weekend.

But that certainly didn't mean that I had forgotten about Bill and his question.

In fact, as soon as I woke up the next morning, I knew exactly what I had to do. The question that Bill had asked me was indeed a tricky one, and I was genuinely disappointed that that had never crossed my mind; however, I knew that I would have to find the right person for the answer to a question as complicated as this.

And I knew just who that would be.

The man who I thought of approaching was none other than Scott, the president of the executive search area of a well-known recruiting company. It took awhile to get ahold of this busy man, but the wait was completely worth it. Besides, I had a few days before Bill would get in touch with me, as he said, so waiting a few extra days to learn something new and extremely important was fine.

We met about a week and a half after I told him that I needed some important answers from him. This humble man was kind enough to apologize and kept explaining that he had been a bit busy over the past few days, which is why he was unable to meet me sooner.

After the initial greetings and catching up, we got straight to the point.

"So, what brings you here today, Joe? I haven't seen you in quite some time. I hope everything's all right," Scott said, in his pleasant voice.

"All's good, my friend. I just wanted some really important information from you," I replied.

"Anything. Just make sure it's not something confidential that I can't share," Scott chuckled.

"I would never put you in a position like that, Scott," I replied.

Scott smiled warmly at me.

"There's something very important that I need to find out from you," I told him. "Now this may sound as if it's irrelevant, or it might sound weirdly out of context, but it's basically something that I was talking about with a student of mine—a young and intelligent former student, if I may."

"Sure. Go ahead," Scott said, evidently curious and concerned about what the question might be and why I had given him such a big back story if I just needed information.

"So, Scott," I said, "how do you select candidates for your clients? Are there any requirements or a certain level of agility that you think they require to be eligible for a particular job?"

Scott had a smile on his face. He assured me that this wasn't an irrelevant question at all and that this was probably one of the questions that he is most commonly asked.

Instead of answering the question straightforwardly, Scott decided that it would be best if he used a completely different approach in helping me to understand the importance of agile abilities and competencies when hiring new candidates.

"Since you gave me so much information before you asked me the question, I think I should do the same before I give you the answer that you're looking for," Scott continued. "Since you and your former student are so interested in how the hiring process works and what's necessary for it, I think that giving you some extra information is the best thing that I can do. I hope you don't mind that."

"Not at all," I replied. "In fact, I'd appreciate it."

"Very well then," Scott said. "What do you think is the major problem in the corporate world these days?"

"I personally feel like it's the lack of agility that's causing all of the problems that we see in businesses, companies, and organizations of today," I replied.

Scott smiled warmly again.

"I agree completely," he said. "There are no second opinions about the fact that that is indeed one of the biggest problems out there. But why do you think so many businesses, companies, and organizations these days feel like they're stuck?"

I wasn't sure what he wanted to hear as an answer so I decided to remain silent. Scott got the hint and decided to answer his question by himself when I didn't respond for awhile.

"To me, I think that problems with their thinking are the root causes of all of the other problems that businesses, companies, and organizations face today," he said.

Even though I understood where he was going with this, I wanted him to elaborate further on this point.

"That's an interesting thought," I said. And I really was interested in hearing a completely different viewpoint. "Could you explain a bit further?"

"I shall," Scott replied.

Scott told me he felt that managers and senior leadership in most of the businesses, companies, and organizations of today essentially face two major problems due to which progress is halted. These problems, according to Scott, had to do more with the thinking of the leaders and managers in these businesses, companies, and organizations than anything else. He told me that he had seen countless cases in which leaders and managers at businesses, companies, and organizations resisted change within the environment because they felt that the same activities, processes, and operations that led to success in the past can continue to do so in the future as well.

The second problem, according to him, was that although some leaders and managers truly do try to be pioneers of change, what ends up happening is that they don't think that their thinking or perception on the corporate environment within their businesses, companies or organizations needs to change. This, Scott said, is the major reason why no one is on the same page when change is being implemented or when people are supporting transformations that can prove to be beneficial, not only for the progress of the business, company, or organization in question but also for all of the employees that work there and people associated with them.

I agreed with every word he said. It is always great to hear the perspective of someone who has been a professional in the field for so long. Scott has been actively involved in the hiring process for several years now, and hearing the perspective of someone who thinks the same way as I do and has a lot of experience up his sleeve was a pleasant surprise. However, since I wanted to learn more about how he thinks regarding the importance of agility and the implementation of change, I decided not to give any input and just nodded in agreement to everything that he said.

Scott continued to tell me how the teams and leaders of today are under a lot more pressure than they were ever before. It was only when he told me he felt that it was important for people to create more dynamic, sustainable, and robust environments for the success and constant progress of their businesses, companies, and organizations that I told him I feel that the leaders and managers of today have to go the extra mile to help their businesses, companies, and organizations to adapt to the **V**olatile, **U**ncertain, **C**omplex, and **A**mbiguous (VUCA) environment of today.

We shared our thoughts and insights on the VUCA environment for a while before we finally got back to talking about the requirement for agility in businesses, companies, and organizations of today.

"Leaders in most places know that the business, company, or organization that they are responsible for needs to change," Scott continued, "but they don't know where or how they are supposed to initiate this change."

Scott paused and picked up a glass of water from the table that was beside his seat.

Scott's statement immediately reminded me of the countless conversations that Bill and I had had about the topic. I didn't say anything as I waited for Scott to continue talking after drinking his water—and continue he did.

"There are no plans. There are no meaningful dynamic strategies," Scott said. "No wonder more than half of the transformations that people try to make in corporate environments these days fail."

I agreed with every word the man before me said. Too often, he had witnessed damage caused by a lack of planning, and he knew exactly what was wrong with the system and the methods that people have been using to transform their businesses, companies, and organizations in the complex and confusing world of today without really planning for change.

In fact, everything that Scott said during our conversation kept reminding me of the famous quote by Albert Einstein: "We cannot solve our problems with the same thinking we used when we created them."[2] This statement is so true that I felt as if there was nothing that could be more relatable and relevant in that moment.

For businesses, companies, and organizations to effectively bring about change and transformation within their system and their environments, it is imperative for them to think beyond addressing unique things or entities and see how and why it is important to change the dynamics of the business, company, or organization in question as a whole.

Dealing with one entity at a time may seem like a good approach to some people—especially those who are not experienced and don't know much about how change works. However, the unfortunate reality is that treating everything as a separate entity and then trying to bring about change tends to result in a preoccupation with the problems that keep arising within a specific entity, thereby not leaving enough room or flexibility for complete focus on the rest of the business, company, or organization in which change is being implemented or transformations are necessary.

Since transformations and changes that are required for a business, company, or organization to progress in the world of today don't really change much about the way in which our leaders and managers think and make decisions, these transformations fail to produce the results that were anticipated, even when they started off the right way. The main reason why the mindset and perspective of the managers and leaders in these places fails to change is because they aren't supportive of the concept of agility, and they believe that they are right in whatever they are doing.

For the effects of transformation and change to be lasting, it is extremely necessary for leaders and managers of businesses, companies, and organizations in the VUCA world to challenge themselves and bring about change from within. As a leader, there are quite a few things that are essential for you to keep in mind if you are at a business, company, or organization in which you wish to implement change.

Before anything else, however, you should know and understand that although you are fond of your own way of thinking and believe that you are making all of the right decisions, as humans there is always the possibility of mistakes being made. What this essentially means is that you should be open to the ideas and beliefs that other people have and understand that it is completely possible for someone else to have a better approach that could be followed to implement change and transformation in the business, company, or organization that you are leading or managing.

By being open to the ideas and decisions of other people, not only will you be able to share your own viewpoint regarding certain things, but it will also be possible for you to learn from more experienced professionals and understand how other people within the environment think. Although most managers and leaders in the corporate world of today feel as if they know what they are doing and that no one can do their job better than they can, the fact of the matter remains that there is nothing wrong with learning new things from other people, and doing so will not make you any more or less competent in the business, company, or organization in which you are a leader or manager.

Another thing that you should remember as someone who is responsible for change or transformation is the importance of taking the time to understand the ever-changing environment and everything that lies within it. Mindful contemplation and perceiving the corporate environment without prejudices or preconceived notions is something that hardly any leaders or managers in the businesses, companies, and organizations of today do.

As someone who will be the pioneer of change and transformation in his or her business, company, or organization, it is essential for you to leave all of your opinions, notions, and instincts behind and truly understand what it means to mindfully review the environment and the changes that engulf it.

Another thing that is crucial for you as a leader or manager of a business, company, or organization is that any decisions that you make should be based on accurate perceptions of the environment. As mentioned earlier, open thinking and really taking the time to understand what is going on within the environment is extremely necessary for you to make the right decisions at the right time that will help implement change, promote transformation successfully, and avoid the possibility of resistance by the people who will be affected most by it at your business, company, or organization.

Jumping to conclusions is something that you should avoid as much as possible whenever you are responsible for implementing change or leading a workplace. Businesses, companies, and organizations in the VUCA environment of today can't afford to have someone make impulsive decisions because the results of doing so can be devastating.

In fact, it is essential for all employees in any business, company, or organization to live by these rules regardless of whether they have a team of subordinates that reports to them. The reason for this is that no employee anywhere is insignificant, and making the wrong decisions can prove to be extremely costly for a lot of people in the business environment of today.

Employees anywhere in the world must also realize that the business environment of today is not the same as it used to be years ago. What this means is that your mental model must be in line with the current situation and that it is practically impossible for you to progress in today's world if you are not willing to adapt or change your way of thinking.

As Scott continued to tell me all about his experiences over the years and how he noticed that the hiring process has changed since he had started working, I decided it would be best to share with him bits and pieces of my conversations with Bill as soon as the chance presented itself. Part of my reason was to ensure that he didn't feel as if his words were falling on deaf ears. I, therefore, decided that giving my two cents every now and then and sharing my own point of view with him would keep the conversation alive and going for much longer.

More than anything else, of course, my reason for doing so was to see if he approved or agreed with what Bill and I thought and to find out whether we were all on the same page.

I told Scott that I personally thought that it was extremely necessary for executives, leaders, and managers alike to play their part in promoting change in the business, company, or organization in which they work. Even though he agreed with my way of thinking, and he assumed that I knew why and how it was important for change to be implemented within any company, business, or organization to help it keep up with the rest, the person who sat before me was interested in hearing the plan that I had in mind for implementing change. At that time, since I thought that Scott had already told me everything that he had wanted to speak about, I decided that I should share my viewpoint with him.

In line with the conversations on this topic that I had had with Bill earlier, I told Scott that I felt as if the approach and strategy that should be used by each company, business, and organization to implement change and successfully initiate transformations depends on quite a number of factors. When asked what I thought these were, I told Scott that I felt as if the approach and strategy may differ depending on the industry that the company, business, and organization that was trying to transform and implement change was a part of. Since Scott himself had years upon years of experience and knew exactly what must be done, I didn't have to say much for him to completely understand what I was thinking.

He did, however, have something else in mind—something that I hadn't given much thought to.

"Do you know what innovation hubs are?" Scott asked me. His face carried no particular expression, which is why I gathered that he was genuinely interested in whether I knew about the concept.

I told Scott that even though I had heard of them, I didn't know too much about innovation hubs, and that I would love to hear more about how they worked. As mentioned earlier, I loved hearing the perspectives of other people, and having someone as experienced as Scott inform me about something as important as innovation hubs and initiating change successfully was truly a pleasure.

Scott was evidently very glad to hear that I was genuinely interested in learning more about innovation hubs and how they worked. Apparently, he supported the idea of innovation hubs completely and was more than willing to share anything and everything that he knew about them.

Much like me, Scott was of the opinion that transformation, creativity, and innovation needed space. Innovation hubs, according to him, were the best option to provide these spaces. According to Scott, innovation hubs were skillfully designed with the sole intention of fostering creativity and promoting change that would be accepted by everyone. Scott believed that this is why they were becoming more popular with each passing day among countless businesses, companies, and organizations from various industries. As soon as he was done saying that, Scott had a smile on his face—and I couldn't figure out whether he was just too excited to talk about innovation hubs or if he had remembered something that he would like to share.

Fortunately, I was saved the trouble of having to think of the right words to say when I wanted to ask him what caused the sudden smile on his face.

"You know, that just reminded me of a quote by the founder of the Visa® credit card association, Dee Ward Hock," Scott said, without me having to ask any questions. The smile on his face, too, didn't disappear. "Make an empty space in any corner of your mind, and creativity will instantly fill it."[3]

Needless to say, a smile naturally developed on my own face as well. It was great to see how passionate Scott was, not only about sharing his opinions but also how eager he was to help me learn about things that I, too, was genuinely interested in.

In the few minutes that I had spent with him, I realized that most people with the amount of experience that Scott had would exude vibes of arrogance—but not him. The best thing that I noticed in Scott was that I didn't find him at all supercilious during the entire conversation that we had, which is another reason why I was becoming even more interested in learning from the experience and knowledge of this professional.

"Since transformations require that a lot of people work together, I believe that it's best if innovation hubs are created in every business, company, and organization interested in transformation or implementing change for the better," Scott said. "I personally believe that this is an essential step that must be taken throughout companies, businesses, and organizations of all industries."

Even though I knew a little bit about innovation hubs and heard the term being tossed around more often than ever before, I never knew that they were such a big deal and would be endorsed and supported by an experienced professional to *this* extent. I wanted to ask Scott why he thought that innovation hubs were such an integral part of businesses, companies, and organizations of the VUCA world of today, but he was so passionate about his insights and perception about the importance of innovation hubs that he barely waited for a response from my end while he spoke.

"Now I know you might be wondering why I'm making such a big deal out of the whole innovation hub thing," he said, "but I feel like they actually deserve all of the importance that I'm giving them and much more."

It was almost as if he read my mind. I had wanted to ask him why he found innovation hubs so important, but it seemed he would continue to explain this, and more, on his own.

"You see, these innovation hubs that I'm talking about are interesting for quite a few reasons. I already mentioned that they are designed skillfully and are constructed and planned with a specific purpose in mind—but that's not all. I think what's more interesting and what makes them even better is that they are facilitated mindfully and that the entire leadership team supports them. When you have that much support, it goes without saying that implementing change and transformation will become the primary focus of quite a few—if not all—of the people within the business, company, or organization in which the innovation hub is being created."

Even though Scott had only said a few words, I immediately began to understand what he meant. I guess all those years of explaining these things to countless people as they were entering the workforce throughout the world, during hiring and otherwise, taught him the art of getting his point across succinctly. Now that I thought about it, brevity looked like something he was particularly fond of—but he didn't look like he would stop talking about innovation hubs at any time soon.

And I didn't want him to.

It isn't often that you get the chance to speak to someone as professional and experienced in his field as Scott, and I wanted to make the most of our meeting. Besides, there were important questions that I was looking for answers to, and Scott seemed to be one of the only people who would be able to help me.

Since I didn't want to cause him to forget what he was saying, I didn't respond with much except a nod. Besides, there wasn't much that I had to say at that point. I wanted him to continue what he was saying before I shared my own opinion with him. However, by the way in which the conversation was proceeding, it seemed that there wouldn't be much that I'd disagree with him about.

"You see, when you have an entire area that is specifically designed for fostering creativity and promoting transformations within the company, business, or organization where you work, it honestly becomes a tad difficult for you to ignore the changes in the environment altogether.

"The support and engagement of leadership teams follow almost immediately after the creation of an innovation hub. With something as great as that going on, I personally believe that innovation hubs allow communities to grow and have the potential and power of making support for transformations important for everyone that works in the company, business, or organization that is interested in adapting to change. The effects of creating an innovation hub for implementing change in any business, company, or organization are far more deeply rooted than what is often evident—or at least that's what I believe," Scott winked at me as he poured himself another glass of water.

I was starting to be convinced about the importance of innovation hubs because they had a lot to offer, and, according to Scott, they had a lot of potential in just about any business, company, or organization where they would be created, regardless of the industry that they were based in. As this experienced man before me drank his glass of water, I felt like asking him how he thought it would be best to get started with creating an innovation hub but thought better of it and kept my question to myself. He would probably start explaining that himself if he thought that it was important.

As soon as he was done drinking his water, he continued to talk about innovation hubs—this time perhaps a bit more passionately than before.

"I feel as if innovation hubs are a great tool for expediting the entire process of having your business, company, or organization transform and adapt to changes for the better. Since there's so much going on at the same time, the quality and speed of innovation is impacted to a great extent."

Even though I didn't quite understand what Scott meant by this, I waited for him to continue what he had to say before I asked him any questions. Apparently, my facial expressions gave that much away, and he started explaining this in much more detail than I thought he would.

"I'm sure you might be wondering what I mean by that," he said, "and I think I'll be able to explain in just a bit."

I simply nodded with a smile. Evidently enough, Scott knew how to read facial expressions pretty well and knew exactly how to explain things to people in a way that they would understand completely.

"I feel like important tools like innovation hubs will be able to expedite the process of transformation and innovation primarily because they will bring about major changes to the way in which the processes, models, and operations work at the business, company, or organization where change and transformation are being implemented. But that's not all. The multifaceted consequences and effects that come about as a result of the creation of an innovation hub may also include affecting the corporate culture in a positive manner, thereby making way for improved collaboration and agility within the company, business, or organization that wishes to implement change and transform to keep up with the environment and ensure that it isn't forced to extinction."

What I understood from all of this was that innovation hubs could help promote innovation and transformation for quite a number of reasons. Changes that innovation hubs have the potential for bringing about in multiple domains and dimensions, such as the attitudes, behaviors, and collaborations that are integral for the success of the business, company, or organization where transformations and innovation are more of a necessity than an option. These changes are essential for survival and growth in the economy, which is why more and more companies, businesses, and organizations are considering innovation hubs.

Since Scott noticed how interested I was in knowing more about innovation hubs, he started asking me a few more questions to find out what exactly I know about them so that he would be able to give me information that would be new and beneficial for me.

"How do you think innovation hubs are formed?" he asked me, in his usual pleasant voice.

"What do you mean?" I replied.

"Do you think there are any factors that need to be kept in mind when creating innovation hubs?" Scott asked me as he picked up his glass of water.

"I'm sure there are," I replied. "But I'm not exactly sure what they are."

"Allow me to explain," Scott replied courteously. "There are certain conditions and factors that absolutely cannot be ignored when it comes to creating innovation hubs that are effective and efficient. Since the primary reason for the creation of an innovation hub is implementing change and transformation effectively and innovating optimally, it is essential for the processes and environment of the business, company, or organization to be kept in mind at all times before it is created.

"There are a few guiding principles that can also not be ignored when it comes to creating innovation hubs that are efficient and effective. The first and most important guiding principle for a successful innovation hub is that it is essential for leadership teams to act as officers for the transformation of businesses. What this essentially means is that it is not only important for leaders and managers to sponsor the innovation hub, but it is also imperative for them to be actively involved in all of the changes that are being implemented and in the entire decision-making process. Without the active involvement of leaders and managers alongside all of the rest of the employees of any business, company, or organization, it is practically impossible for the innovation hub to be successful, regardless of how well the plan of the creation of the innovation hub and execution of the transformation itself is carried out."

I was surprised that Scott and I had opinions that were so similar. Even though he was explaining the importance of the active involvement of leaders and managers in the context of innovation hubs and how they should be a part of them instead of leaving all the work up to the employees and those who are lower in the hierarchy in the company, business, or organization where change and transformation are meant to be implemented, the fact of the matter was that we had exactly the same point of view. In fact, everything he said to me was in many ways similar to the things that I had said to Bill in all of the conversations that I had had with him since I met him at the airport that fine day.

Since I didn't question a word he said, I waited for him to continue. By the looks of it, he wasn't really waiting for any replies or responses from my end either, and he began to talk about what he believed the spaces of innovation hubs should be like.

"Another one of the guidelines that I believe must be kept in mind when creating effective and efficient innovation hubs is that they have to have the right spaces. In my opinion, innovation hubs are best created in spaces and areas that are not too congested and have very high ceilings.

"The way I see it," he said, "innovation hubs also need to have a lot of natural lighting coming in. I feel that natural lighting plays a vital role in improving the performance of employees and can also come in handy for innovation and creativity. This, I believe, is extremely important whenever you are thinking of creating an innovation hub for any business, company, or organization, regardless of the industry that it is based in."

As soon as Scott was done saying this, I started wondering why it was important for innovation hubs to be created in spaces that were very open. Whereas all of the rest of the questions that I had had were put to rest without me having to explicitly ask him about them, I thought it would be best for me to ask him this question since I really didn't expect him to answer or elaborate on that point by himself. I seized the opportunity as soon as he took a break to breathe.

"I understand the whole natural lighting part, and I completely support your views on that, but why do you think it's necessary for these innovation hubs to be created in large open spaces? Why isn't it possible for them to be created in areas that are small and congested?"

A smile appeared on the face of the man before me as soon as I asked this question. The smile was soon followed by a reply in his characteristic pleasant voice.

"I never said it's not possible," he said, with the smile still on his face. "It's just *preferable* if they are made in large open spaces. I feel as if open spaces and the right amount of lighting just create an aura in which spontaneous interactions are welcomed and creativity is fostered. That's pretty much all that's needed for innovation hubs, right?"

I nodded in agreement as I returned the smile.

"Besides, I was almost certain that you'd ask me a question. That's the only reason why I took a pause," he continued, with his warm smile.

"And how is that?" I asked, genuinely surprised.

"You started listening more intently when I got to that part," he replied.

My conversation with the experienced professional before me continued for quite awhile. In the time that we spent with each other, he told me everything that he thought about creating the perfect innovation hub for any business, company, or organization.

According to Scott, everything from the furniture and equipment in the innovation hub to the colors that are used in the place are extremely important. This professional strongly believed that designing an innovation hub shouldn't be a random process and that a lot of thought needs to be put into creating a transformation to ensure that it provides the benefits that were anticipated.

Scott was of the opinion that all of the furniture and equipment that is present inside innovation hubs needs to be mobile to create a more efficient environment for everyone who will be working in them. Since people will come together to share ideas and information with each other in innovation hubs with the sole intention of making the business, company, or organization ready for transformation and help it adapt to change, regardless of the industry that it is a part of, Scott believed that it is extremely important for the perfect work environment to be created in a place where you can be as creative as possible.

To create the perfect innovation hub, Scott believed that having mobile equipment, such as large magnetic whiteboard walls, portable working desks, and technical equipment, was the best strategy for any business, company, or organization that was interested in innovating and adapting to change in an efficient way and to ensure that these innovations and changes won't be resisted.

Scott also shared with me the importance of having dedicated project rooms within innovation hubs. He explained how he had noticed over the years that having a dedicated room for projects promotes productivity and teamwork and makes people more interested in the work that they are doing, instead of discussing important projects and ideas in any random location. Scott told me that this was also one of the major reasons why he believed that innovation hubs are capable of producing remarkable results.

As Scott continued talking about innovation hubs, which he was quite passionate about, I couldn't be more appreciative that he was actually taking the time out to explain these things to me in such detail. The individual before me spoke purely from experience and had learned countless things as he worked tirelessly over the years—things that he is evidently more than happy to share with anyone who he feels is as genuinely interested as he is in learning anything—from the hiring process to transformations to adapting to change in a way that it results in exactly what was anticipated.

Owing to his years of experience, Scott was able to enhance my knowledge to a large extent. One of the things that he taught me was that colors have a major impact not only on one's creativity but also on one's productivity. Scott told me that there have been countless research studies conducted on the impact of colors and how certain colors have been proven to boost productivity.

Scott told me that it's imperative for someone who is experienced in colors and interior designing to design the interior of the innovation hubs of your companies, businesses, and organizations if you want to reap their benefits in their entirety.

"Designing innovation hubs is no easy task," he said. "I believe that creating an innovation hub for any business, company, or organization, regardless of the industry that it is based in and the environmental conditions that surround it, involves a lot of hard work. Just as people come together in the innovation hub itself to share ideas and work hand in hand towards transformations and innovation, it is imperative for a lot of minds to work together when designing the innovation hub itself.

"Innovation hubs are multifaceted tools, and their creation and designing is a trans-disciplinary project that needs to be pulled off in the right way to ensure that the innovation hub proves to be as beneficial as was hoped."

Getting the opportunity to speak to and learn from someone who is as extremely passionate and experienced at what he does is not something that happens often. However, as happy and pleased as I was to be learning from someone as professional and experienced as Scott, I couldn't wait to tell Bill all about my meeting with this great individual.

Since Bill was in a bad place and wasn't completely certain about quite a few things that were extremely important for him when he was starting his search for a new job, I knew for a fact that I had learned a great deal of new things myself during this long meeting with Scott—things that would be far more important for someone like Bill than they would be for myself.

Just as Scott was interested in sharing all of this vital information with me, I thought it would be best to share everything that I had recently learned with Bill as soon as I got the chance. I was not only a strong believer in the fact that you should share important information with others, but I knew that it would be extremely beneficial for Bill, who was now more in need of a job than ever before.

Once he was done explaining the guidelines that he thought it was essential to keep in mind when creating innovation hubs, Scott continued to tell me more about how he thought innovation hubs could be beneficial to the companies, businesses, and organizations at which they are created. More than anything else, I understood that he was a fan of the involvement factor that came with innovation hubs.

"I feel like innovation hubs are very inviting," he told me, looking at nothing in particular before shifting his focus to me. "It's like everyone can just come and work together and change the space according to their own needs and requirements."

"These tools are just that versatile," he continued. "Instead of having a predefined structure that doesn't change regardless of the conditions and the requirements of the people that will be working in the innovation hub, the space provided by the innovation hub can be leveraged by people according to their own requirements, and the structure can be modified in a way that guarantees optimal results and maximum efficiency for whoever is using the space for any particular projects or to discuss ideas and share information."

Even though I knew that Scott was talking about all of the benefits that innovation hubs have to offer extremely passionately, I was starting to draw parallels between innovation hubs and co-working spaces. To ensure that I didn't end up reaching any inaccurate conclusions after our conversation, I thought it would be best if I asked Scott if they really were similar.

"I'm sorry if this question comes across as a bit immature, but isn't the atmosphere in innovation hubs a lot like co-working spaces?" I asked.

"Yes and no," he replied. "But first, remember to never hold back on any questions just because you feel that they are too immature or obvious. We're all learning," he continued, with the warm smile of a lenient teacher.

"Care to explain?" I asked.

"I definitely will," he replied, without letting the smile disappear from his face.

After a short pause, he continued talking. "You asked if innovation hubs and co-working spaces are similar."

Since I didn't quite understand whether this was a rhetorical statement, all I did was nod in return.

"Well, as I told you before, innovation hubs are created for a specific purpose. The primary intention behind creating these hubs is to ease the transformation process and promote changes and the adaptation to them without creating any resistance. Since adapting to change is essential for companies, businesses, and organizations of today to ensure that they aren't forced to extinction, these innovation hubs prove to be highly advantageous in the VUCA world of today."

Even though both Scott and I had become engrossed in our conversation about transformations and adapting to change, I was immediately reminded of my reason for having that meeting with Scott as soon as he stated this last sentence.

Considering how important agility and being able to strategize effectively is in the VUCA world of today, Bill had asked me whether it would be possible for someone to learn or develop agile qualities if they didn't already possess them when they entered the workforce—and finding the answer to that question was essentially the purpose of the meeting that I was having with Scott. It was only when I thought about this question again that I understood why Scott had told me everything that he did.

Throughout the conversation that I was having with Scott, I understood that he was particularly fond of both brevity and conciseness, but he had given me a lot more information than what I had asked for. It was only then that I realized that he had given me all of this extra information to answer the question that I had asked him.

From what I gathered, Scott believed that it really was possible to develop agile capabilities and qualities, given the right circumstances. After he was finished discussing the benefits of innovation hubs, I thought it would be best to find the right words to ask him whether the conclusion that I had reached was correct. All Scott did was respond with his characteristic warm smile as he nodded slightly.

"I'm glad you were able to figure that out," Scott said without the slightest tinge of sarcasm. "However, it doesn't just end at that."

"What do you mean?" I asked him, just as I did several times earlier on in my conversation with him.

"Now what I tried explaining to you during this time was that it is indeed possible for people to learn and develop agile qualities and capabilities if they join the right business, company, or organization, which is equipped with all of the tools that are essential for it to keep up with the changes of the environment and transform effectively and efficiently. The fact of the matter, however, is that just having these tools but not knowing how to prepare your business, company, or organization for change and transformation is a surefire recipe for disaster."

After he had explained everything at length, I understood how and why it was necessary for companies, businesses, and organizations to invest in creating the perfect innovation hubs that will allow them to adapt to change, foster creativity, and innovate, unlike their counterparts. However, what he said about preparing your business, company, or organization for transformation was beyond me. *"Isn't creating an innovation hub enough?"* I thought to myself. Fortunately, just as before, Scott went on to explain everything.

"Do you know how businesses, companies, and organizations can prepare for transformation?" Scott asked out of the blue.

"I'm not particularly sure about that," I replied.

"Well, that's what I'm here for," Scott replied like a teacher who is always willing to help.

"I personally feel that it isn't enough if you have the tools for innovation, such as innovation hubs, if the place where you work isn't ready for transforming or adapting to change," he continued. "Having tools but not knowing how to use them effectively and efficiently for the benefit of the business, company, or organization that you are a part of doesn't do quite enough. Unfortunately, however, most people are of the opinion that their job is done by having tools and implementing certain strategies, and they end up feeling disappointed and disheartened when they find that it wasn't enough after all.

"Pulling off a transformation is a difficult task that requires a great deal of effort on the part of everyone who is involved in the business, company, or organization that is trying to change and progress. The workforce of today comprises many young people. Unlike in the past, however, the younger generation today has a very different approach to working and getting things done. Personally, I feel that it's important to cater to their requirements and preferences more than anything else if you want your business, company, or organization to transform successfully."

Even though I didn't completely understand what he meant by all of this, I decided that it would be best to take his word on everything he was saying and respect his opinion on transformations and how they should be prepared for. After all, considering that the professional before me was far more experienced than I was, and he had been actively involved in the hiring process for quite a few years, I concluded that he would really know much more about the workforce and how it has changed than I would.

Scott believes that it is essential for businesses, companies, and organizations of today to revise their human resources (HR) business model so that it will be more in line with the requirements of millennials and the younger generation. When asked why he thought that was necessary, Scott replied that there haven't been any major changes in the way in which HR has worked over the course of several years, and that for transformation to occur, it is essential for businesses, companies, and organizations to start by bringing about changes to their own HR departments. Changing the business model for HR, Scott said, is the essential stepping stone for a successful transformation.

Scott is of the opinion that businesses, companies, and organizations can only keep their competitive edge and innovate if they experiment with business models that will change the way in which their processes, operations, and activities are carried out for the better. In this way, Scott said, it would be possible for these businesses, companies, and organizations to deliver and capture value.

"Over the years," he continued, "I've noticed that quite a large number of businesses, companies, and organizations are not able to keep up with changes in the environment for a few fundamental reasons. As unfortunate as it may sound, the reasons for the failure of these businesses, companies, and organizations don't change much. It's just that no one these days is willing to learn from the mistakes of others."

Scott explained to me that recently most major domains and departments, such as HR, Finance, and information technology (IT), haven't been given the importance that they deserve, which is why such large numbers of businesses, companies, and organizations have failed over the last few years even when the leaders and managers that were responsible for transformations believed that they were doing everything right. According to Scott, it is imperative for leaders and managers to give these areas and departments their due importance to ensure that the needs and requirements of customers and clients are being taken care of at all times and to guarantee that the company, business, or organization rises to new heights every day.

"In addition to many young people joining the workforce, it is important for businesses, companies, and organizations to understand that quite a large number of people from older generations are retiring, which means that departments—especially those such as HR—need to deal with the requirements of people from different age groups. And to make things more challenging for the HR department, it must be understood that the competition for talent is more fierce now than ever before, which means that it is essential for regulations and policies to be revised."

When I asked Scott how he thought the business model for the HR department could be changed, he proposed quite a few changes.

"It isn't possible for the HR department to do its job without any external help anymore," he said. "I believe that it's essential for HR departments to partner up with others to acquire talent and promote learning in ways that can't be categorized as traditional."

HR departments in companies, businesses, and organizations that are interested in transforming for the better and adapting to change to ensure that they progress in the right way need to partner up with associations and organizations that will make their task much easier. Additionally, since the millennial work-force is all about diversity and versatility, partnering up with different organizations and associations will ensure that the human resources departments of the companies, businesses, and organizations that are interested in change manage to acquire all of the right talent and keep potential employees engaged.

Scott informed me that he believes that HR departments now are less competent than before because the ways in which they carry out their operations, processes, and activities have more or less become static. The experienced professional before me believes that the HR departments of companies, businesses, and organizations that are interested in not only attracting but also retaining talent from the younger generation needs to focus on branding, recruiting, development, and social media promotion.

Scott believes that since people in the HR departments aren't focusing on these aspects and domains as much as they should, it will not only become difficult for the companies, businesses, and organizations of today to find the right employees for a variety of positions, but it will also be problematic for them to try and retain competent and hardworking individuals and transform in a way that is necessary for them to survive in the VUCA world of today.

Scott is also of the opinion that it is essential for companies, businesses, and organizations of today to focus on face-to-face interactions far more than digital interactions. Millennials, according to Scott, are more fond of talking and conversing with other people and sharing ideas in person rather than through digital platforms and forums.

Scott sat up straight soon after he gave me all of the aforementioned information about the importance of changing the HR departments of companies, businesses, and organizations and how millennials work in a way that is much different from the way in which previous generations worked. The look on his face gave me the impression that he had something very important to say.

"I know that you didn't come here to hear any of this. And I'm sure that you already knew most—if not all—of the things that I told you today," he said humbly. "The reason for me to tell you all of this right now was that even though learning agility is possible, the environment of the workplace that you join plays a major role in whether you'll be able to learn agility or pick up on any other qualities that you would like.

"With that said," he continued, with his characteristic warm smile, "I'm very glad that you've grown into the mentor that you are today. And since you took out the time to come here to ask me all of these questions, I think I should summarize everything in one little sentence: 'Your student should be able to develop agile qualities, but that will only be possible if he joins the right workplace. Tell him to keep his eyes wide open when he's searching for a new job.'"

I thanked Scott for all of his generosity in telling me everything that he did.

"I'll be here whenever you need me," he replied. "I hope I have been of help to you and your student."

References

1. Highsmith, Jim. (n.d.). AZQuotes.com. Wind and Fly LTD. Retrieved from http://www. azquotes.com/quote/822295.
2. Einstein, Albert. (n.d.). Albert Einstein Quotes. BrainyQuote.com. Xplore Inc. Retrieved from https://www.brainyquote.com/quotes/albert_einstein_121993
3. Hock, Dee. (n.d.). Dee Hock Quotes. BrainyQuote.com. Xplore Inc. Retrieved from https://www.brainyquote.com/quotes/dee_hock_285469

Chapter 8

Searching for Problem Solving and Decision Making

There are not more than five musical notes, yet the combinations of these five
  give rise to more melodies than can ever be heard.

There are not more than five primary colors, yet in combination
  they produce more hues than can ever been seen.

There are not more than five cardinal tastes, yet combinations of
  them yield more flavors than can ever be tasted.

— *The Art of War*, Sun Tzu[1]

It wasn't long after my meeting with Scott that I decided that I should pay a visit to my former student and share with him everything that I had learned from the experienced professional who had very generously taken so much time out of his extremely busy schedule just to help an old friend and his student.

"It isn't often that you find people who are as humble and selfless as Scott," I thought to myself.

Since Bill had already talked with me about his schedule quite a number of times, I knew that Bill wasn't particularly fond of partying or wasting time on the weekends like other people of his age. I, therefore, decided it would be best if I asked him to meet me on a Saturday afternoon. Besides, he probably didn't even have much to take care of at work because he was almost done serving his notice period at his former toxic workplace.

After one of my lectures on a weekday, I headed home and gave Bill a call. It didn't take him long to pick up the phone.

"Hey, professor," he replied with a jovial voice.

"How's it going Bill?" I replied.

"Define 'it,'" Bill replied with a laugh, before he got serious.

"Well," he said, "I'm pretty happy that I've made it to the last few days of my notice period. The job search, however, is something I'm not too proud of. I'm still trying my best though."

"Well, there's something I need you to hear," I replied.

"When and where are we meeting?" was all he said in return.

"Are you free this weekend?" I asked Bill. "And I think the location's a given." Bill laughed on the phone.

"Saturday afternoon at 2?" Bill asked.

"Sounds good to me."

When Saturday finally arrived, it started drizzling—much like every other time that we had met at that small restaurant near my house. For once, I wanted to be there on time and decided to leave about 40 minutes before 2, to avoid traffic. Luckily, there wasn't much traffic on the road, and I figured that I'd reach there much sooner than planned. At about 1:40 p.m., I reached the little restaurant, which was almost as crowded as it was during my last visit.

As expected, I started receiving special loyal-customer treatment as soon as I walked through the door. Even though there already were quite a few people in the restaurant, the manager directed me toward the table where Bill and I usually sat. Immediately after I was seated, the tall waiter who always served us brought two menus to the table and placed one before me.

"Will you be waiting for your friend?" he asked with a smile on his face, as he held the second menu in his hand.

"I'm sure he's on his way right now," I replied, returning a smile to the waiter.

The waiter nodded lightly and placed he second menu on the table. "Whenever you're ready, sir," he said, before he left.

I fiddled with the menu in my hands for a few minutes before I actually opened it and browsed through my options. I had only read a few of the options on the menu when there was a knock on the table.

"You're here early today, I see," Bill said, as I looked up to see who was demanding my attention.

"Thought I'd welcome you for a change," I replied as I extended my hand for a handshake.

Bill returned the greeting before he sat down before me.

"So, what were you looking at, professor? Let's order something quickly. I'm starving!" Bill said.

"Nothing special," I replied. "I just arrived here myself. See what you want so that we can order and get straight to business."

Both Bill and I were in the mood for pizza so we decided that that's what we should get. Besides, we had been at the restaurant several times before but had never ordered pizza, despite recommendations from our kind waiter on multiple occasions.

We signaled the waiter and he kindly obliged.

"We've finally considered your recommendations," I said. "We'll go with pizza today. Get us your best flavor, please."

"I'll make sure you love it," the kind waiter replied as he picked the menus up from the table and left.

"So, what is it that I should hear?" Bill asked inquisitively.

"I think you forgot but you had asked me a question the last time we met here," I replied.

"I honestly don't remember. I'm sorry," Bill replied.

"Well," I continued, "I met with someone who is very experienced a couple of days ago. The humble man who I met has been involved in the hiring process for quite a few years now. Needless to say, he knew a lot that you and I can learn from."

"Let's hear it," Bill replied.

"Well, I remember that you asked me last time whether or not agility was something that could be learned. When I met this person I was just telling you about, I found out that it is indeed possible to learn and develop these capabilities. One thing, however, that he mentioned explicitly was that it's impossible to do so without the right setting and environment."

"I just remembered that I asked you that question. But I'm sorry to say that I'm not too sure what you mean by that," Bill replied.

"I wasn't either," I smiled at Bill. "But Scott was kind enough to explain. He told me that even though quite a number of companies, businesses, and organizations in the **V**olatile, **U**ncertain, **C**omplex, and **A**mbiguous (VUCA) world of today are interested in transforming and showing their competitors how they can adapt to change much better than their counterparts, the fact of the matter is that people these days don't know how to leverage the tools and information that is available.

"Most companies, businesses, and organizations of today are shackled by the thought that they'll be able to progress if they continue to carry out processes, operations, and activities as they did in the past. As unfortunate as this may sound, this is the very thought that is preventing them from moving on and progressing."

Bill simply nodded in return.

It had only been about 15 minutes since we had placed our order, but I saw our waiter coming to our table with a steaming hot pizza.

"Bon appétit," he said, with a smile on his face. "Can I get you anything to drink?"

"Just the usual," Bill replied.

"I'll get you your water and wine in a bit," the waiter said, before he headed to the table next to ours to take an order.

Both Bill and I placed a slice of pizza on our respective plates before we continued talking.

"How does that affect the possibility of learning or developing agile qualities?" Bill asked, as he took his first bite.

"What Scott tried to explain to me was that since companies, businesses, and organizations of today don't really know how they should strategize when they are trying to implement change, the morale is often low and people are resistant to change. Scott used a very different approach and told me about the need for innovation hubs to explain how people can work together and modify spaces within the company, business, or organization where change is to be implemented to ensure that the results are as positive as anticipated."

"How an innovation hub alone can change everything for these places is something that I fail to understand," Bill replied.

"That's exactly what I'm trying to tell you, Bill" I said.

"I didn't know much about innovation hubs before, either, and that's why I couldn't explain things to you in much detail. However, now that Scott was kind enough to tell me everything that I needed to know, I'm more confident that a lot of preparation needs to be done to ensure that anticipated results and goals are reached even when you have an innovation hub in your business, company, or organization."

I went on to explain to Bill that people have considered innovation hubs to be synonymous with elixirs for far too long and that it is essential to ensure that the right space is used and the perfect atmosphere is created for innovation hubs.

"Scott told me that everything from the colors used to decorate the interior of innovation hubs to the amount of natural lighting that comes into these rooms as well as the nature of the furniture used in these places are all extremely important and must be carefully planned when you're talking about innovation hubs," I continued. "They aren't just the co-working spaces that you and I always thought they were—they're far more than that."

The waiter brought both of our drinks and placed them on the table before us.

"How do you like your meal?" he asked courteously.

"I haven't had pizza this good in a very long time," Bill responded with a smile, and I agreed. There was something different about that restaurant ever since they revamped it and changed their menu, and I loved everything new that they had to offer.

"I'm glad that the two of you finally took my suggestion seriously," our waiter replied with a smile. "Feel free to ask, if you need anything else."

Once we had both acknowledged how good the food was, we were unable to continue our conversation until we were done with our meal.

"I'm sorry but what do you mean by saying that they're much more than just average co-working spaces?" Bill asked, as he wiped his face with his napkin.

"I never considered this before either, but Scott was kind enough to elaborate on the difference for me," I said. "The thing with co-working spaces is that they have what you can call a predefined structure that can't be changed. In co-working spaces, you just have people who come in from many different places. On the other hand, when you have an innovation hub, you can have anything from a new idea to a project that people of all ages and who fulfill diverse roles in the business, company, or organization will come together to discuss.

"The best thing about innovation hubs is that there is so much positive energy and there are so many hardworking people who come together to get something done that they have an impact on everyone else. *This* is what promotes agility and helps new people learn and develop important capabilities."

I could tell that Bill understood everything that I was saying while I tried my best to explain the importance and benefits of innovation hubs to him in the same way that Scott had explained these things to me.

"And before I forget," I continued, "my friend had some advice for you."

"Oh, yeah?" Bill replied, with a smile on his face. "And what is that?"

"Keep your eyes open when you're looking for a new job. The last thing you want is to be stuck in a workplace that is as toxic as your current one."

Bill laughed. "Speaking of my *current* job," Bill said, "I just have three more days to go for my notice period to end."

"Have you found anything yet?" I asked, genuinely concerned.

"There's this one job that I'm considering. It's an offer that I got from a startup. It doesn't look like anything too special, but the work is something that looks interesting to me. I think I might just give it a shot, starting the 1st of next month," Bill said.

I checked my calendar. It was the 23rd. That meant that Bill would be starting at his new workplace in a week.

"I wanted to meet you to give you this news but I got a little caught up with some work," Bill continued.

"That's all right," I replied. "But I can only hope that you keep all of my advice in mind when you say yes to them."

Bill said nothing in return for quite awhile. Our tall waiter came back to see if we needed anything else, and I asked him to bring another round of drinks for us.

"No dessert?" he questioned.

"We'll let you know in a bit," I replied. I smiled at the waiter, and he left.

"I did try," Bill replied almost as soon as the waiter left our table. "But I didn't really have many options open. I guess we'll just have to wait and see how it goes."

Bill picked up his glass of wine and started twirling it in his hand as he looked across the entire restaurant. I could tell that he was starting to get nervous about his new workplace and how he would like it. Since I didn't want him to start his new job on a skeptical note and didn't want him to be confused or worried, I tried my best to help him feel relaxed and confident in the decision that he had made.

"You're a smart young man," I reassured Bill. "I'm sure you've tried hard enough. Besides, if it doesn't work out for any reason, you know that I'll always be there to help you out."

All Bill did in return was look at me and smile a nervous little smile.

"I know, professor," he finally said. "But I really hope it does work out. I've already bothered you so many times and troubled you with so much. I wouldn't want to do that again."

"This isn't trouble. I feel like it's my responsibility to help my students out. Besides, I think we're friends more than a teacher and student now," I laughed.

"Well, that's true," Bill said, with a smile on his face.

Once both Bill and I had finished our drinks, we called the waiter and asked him to bring us the bill.

"We'll be back for dessert soon," I told the kind waiter, who laughed as he cleared the table.

Bill started taking out his wallet, as he did last time, but I told him that it wasn't necessary for him to pay every time. When he told me that he wouldn't let me pay the entire amount, we decided that we should split the bill. Bill and I headed out of the small restaurant as soon as we were done paying the bill.

"Come back soon," we heard the manager say, as we walked out.

We had completely forgotten about the fact that it had been drizzling when we had entered the little restaurant. Fortunately, however, the rain had stopped by the time we stepped outside, and the clouds had started clearing. Bill and I decided that we should take a walk on the sidewalk as we had done after our last meeting at the restaurant not too long ago.

"You know, Bill," I said to Bill, "I have multiple sources and contacts in various industries. I could have helped you get a job in just about any place that you wanted, but I wanted you to learn how to do things and make decisions for yourself. With all of the advice and information that I've given you, I'm sure that you'll do just fine. But just remember, if you feel like the new workplace that you're all set to join in the next few days is equally—or more—toxic than your current job, don't hesitate to ask me for help again. I've seen you go through a lot already. Don't ever feel as if you're burdening me with too much in case you need my help again."

Bill was walking with his head down as I spoke to him. When I was done, all he did was stop walking, turn to me, and give me a hug.

"I never thought we'd ever be this close, professor," Bill said to me as he looked me in the eye. "You know, I used to hear people praise their teachers, professors, and mentors and always wondered how someone could ever become friends with someone who taught them a course or two at a university. I guess I have my answer now, Joe."

"I hope things work out for you, Bill."

We walked on along the same route that we had taken a couple of days earlier, chatting about everything under the sun. Bill told me how more people at his current workplace had finally understood that there was something wrong with the company and that sticking around for too long would only continue to have more of a negative impact on their capabilities. Barely anyone at Bill's current workplace was willing to be that complacent. The only people who were ready to continue working at the job were not brave enough to look for different opportunities.

When we had walked a couple of blocks from the little restaurant, we decided that it would be best if we picked up coffee from the café that we had gone to previously. After we got our coffee, we headed to the same bench as before as well.

"This feels like a rerun of our last meeting," Bill pointed out, as we sat down on the bench. "Except that this time, I actually have a job to look forward to."

Both Bill and I laughed heartily. I knew, however, that I had something very important to tell Bill before we called it a day.

"I can't tell you how happy I am that you finally found a new job, Bill," I said to Bill, as he sat next to me on the bench and sipped his coffee. "But there's something that I need you to do."

"And what is that, professor?" Bill asked me inquisitively.

"Well, I think I've given you a lot of information since we met that day at the airport."

Bill nodded, evidently waiting to hear what I had to say. I thought it best to cut to the chase and not waste anymore time.

"Now, I think you'll be able to know what's good and what isn't all that great for you as a person and for your career. With that said, I really want you to apply all of the advice that I've given you during these meetings. I know nothing about the new place where you'll be working except what you've told me today. Since I want you to figure things out for yourself, I won't even be doing any research on my end. Besides, I don't think I really should at this point because you've already made your decision. I just want you to know what you're looking for in life and in your career and make sure that your new workplace has great opportunities for you."

"I'll definitely keep your advice in mind, professor," he said, with a smile on his face. "And don't worry, I'll contact you if I feel like something's amiss."

I patted Bill on the back, and he smiled.

"And yes, I tried to keep all of your advice in mind even when I was looking for this new place. I just hope that it works out for me," Bill said.

"I hope the same for you, too, Bill."

Bill glanced at his watch and was surprised at how much time had passed. It was now almost 5 p.m.

"I think we should head back, Joe," he said to me. "There's some work that I need to take care of."

"I was just about to say the same thing."

We continued chatting about various things as we walked back to the little restaurant where our cars were parked and only stopped talking a few steps before we reached the restaurant. I could tell that Bill was getting nervous again, so I gave him a hug as soon as we approached our cars.

"It'll go great," I told him.

"I'll tell you all about it," Bill replied.

I didn't want Bill to be too skeptical about his new workplace and to become overly critical about everything he found there, so I decided I should give him about a month's time to decide how he *really* likes it.

"I'll see you in a couple of weeks, Bill," I said to him.

Since I didn't want Bill to feel as if he wasn't welcome and couldn't talk to me if something went wrong, I asked him to feel free to contact me in the meantime if he needed any type of help. He said that he definitely would, and we called it a day.

* * * * *

As I headed home that evening, I couldn't help but feel as if Bill was making the wrong decision regarding this new job. To me, it sounded as if he hadn't given it much thought and just said yes to this prospective employer simply because he was sick and tired of the way he was being treated at his current workplace. Besides, whenever I tried to start a conversation with him about his new job and what it was all about, he really didn't have much to say except for the fact that he would wait and see what he's expected to do there and what it's like.

Since I had told Bill that I would give him the time he needed to do so, without trying to influence his decision or opinions, I decided not to talk to him about his new job for at least a few weeks. However, as much as I hated it, Bill and his new workplace were the only things that were on my mind over the next few days.

Many questions crossed my mind during this time. I kept wondering whether he would be able to adapt to the atmosphere and environment at his new workplace, whether he would like the work, and how his coworkers at this startup organization would be. The one thing that bothered me more than all others, however, was whether the new startup organization that he had joined would be innovative and agile because that's essentially more important than anything else for any company, business, or organization—and that's especially true when talking about a startup. Besides, lack of innovation was the primary problem with Bill's current workplace as well, which had caused so many people to feel miserable and shackled, despite all of their efforts.

As mentioned earlier, the major problem with the companies, businesses, and organizations of today is that they fail to innovate and strategize the way they should. Although innovation and agility have always been vital for companies, businesses, and organizations, their importance has increased tenfold in the VUCA corporate world of today. Innovation is the major driving force that motivates employees, leaders, and managers in any setting to continue to give the company, business, or organization where they work their all. Without innovation or the freedom to be creative, work feels extremely monotonous and employees often feel as if they don't have any reason to continue working hard.

One of the major advantages of innovation is that it helps give direction to employees and managers in any company, business, or organization. People generally pay more attention and put in a lot more effort when they are doing something new or being creative with their work. It goes without saying that one won't feel the need to go the extra mile or put in their all if the company, business, or organization where they work isn't ready to innovate or refuses to be creative with the way in which work is done.

Innovation has become so vitally important in Europe and other places worldwide that it is being focused on in science and technology, in certain regions. The primary intention behind focusing on innovation and creativity in these places is to ensure that people enjoy their work. When innovation is focused on in the workplace, the direction that is used to carry out operations and processes does not only become more efficient and sensitive, but it is also far more result driven than otherwise.

Employees, leaders, and managers in a business, company, or organization that is creative and innovative also appear to be more ambitious in their efforts to try out new approaches and experiment with new and effective approaches to work and achieving goals. Professionals in the corporate sector throughout the world now unanimously agree with the fact that innovativeness is a prerequisite for companies, businesses, and organizations of today to progress and succeed.

In addition to innovative systems, innovative environments have been discussed increasingly over the past few years. Since people these days are more educated than ever before, mobility has become more of a possibility than it was earlier. The vast availability of knowledge has made it possible for companies, businesses, and organizations to be more creative with what they do and to search for ideas outside of the workplace. Additionally, the increased availability of venture capital now allows ideas to be developed outside of organizations, which was not seen in the past.

People from companies, businesses, and organizations throughout the world now understand that it is possible to work on ideas and optimize processes, operations, and activities even from outside of the workplace. For this, it is essential for the businesses, companies, and organizations of today to foster creativity and innovation to the greatest extent possible. It is not only imperative for these businesses, companies, and organizations to implement new and effective strategies and policies wherever possible, but they are also required to leverage all of their assets and available technologies as much as they can to ensure that they don't become extinct in the competitive world of today.

Even though people in most of the businesses, companies, and organizations of today are fully aware that innovation has become extremely important and that it is impossible for them to progress and survive without innovation, it is often seen that they aren't willing to innovate or change their structure and the way in which their business processes are carried out. "We develop products first and worry and change business processes later." You can hear statements like this very often.

This is especially true for new businesses, companies, and organizations as well as startups, which is why I was even more afraid of what Bill might experience at his new workplace.

Even though this is surprising, the reason why these new firms and corporations refuse to innovate is because they aren't ready to take the risk associated with it. However, as unfortunate as it may sound, if new companies, businesses, and organizations aren't willing to take the risk now, it will be even more difficult for them to innovate—and eventually survive—later on. Needless to say, "innovate or die"—one of the most popular phrases in the corporate world—holds true today more than it ever did before, and businesses, companies, and organizations of all sizes and in every industry need to understand that to ensure that they aren't forced to extinction simply because they weren't ready to take risks.

Although it may be difficult and risky for small and new businesses, companies, and organizations to think about and start being innovative at first, once they muster the courage to take on the challenge and aren't afraid of the risks anymore, it is extremely likely that they'll be able to learn from the experience and make their way forward toward success. Another plus is that they'll also be able to develop agility in the process.

I found myself becoming increasingly interested in innovation as I thought about how Bill must be doing at his new workplace. To channel my interest in this domain in the right way, I decided to start incorporating it in the lectures that I delivered to my students for MBA strategy classes. I found myself researching innovation, creativity, and agility more than ever before.

Since innovation is something that is frequently spoken about in several classes, I decided that it would be best if my take on this domain was different from the rest, to ensure that my students didn't get bored from hearing the same examples over and over again. Contrary to popular belief, people have been trying to be innovative in their processes and operations for a very long time. A little research was all it really took to figure that out.

From my research, I found out that people have been innovating in their own ways since the beginning of time. One of my favorite examples of innovation dates back as early as 1830, when a French diplomat based in Cairo, Ferdinand de Lesseps,[2] thought of creating a link between two of the most populated continents, Asia and Europe. Lesseps' idea was to create a canal by cutting about 118 miles of arid land. The entire project was expected to cost about FRF 200 million. The Suez Canal officially opened on November 17, 1869, but the outcome was nothing short of disappointing. During the first complete year of operations of the Suez Canal, less than 500 ships passed through it. This was not only far less than the expected return on investment, but dividends weren't materializing either.

Since the government of Egypt at the time was extremely in need of cash, they sold the shares of the project to Great Britain. Even though shares were sold for GBP £4 million, this proved to be one of the best moves for the project. In the year 2002, about 15,000 ships passed through the Suez Canal, ultimately generating the equivalent of USD $2 billion for Egypt.

Since Lesseps really wanted his idea to work out, he decided that it would be best if a project of a similar nature was initiated in Panama as well. Again, all of the efforts that Lesseps and his team made went in vain, due to the weather and diseases such as malaria, cholera, and yellow fever, which ended up claiming the lives of nearly 22,000 people who worked tirelessly on the project. In the year 1904, work on the project in Panama started once again thanks to US President Theodore Roosevelt.[3] The US Army Corps of Engineers began working on the project, which ended up costing about USD $352 million.

Even after 5,609 lives were claimed while work was done on the project, less than five ships passed through the Panama Canal per day when the project was finally completed in 1918. With some tweaking and changes in the structure and management, the number of ships passing through the Panama Canal daily went up to 15,000.

But that's not all. The stories of the Panama and Suez Canals are just two out of countless examples that demonstrate how innovation and agility made a difference and resulted in unprecedented successes. However, being able to pull off the right innovation strategies and decisions requires a lot of hard work on the part of all of the individuals that are a part of the company, business, or organization that is trying its best to succeed and rise to new heights every day.

The fact of the matter is that innovation is impossible and can't be pulled off without systemic vision. To successfully, resourcefully, and optimally innovate processes, activities and operations, it is imperative for companies, businesses, and organizations in the VUCA world of today to hire individuals who will not only be able to foresee and visualize problems and issues of the future through a practical lens but also come up with solutions that are based on dynamic and analytical decision-making skills. One such person who thought outside box was General Billy Mitchell[4] who was considered to be the father of the US Air Force. The proposition that this innovative man made in the year of 1920 was that airplanes should be used to drop bombs on and sink battleships.

As is seen on many similar occasions, Mitchell was ridiculed not only by those that he reported to but also by his subordinates. "That idea is so damned nonsensical and impossible that I'm willing to stand on the bridge of a battleship while that nitwit tries to hit it from the air," the US Secretary of War at the time, Newton D. Baker, said.[5]

On July 16, 1910, the Scientific American, too, offered an opinion on the proposition with the following words: "To affirm that the aeroplane is going to 'revolutionize' naval warfare of the future is guilty of the wildest exaggeration."[6] Now, more than a century later, it is evident that Mitchell's idea was, indeed, one of the most revolutionary propositions of his time even though the masses were not only against it but also thought of it as absurd and impossible.

Another extremely important thing that I learned while I was doing my research on innovation and the different ways in which people try to create an environment to foster creativity was the concept of the Triple Helix model for innovation. Even though the concept is not really new, it has great potential, and a lot can be achieved through the concept.

The idea behind the Triple Helix model[7] was cooperation between universities, industries, and the government to promote the sharing of thoughts and ideas among people and ensure that fostering creativity and innovation is possible more than ever before. Earlier, companies, businesses, and organizations relied on closed innovation, for the most part. What this meant was that, in the past, the companies, businesses, and organizations believed that they already had all of the information that they could possibly need in order to progress and innovate successfully.

Although the Triple Helix concept was quick to be adopted by several companies, businesses, and organizations, most people now believe that it is best if National Open Innovation Strategies[8] are focused and concentrated on more than promoting closed innovation and relying on temporary fixes, instead of dealing with the problem at the root level.[9]

Open innovation strategies are now becoming increasingly popular for quite a number of reasons. They prove to be highly beneficial, especially for small economies that struggle in the face of turmoil. Since the implementation of new and improved strategies for open innovation has increased with time, people throughout the world have now learned much more about the open innovation strategies than was ever possible in the past.

When it comes to open innovation, the most important thing that people understand now is that this is not a solution *per se*. In fact, open innovation is simply a concept that can attract more stakeholders when openness is promoted in the way that it should be. While open innovation is not a solution in and of itself, the concept is essentially all about using all of the right tools, principles, and strategies to not only address issues within the system but also to be able to improve the system as a whole and address failures that are hindering progress.

Another very important thing to remember when talking about open innovation or National Open Innovation Strategies is that the concept is extremely important in this day and age. With digital transformations underway in nearly all industries and domains under the sun, it's fair to say that a lot of people who are actively involved in the workforce have the need for collaborative and innovative ecosystems that promote sharing ideas and discussing solutions. Unlike in the past, policy and decision making today is no longer a static process, and it requires a lot of collaboration.

Since innovation and agility are both requirements of today, it is fair to say that there couldn't have been a better time for open innovation strategies to be focused on than now. People in the workforce—both young and old—are now aware of the difference that agility and innovation can make, and they are all firm believers in the fact that it is impossible to rise to success if the right strategies aren't implemented at the right time. With that said, it is imperative to realize that it is practically impossible for people to implement open innovation strategies top-down. The primary reason for this is that it is difficult for the plan to be rolled out all in one go with the help of a larger federal initiative. Instead, it is best if stakeholders are invited to own their own respective ecosystems and take action as necessary.

The best part about concentrating on one domain at a time is that it not only allows deeper learning but also creates bottom-up ownership, which is something that has become extremely rare in the businesses, companies, and organizations of today. Another important advantage of using the bottom-up approach for implementing open innovation strategies is that it is possible to create unique and diverse innovation ecosystems that are not uniform and can also get the job done.

Even though open innovation is a great new technique that should be increasingly focused on, it is unfortunately true that developing the right open innovation strategies will take a lot more time than we think. Implementing strategies and deploying perfect open innovation systems will not be possible unless there is a shift in our current policy-making paradigm. Although this may sound extremely dangerous and risky, it is essential to keep room for experimentation in innovation ecosystems to ensure optimality. Since creating the right culture and ecosystem in which innovation and new strategies are promoted will take time, it is incumbent on the current workforce and active employees of the companies, businesses, and organizations of today to play their part in promoting diversity and innovation by themselves to the fullest extent that they possibly can.

Since innovation environments are also being talked about more often now than ever before, I thought that it would be best if I learned an additional thing or two about them as well before I tried to explain the concept to my students. During my research, I realized that other people, too, believed that the business environments of today are far more VUCA-like than they were in the past. Although this makes the need for improvement and innovation more prominent than ever before, the fact of the matter is that companies these days are also more afraid of taking risks and worried about what the future holds.

Owners, leaders, and managers in the businesses, companies, and organizations of today are uncertain what strategy to choose in order to maintain their competitiveness. In the past, whenever we talked about innovation and fostering creativity, these were concepts that were limited to the confines of the room or building in which the company, business, or organization operated. With that said, the introduction of open innovation and all of this talk about innovation systems and innovation environments has allowed leaders, managers, owners, and all other employees of businesses, companies, and organizations to think outside of the box—literally.

Although business environments of today are far more VUCA than they were in the past, the reality is that our environments now are also hyperconnected. The greatest benefit that being more connected than ever before gives companies, businesses, and organizations is that they are now able to innovate in a way that wouldn't have been possible in the past. Since businesses, companies, and organizations are now more open to the idea of gaining information and sharing ideas with those who are not within the confines of the entity that they call their own, people are not only able to learn and understand how others think, but it has also become possible to learn from the mistakes of others who are on the same page and based in the same industry.

One of the best examples of innovation in recent times is that of General Electric® (GE®). Contrary to popular opinion, the leaders and managers there knew that there is nothing wrong with asking for help from someone. Since Bill Ruh[10] knew many people at Cisco®, he thought it would be best to contact them in order to expand and venture out.

Fortunately for many people who are interested in seizing new and exciting opportunities, closed innovation is slowly and gradually becoming a thing of the past. As a result, people understand that there is no real reason for them to limit innovation and creativity to the confines of a small building or room when there is the potential for so much more. Since the mobility of these educated people has increased, it has become possible for them to share thoughts and ideas with like-minded people in order to achieve bigger and brighter things, not only for themselves but also for the company, business, or organization at which they work.

Looking for new tools and technologies from external sources that can help provide benefits unlike any other for their workplace and help give them an edge over the competition, innovators from the companies, businesses, and organizations of today have also started contacting and cooperating with suppliers and competitors to ensure that they are able to optimize processes, activities, and operations in a way that creates value for the customer and affects the workplace in a positive manner.

While most people may still feel that reaching out to external sources for help is a sign of weakness, this notion is far from reality. In fact, the increasing popularity of the open innovation model proves that people have now understood how dangerous it is to continue shackling people and their thoughts and ideas within the confines of a small area or building. With that said, the steady erosion of the closed innovation model has made it clear that people are more impressed and satisfied with the results of the open innovation model that has become more popular now than ever before.

Seeing the way in which the companies, businesses, and organizations of today are saying goodbye to the closed innovation model and relying on open innovation to change the way in which they manage their processes, operations, and activities instead, it is fair to say that a lot more people are now strong believers in the fact that it is not possible to progress and grow when you limit yourself for any given reason. Although there are still quite a number of leaders and managers who think that they know better than the rest and fear consulting or cooperating with the world outside of their business, company, or organization, the fact of the matter is that sharing ideas helps people learn and grow in a way that would otherwise not be possible.

Since I needed something substantial as my basis to prove my point to my students, I continued doing my research about innovation models and why are they important. I found something in one of the online papers[11] I had read years ago that really caught my attention. The paper included an outline on the problem-solving process. When I saw this again, years later, I knew that I absolutely had to share this information with my students.

This paper states that there are about seven steps that are involved in solving problems of any kind. Since innovation was only necessary to solve a certain number of problems, I thought that it would be best for me to share this information with my students at the same time as I discussed innovation models with them. The first step in the problem-solving process, according to the paper, was understanding the problem and defining it as a challenge or opportunity that needs to be dealt with as soon as possible.

According to the paper, a problem is nothing more than understanding that you have an opportunity to create something better than what is already available in the market. It also states that it is not possible to solve any problems or seize any opportunities without having a particular vision in mind.

A major issue that countless people in the businesses, companies, and organizations of today face in the problem-solving process is that they often fail—or refuse—to acknowledge that there is actually a real and substantial problem that exists. The first phase of the problem-solving process, therefore, makes it clear that it is imperative for one to not feel personally responsible and realize that accepting the fact that there is a problem that exists is the first thing that will help people initiate the problem-solving process in the way that it should be dealt with.

Once people understand and acknowledge the fact that there is something wrong or that certain processes, operations, activities, or products can be improved, only then will they be able to really brainstorm ideas and solutions to deal with the problem. The paper that I was reading explicitly mentions that intuitive knowledge should be taken into consideration at all times, especially during the initial phase of the problem-solving process because you never know when you'll be able to find the right solution for any type of problem. With that said, it is essential to create an outline that you will be using not only to identify the problem but also to solve it in the most optimal way.

According to the paper, the next phase involved finding out all of the facts that are related to the problem. What this essentially means is that it is impossible for the leaders, managers, owners, or any other employees at any business, company, or organization to figure out a practical solution to any kind of problem if they don't have all of the correct and essential information that is required to reach any solutions or to draw appropriate conclusions. Once you have all of the correct information and facts regarding the problem and what caused it, you will naturally be able to find more practical solutions and know the right direction that you should be brainstorming in in order to reach the most optimal, effective, and efficient solution for the problem at hand.

The third phase is called the problem phase and is highly related to the second phase. Once you have the right outline and all of the facts regarding the problem, you will be able to discover more about the problem itself and describe it in greater detail. This, according to the paper, must be done in the third step. People who work in the companies, businesses, and organizations in the VUCA world of today are fully aware that problems may be much different in reality from what they appear to be. For this reason, it is essential for owners, managers, leaders, and all other employees who are a part of today's companies, businesses, and organizations to truly identify what the problem that they must deal with is all about to ensure that they don't end up making the wrong decisions or proposing solutions that are not in line with the problem at hand.

The next phase, namely, the idea phase, is also one of the most important stages in the problem-solving process. Every problem solver knows and acknowledges the fact that it is always best to look for alternatives and have a contingency plan in case things don't go as you had intended. Alternative solutions and plans are, therefore, essentially what the idea phase is all about. Even if you have a solution to any given problem thought out in your head, it is essential for you to think of ideas and other solutions that you can fall back on in case your initial plan or solution doesn't work out the way you thought it would.

The possibility of unforeseen factors that can come in the way of your ideal solution should never be ruled out, which makes these alternative solutions even more important. Additionally, it is necessary for you to also consider the fact that there can be limitations and restrictions that come in the way of your intended solution that you never considered before, which is why it is always necessary for you to have a practical backup plan to ensure that you can deal with the problem effectively, as soon as possible.

Once you have a number of possible alternatives for the problem at hand and you know for a fact that you won't be left without any solutions to the problem in case something is amiss, you'll be able to focus on refining the ideal solution even more to ensure that it is perfect for the problem. In the solution phase, you are supposed to polish and refine the solution that you have chosen in order to make it implementable and usable for the problem that you are facing. Refining solutions to make sure that they are in line with the requirements of the problem is essential in order to ensure that complications don't have to be dealt with in case the required amount of effort was not put in to improve the quality of the solution.

After the chosen solution has been refined, you should then focus on all of the actors that are important for the actualization of the solution. This is what needs to be done in the approval phase. Regardless of the type of solution that you have chosen for any given kind of problem that your company, business, or organization is facing, the fact of the matter is that there are quite a few different factors that are involved in the seamless execution of any solution. This holds true irrespective of the industry that your business, company, or organization is based in. Before you begin the execution of your solution of choice, it is imperative for you to understand that all of the actors that need to be involved in the execution of the solution need to be in the right place at the right time to ensure that nothing goes wrong due to a lack of cooperation or because an important factor or two were neglected at the time of execution. Once all of the actors are in the right place and all of the factors are taken into consideration, you are all set to begin the actualization of the solution that you chose for the problem that you are dealing with at your company, business, or organization.

The last phase of the problem-solving process, according to the paper, is the realization phase. Since the realization phase is the last stage of the problem-solving process, there is a lot that needs to be done in this phase to ensure that no problems arise during the execution of the solution that was chosen and refined according to the requirements. As the name suggests, the realization phase is basically all about realizing new problems that may have arisen or identifying parts of the problem that weren't initially considered in the previous phases.

Since this is the last phase of the problem-solving process according to the paper that I was reading, a lot of emphasis was placed on how important it is for leaders, managers, owners, and all other employees that are responsible for solving problems to understand that this phase may even require certain phases to be repeated or started anew to ensure that the solution is executed seamlessly and the anticipated or expected results are reached. Additionally, it is also extremely important for people to understand that, depending on the situation, it might even be possible that the entire process may have to be restarted in case certain steps or phases weren't executed properly. In fact, it is also entirely possible that multiple steps and phases will have to be repeated more than once to actually reach the realization phase and achieve the desired results.

Once I was finished doing my research on the problem-solving process, I thought that it would be best if I did a little in-depth research on innovation itself. I had a habit of tackling any topic or piece of information in several different ways to ensure that I would be able to deal with unusual circumstances and also be able to answer any questions that my students had, without any problems. I knew for a fact that innovation was something that a large majority of my students would be interested in and that they would ask me for more information. Even though most students probably didn't think of me as much more than a professor or a teacher that they have to take a course or two with while they are enrolled at the university, I believe that I am the teacher and mentor who should be able to help them with any and every type of question that they could possibly have.

Even though I was already aware of a lot regarding innovation and how it should be dealt with, I knew that there was no harm in doing a little research. I am a strong believer in the fact that you will always be able to find something new or important that you might have missed, even if your research material is limited to books, articles, or websites that you have gone through several times already. I believe that one is always wiser and thinks differently whenever they are rereading any piece of information, which is why important books or other sources of information should never be discarded. You never know what you'll learn, when you refer to one of these resources again. Besides, since I was now looking in entirely different areas, I knew that I would certainly be able to find something of use to share with my students if they ask for more information or seem more interested in the concept than I remembered.

The amount and type of effort that companies, businesses, and organizations have to put into innovation largely depends on the type of innovation—that much I already knew. One thing that I didn't know, however, was that these types of innovation are actually classified into two major categories—namely, disruptive innovation and incremental innovation.

Through my initial research, I found out that incremental innovation is essentially all about making improvements in features of the products and services that already exist. Disruptive innovations, on the other hand, focus on something entirely different. Disruptive innovations create dramatic changes and primarily deal with changing entire markets or industries. According to the initial research that I did, I discovered that disruptive innovations may even involve creating or launching new products or services that were unheard of in the past.

Even though I had derived a lot of information from my initial research, I just had to know more to quench my thirst for knowledge. As a result, I started exploring several different avenues to find out more about these two different types of innovation and why they mattered so much. Fortunately, it didn't take a lot of time or effort to understand the significance of these two types of innovation.

Apparently, incremental innovation deals primarily deals with improving the quality and increasing the competitiveness of existing products and services. This is done in a number of different ways. The cost of the existing product or service can be reduced to ensure that more and more customers are interested in it, hence increasing the competitiveness factor. Additionally, it is also possible for companies, businesses, and organizations to add new features or improve existing features and optimize the functionality of existing products or services to ensure that people have more reasons to buy or invest in the product or service that is being innovated.

In my opinion, one of the best examples of incremental innovation that has been seen in recent times comes in the form of the most popular email service in the world, Gmail™. With time, people became interested in this email service, which is provided by Google LLC, for its simplicity. Once the email service had a strong and loyal following, Google LLC slowly and gradually started adding features to the email service. What happened next is no mystery. Loyal users loved the idea and continued to use the service, whereas plenty of new users became interested in the service as well. With that said, all Google LLC essentially did with Gmail was use the incremental style of innovation. Since people had already become interested in the prime features of the simple service when it was launched, they didn't mind additions. In fact, some even appreciated how the company was growing and offering greater value to users with time.

The same style of innovation has, since then, been used multiple times with other products of the company as well. Google LLC is now known to launch simple products or services to win the hearts of loyal users and potential users alike, after which the company continues to add to existing products and services to ensure that users not only remain interested in the product or service that they have grown to love but are also constantly looking forward to what the company will think of next. Google Maps™ and the Google Chrome™ internet browser are great examples of how the company initially launched something that, in my opinion, only looked like it was enough to get the task at hand done; however, with time, these products, too, have seen more than their fair share of improvements and tweaking that have fortunately proven to be beneficial for the company.

As unfortunate as it may sound, there are still quite a few risks involved with incremental innovation. This is especially true if the incremental innovation is the only thing that you're relying on. Kodak®[12] was one of the most popular companies in the photography industry in its time. However, relying solely on the incremental style of innovation led the company to destruction. The photography giant enjoyed years of success before things started to go downhill. For years, Kodak slowly and gradually made improvements to traditional film. That approach was perfect and helped the company rise to new heights every day until disruptive innovation came into the picture. Since Kodak had such a linear approach and was solely focused on traditional film, the introduction of digital imaging left the company with no alternative except to be lost in the pages of history.

Businesses, companies, and organizations throughout the world are trying their best to learn from the mistakes that Kodak and countless other companies have made and are now investing a lot more time and effort into learning about and executing successful disruptive innovations. Quite a number of people in the corporate world are strong believers in the fact that Kodak would still be an important player in the photography industry, had the leaders and managers of the company known how to think outside of the box and let go of the linear approach that they had religiously been following every once in a while.

Although people unanimously agree that incremental innovation is all about playing it safe, disruptive innovations are something different altogether. In fact, most people consider the phrase "all or nothing" to be the best way to describe the process that is involved in executing successful and efficient disruptive innovations. The reason behind this is fairly simple: When talking about disruptive innovations, you no longer have the option or freedom to improvise on existing products or services. In fact, if you are a leader or manager who is in charge of disruptive innovations to ensure that the business, company, or organization that you are a part of isn't forced to extinction, you will most definitely have to explore new ground to help broaden the horizons of the place where you work.

The best part about disruptive innovations is that you get to learn a lot more when dealing with disruptive innovations than you would with incremental innovations. But there's a catch. When dealing with disruptive innovations, it is imperative for you to have a team of highly passionate and skilled people who are truly interested in making the business, company, or organization rise to new heights.

Since disruptive innovations are essentially all about being creative and doing something the likes of which has never been done before, people often enjoy working on disruptive innovations far more than incremental innovations. Individuals who are passionate about creating something new and having their ideas known by the entire world work tirelessly to turn their dreams into reality when they are given a chance to work on disruptive innovations.

However, needless to say, it isn't all fun and games.

The problem with disruptive innovations is that, unlike incremental innovations, you really have nothing to hold onto. What this means is that, since you have no substantial ground in the form of an existing product or service that you can work your way up on, everything in disruptive innovations needs to be done from scratch. Even though this may excite certain people and be their motivation to work harder than others, the amount of uncertainty and risk involved in disruptive innovations is downright ridiculous.

It is, however, important to note that much like any other situation that has a very high level of risk associated with it, disruptive innovations also have great potential for success. Since disruptive innovations are essentially all about creating something new, from scratch, there is always a considerable possibility that the idea that you have in mind will be loved by the masses if you introduce people to it the way you should.

One of the best examples of successful attempts at disruptive innovation in recent times is that of the transportation technology company, Uber Technologies, Inc. Although taxi companies worked tirelessly to improve the service that they were providing to their customers for several years, the ride-hailing application brought a shift in the industry that was unheard of in the past. This transportation technology company was able to grab hold of a large market share almost immediately after it was introduced to the general public and now operates in over 80 countries across the globe.

A great advantage of using disruptive innovations to help your business, company, or organization reach unprecedented success is that the process that is involved in implementing disruptive innovations is generally very informal. The reason for this is that it is impossible to have a generic process for disruptive innovations because every idea is different and is best implemented in a unique way that is in line with the idea and maximizes the chances of it being successful.

One thing about disruptive innovations that people generally find extremely funny is that they are often implemented in the form of several incremental improvements. Startups and other small businesses, companies, and organizations are considered to be important players in disruptive innovations because of the risk that is involved in disruptive innovations.

It is generally believed that the major reason why people at the businesses, companies, and organizations of today are still interested in disruptive innovations in spite of all of the risks associated with them is that you don't always have to compete for the market share when you are using this approach to innovation. Instead, it is possible for businesses, companies, and organizations practicing disruptive innovation to branch out and create an entirely different market altogether.

With the difference between the incremental and disruptive styles of innovation clarified above, you might be of the opinion that you should go for either one of the two approaches, depending on the type of innovation that you would like to implement and the nature of the industry that your business, company, or organization is based in. While choosing between the two would have proven to be beneficial for innovative processes of the past, the same doesn't hold true for the innovative processes that need to be implemented in today's world.

We have seen examples of failed innovation far too often in recent times, which demonstrates that innovating in the world of today isn't as easy as it used to be in the past. The VUCA corporate world of today is dealing with a lot more than ever before. With that said, it is practically impossible for a business, company, or organization to innovate successfully by relying solely on one of these two methods or approaches.

Since technological changes and other types of changes that are important for any business, company, or organization vary greatly between industries, it is imperative for you to consider and truly understand the factors that can influence the rate of success of your innovation idea before you make a decision. Since there is a lot of risk involved in both styles of innovation, the leaders and managers of businesses, companies, and organizations today are trying not to keep all of their eggs in one basket. Instead, an increasing number of people are opting for the middle path and trying to find the right balance between both styles of innovation.

These days, businesses, companies, and organizations are focusing on having a comprehensive view of their initiatives to ensure that they don't overwhelm or underwhelm the market. By using a combination of both approaches while keeping external factors and industrial changes in mind, businesses, companies, and organizations of today are able to innovate in the way that is required.

But what if you feel like the risk is greater than the potential for success?

As hard a pill to swallow as this may be, the fact of the matter is that innovation cannot be ignored any longer just because you feel as if there are too many risks associated with making a move or taking a step that is unheard of. It is unfortunate that there are still countless people who believe that their businesses, companies or organizations can survive in the highly competitive world of today without making any extra efforts. Although this may have been true in the past, the same doesn't hold true for the businesses, companies, and organizations of today.

The workforce today is full of competent and passionate individuals who are ready to go the extra mile just to leave a mark on the world. With the majority of people these days being as passionate and focused as they are, it is absurd for one to still believe that their business, company, or organization will remain safe in the wake of industrial disruption—and the fact that disruptions are not just a passing trend but rather the new normal makes things even more challenging for such people.

> *Why have disruptions in the business environments*
> *of today become so common, you ask?*

Although the answer to that question is multifaceted, it is still simple. The first factor that has contributed to the increase in business disruption to the extent that it is now being deemed normal is the rapid expansion of technology. Additionally, the vast majority of the population of today is quite tech savvy, which has allowed businesses, companies, and organizations of today to not only explore new and emerging technologies but also experiment with them.

Globalization is another factor that has played its part in making business disruption the new normal. It has made it possible for new and improved business models to be introduced in the market, ultimately giving rise to competition within the corporate world. What's more is that costs, too, are being decreased at a steady rate, allowing businesses, companies, and organizations to innovate and get their ideas out in the market more quickly than ever before without being shackled by financial constraints.

Experts throughout the world are convinced that the external environment is not only changing at a rate like never before, but that it will continue to change at lightning speed for a number of years to come. One way to survive in an environment like this, they say, is by changing the game within your own business, company, or organization. However, as you might have guessed, changing the game internally isn't as easy as it sounds.

To successfully bring about change internally in a way that your business, company, or organization is able to counter and rise above the changes in the environment, it is essential for you to do two things. The first thing that must be done in order to thrive when you are submerged in disruptive changes in the environment is to accelerate the speed at which you execute your plan. It is best for you to increase the speed of execution of your ideas and implement them as soon as you can in order to prevent any problems that are caused by pointlessly delaying the matter. This, however, certainly does not mean that you shouldn't plan every move before you make it. Once you have an idea that you *believe* will work in your favor, you are required to plan every step of the execution and implementation of your idea to rise to success. As always, you can't afford to ignore potential complications and limitations of the system in this step. Once the planning phase is complete, you're good to go.

The second most important part of your game plan should be—you guessed it—to increase the agility of your business, company, or organization. As I continued to do my research on how this phase works, every word that Scott had said to me just a few days earlier resonated with me. As always, I made it a point to do my research from a number of different sources, including books, articles, and blogs on the internet written by experienced professionals just like Scott, and I was impressed to see that every single one of these sources pointed out the exact same requirements and mistakes to avoid that this kind man had generously shared with me.

The primary reason why it is essential for businesses, companies, and organizations of today to focus on increasing their agility is so that they will be able to hit the ground running and seize opportunities at the best possible moment. Without developing agility and constantly being on the lookout for ways in which they can succeed or rise above the competition, it is practically impossible for the businesses, companies, and organizations of today to rise to unprecedented success.

Once businesses, companies, and organizations are able to increase the speed at which they execute their plans for innovation and are able to increase their agility in order to seize opportunities at the right moment, they will be able to do a lot more than simply survive. As a matter of fact, once the businesses, companies, and organizations of today successfully increase their agility and the time that they take for implementing a well-thought-out and properly planned strategy, they will also be capable of disrupting the entire business environment as a result of the success that they will achieve.

Since there is a lot that needs to be kept in mind and considered at all times when you are trying to innovate resourcefully, most businesses, companies, and organizations end up falling prey to the barriers and limitations that come in the way, resulting in their failure. People often fail to realize that the set of skills required to properly and successfully pull off disruptive innovation is in many ways different from the type of skills that are required for management. Since it isn't everyday that businesses, companies, and organizations of today think of innovating and disrupting the business environment, most of them are usually not even equipped with the set of skills that is required for them to successfully implement innovative ideas. For this reason, the leaders and managers of today also have to work extra hard in order to overcome all of the barriers and obstacles that they will inevitably face when they are trying to innovate and take the market by storm.

Once I was done doing my research on the different types of innovation, I decided that it was finally time for me to share all of this information with my students through my lectures.

"I know that most of you will find this question a bit absurd," I said to them, "but what do you guys know about innovation?"

Silence took over the classroom. It was probably too early in the morning for a question like that.

"Is this one of those Sun Tzu classes again?" one of the students seated in the first row asked, with a smile on his face. The response was followed by muffled giggles from every direction.

"I can turn it into one of those if you'd like," I replied, returning the smile.

My students soon became interested in what I had to say to them. Questions were asked about the different approaches to innovation and examples were shared.

"I feel as if it isn't even necessary for you to improvise your product or service into something that is absolutely new and unheard of with the incremental style of innovation," one of my students said. "Isn't The Coca-Cola Company a good enough example of the incremental approach in itself? I mean, they did change their formula slowly and gradually to win the hearts of customers who became interested in different flavors, over time. Look how many different flavors they have now!"

"I've been waiting for someone to point that out all day," I applauded. "The Coca-Cola Company really is one of the best examples of our time."

And we ran out of time . . . The students had a look of disappointment on their faces. They were finally enjoying the lecture and were keen on learning how industry giants rose to success.

"We'll continue talking about more great examples in the next class," I said to them.

My students headed out of the class talking and being amazed at one example after the other as I packed my bag at the table in the front of the class. Once all of them had left, I took out my phone from my pocket to see if I had any calls or messages that had to be responded to. I had a habit of keeping my phone on silent mode during my lectures so that I am not disturbed by unimportant notifications.

Most of the people that I was in contact with knew my class schedule and tried their best not to contact me during my lectures unless there was a really important reason to do so. They knew that this was a pet peeve of mine. For that very reason, I was surprised to see three phone calls and a text message that came in during the last one hour—all of them from the same person.

"Hey, professor, I tried calling you a bunch of times but you didn't pick up. I know that you're probably busy right now, but we need to talk. Let me know when we can meet," read the message from Bill.

I thought it would be best for me to head straight to my office before I gave him a call, but Bill apparently couldn't wait that long. I received another call from him almost as soon as I was done reading his text message.

"Hi, professor. I know that you are busy, and I'm really sorry but I don't know what happened. I need to see you as soon as possible."

It wasn't like Bill to panic this way. To the extent that I knew the young man on the other end of the phone, he was resilient and wouldn't make a fuss out of something unless it was absolutely necessary.

"Let's meet today," I replied without any greetings. "But can you at least tell me what happened? Are you all right?"

"I'm fine, I guess," Bill replied. That certainly wasn't the answer that I wanted to hear. Bill left me feeling more skeptical and curious than before.

"All right, when do you want to meet?" I asked Bill and avoided asking any more questions about how he was doing, to avoid stressing him out even more.

"6 p.m. sounds good to me. I hope you're free then." *Where are we meeting?* wasn't even a question that we asked anymore.

"I'll be there, Bill. I really hope you're all right," I replied.

"Thanks, professor. I'll be fine."

Needless to say, I started feeling very concerned about Bill. Over the last few weeks, the only thing that was on my mind were questions about how Bill was doing at his new job. Was he satisfied? Did he like the work? Did he find the environment better than at his previous workplace, which had gradually become more and more toxic?

I had wanted to give him time to decide how he liked the new place without any external factors or my advice influencing his decision. After the phone call, however, the only thing that I wanted to do was meet Bill and ask him what was going on with his life. Never before had he called me like this in the middle of my lectures, which is why it was becoming impossible for me to shake off the feeling that something was very wrong.

Once we were done talking on the phone and had decided that we would be meeting that evening, I packed my remaining belongings in my bag and headed straight to my office. Placing my bag on my desk, I leaned back on my chair. All the while, there was nothing that I could think of except Bill. I wasn't sure whether I was imagining things, but now that I thought about the conversation that we had just had on the phone, I slightly remembered his voice being shaky.

The worst part of the situation that I was facing was that I didn't even know what the exact problem was. Naturally, my mind started thinking of the worst possible situations. Was there legal trouble involved or was he going through some other kind of difficulties and problems in his life that he could only talk to me about in person? There was no way that I could find out before 6 p.m.

About half an hour after I reached my office, it suddenly occurred to me that I had just a few minutes left before my next lecture. I tried to collect myself, grabbed my bag (which I hadn't touched since I entered my office), and rushed straight to the classroom.

About five students were already present in the room when I walked in. Soon after, students of all ages started storming in. "Hey, professor," most of them said, as they walked past me. All I could do was fake a smile in return.

I was surprised to see that one of the last students to enter the class was able to look past the façade and saw the concern in my eyes.

"Is everything all right, professor?" he said, as he put a hand on my arm.

I was startled, but I managed to regain my composure.

"Yes," I said with another fake smile. "I was just thinking about something important. Sorry to scare you like that," I lied.

"I hope you're telling the truth, professor," he said, as he walked on to take a seat. I could tell by the look on his face that he wasn't buying a single word that I said. My student, however, didn't say much because he could probably tell by the look on my face that I wasn't in the mood for small talk or explaining things to anyone.

Once all of my students finally took their seats, it was time for me to offi-cially start my lecture. Unfortunately, however, the phone call with my student was the only thing that kept running through my head. Even though I tried as hard as I possibly could, it was becoming impossible for me to concentrate on anything except my conversations with Bill. Instinctively, I tried to make the most of the situation that I was facing and decided to revolve my lecture around most of the topics that Bill and I had covered during our conversations. Besides, the class that I was giving was only supposed to be an hour long. Bill and I had had a lot more conversations and had covered far too many topics to be covered in a single hour.

Gathering all of my composure once again and trying my best to look nor-mal, I began my lecture.

"How's everyone doing today?" I asked my students, in a fake cheerful tone.

"Great," replied several different voices from a number of areas in the classroom.

"So, I'm thinking of changing things a bit for today," I said to them, almost as soon as they responded.

"Oh boy!" replied a young man from one of the first rows of the classroom.

"I was hoping for that," replied one of the more silent students.

"What do you mean?" asked one of the girls in the class.

"Well," I smiled, "instead of just presenting a boring lecture, I thought of trying out something new today."

"And what is that?" a voice from somewhere in the classroom questioned inquisitively.

"I feel like we've already talked a lot about a number of different topics and covered a lot of strategic concepts in our classes throughout the semester. For that reason, I'm looking for suggestions from you guys now."

My students were evidently confused. Even though I did innovate in my lectures and change things around often, never before had I asked them for suggestions so explicitly. Besides, until that time, they never knew why I wanted to hear their feedback, suggestions, and opinions. Since it felt like that question was lingering in the minds of many but they weren't putting it into words, for one reason or another, I decided to take it upon myself to break the ice.

"Won't any of you ask what I need suggestions for?" I questioned, with a smile on my face.

"I was just about to," said one of the pranksters of the class. There was laughter in the entire classroom.

"I'm sure you were," I winked at the student.

"Now," I continued "what I wanted your suggestions for was something that should be quite simple for you guys. You're all MBA students in your last semester. I think it's time for me to be asking you questions that will help you in your professional careers."

All of the students in the classroom listened intently to what I had to say.

"But before I ask you the question, I need you all to promise me something," I said.

My students had a puzzled look on their faces. It isn't often that a university professor goes around asking students to promise him or her something.

"What is that?" asked a number of students seated throughout the classroom.

"Promise me that you won't hold back on any answers just because you feel that they are immature or are not as good as the answers that other students are giving."

The atmosphere within the classroom suddenly became more relaxed. It was evident that most of the students felt more self-confident now and believed that they could finally participate in the class no matter how absurd their thoughts or ideas might sound to other people.

"And there's a strict rule that we'll be following for today's activity," I continued. "No one will laugh at or ridicule anyone else in any way for their questions or suggestions."

The vast majority of students were apparently quite impressed with these rules. "Deal," they unanimously agreed.

"Perfect!" I said, from the front of the classroom. I could tell by the looks on the faces of my students that they wouldn't be able to contain their excitement for the activity any longer. They awaited the question so impatiently that they almost demanded to hear what the activity would be all about.

"And now for the question," I continued, after finally creating enough suspense. "Since we have had multiple conversations about the businesses, companies, and organizations of the VUCA corporate world of today and all of the problems that leaders and managers face, I wanted to ask all of you what you think the best way to overcome all of these problems could be."

This was it. The opinions of my students would finally be heard. Since feeling ignored and not feeling that their thoughts are important is one of the things that students throughout the world complain about most often, my students were apparently very happy about the activity. Even though I had spontaneously decided on having that activity in the classroom that day only because I couldn't get the conversations with Bill out of my mind, I suddenly realized that all my students really wanted was to be heard, and to feel as if their opinions mattered every once in a while.

One by one, almost all of the students in the class started raising their hands.

"Is this response because you are genuinely interested in this activity or just because none of you feels like taking an actual class today?" I questioned, as soon as I saw the response in the classroom.

"We'll let you take your pick, professor," the prankster of the class was back at it again.

"Well played," I said. I was actually feeling a bit happy that I had all of my students around me to help me get my mind off of the conversations and the meeting that I was supposed to have with Bill that evening. Besides, since my students were so excited about the activity that was taking place in the classroom, I decided that it wouldn't be fair to them if I was only barely interested in what was going on there and just focused all of my energies on finding a solution to a problem that I didn't even know the nature of.

I could tell that most of the students were getting tired and might even have been having second thoughts about what it was that they were doing, so I decided that I should start asking them for their answers.

One of the students from the first row slowly lowered his hand down as he thought that he would never get the chance to speak. I noticed this and immediately called out to him.

"Yes, young man. What do you suggest?"

"Me?" he asked, pointing at himself. It was evident that he didn't think I noticed him slowly get disappointed and lower his hand.

All I did was nod in return.

"I think they need to up their agility game. I mean, that's what you always taught us."

By this time, the rest of the students in the class, too, had lowered their hands. Almost all of the students present in the classroom at that moment started listening intently to the conversation that I was having with my student—all of them except for the prankster who was busy watching a video on his phone and giggling.

"That's true," I nodded, showing appreciation for his answer. "But how do you think they can do that? Do you have any personal suggestions?"

The way in which his expression changed was proof that he was starting to get nervous. I could almost swear that he was also starting to sweat.

"Umm, I guess they just have to keep an eye on changes in the environment. But like, since there's a lot that is going on the business environments of today, I guess that they'll have to create proper teams."

"Functional teams. Very good," I summarized his statements for the entire class to take notes as the nervous young man before me sat back down on his seat.

"Does anyone else have any other suggestions?"

"Dedicated places to share creative ideas!" a girl from the last row of the class exclaimed. All 50 heads turned to her.

"I'm sorry, was that too loud?" she blushed.

"It's all right," I smiled at her warmly.

"Dedicated places?" I asked inquisitively, giving her a chance to refine her suggestion.

"I think there's a name for them. A place where people can come together and talk to each other and share ideas."

"Are you talking about co-working spaces?" another student asked her.

"Definitely not those," she told him. "They're called something else but I can't remember the name right now."

Since I hadn't told the students in this particular class about innovation hubs, I was actually quite impressed that some of them were actually familiar with the concept. I was actually hoping that they would get into a conversation about innovation hubs as everyone tried figuring out what they were called.

It didn't take too long for my wish to be fulfilled.

"Innovation hubs! I think that's what they're called," she yelled out in the class, as she was evidently very excited. Once again, all heads turned to her.

"I should probably stop doing that," she continued, with a shy smile on her face.

"That's right, they're called innovation hubs," I confirmed.

"I thought so," she said, this time in a much lower voice.

"So, what else do you know about them?" I asked her so that she didn't stop answering or providing her feedback.

"Not much, honestly," my student responded softly. "I just know that teams of all kinds can come together in those places and have discussions about whatever they think is the best way to innovate and create something out of the box. And I think I read somewhere that they're actually pretty different from co-working spaces because of certain features that they have. I'm not too sure what those are though."

To help her and everyone else in the class, I decided that it would be best for me to give them a brief overview of the information that I had regarding innovation hubs. Additionally, I decided that it would help everyone if I would share with them my thoughts about how the businesses, companies, and organizations of today can make use of innovation hubs effectively and efficiently.

The best part about that class was that there was already so much positive energy flowing that the students barely even noticed how I taught them concepts such as the importance of innovation hubs—all within the context of the conversations and discussions that we were having. Seeing the results, I concluded that it would be best for me to use this approach more often. Not only were all of the students present in the class more interested than ever before, but I, too, was enjoying the class just as much.

Once the entire discussion about innovation hubs was over and I had successfully explained to them how innovation hubs are far more than the average co-working space and why they need their fair share of natural lighting and large, uncongested areas, we were finally able to proceed with the discussion that was initially taking place in the classroom.

I noticed that another one of the students in the front row was waiting for quite some time for his turn to speak so I decided to give him the chance as soon as the discussion about innovation hubs was over.

"So," I said, signaling to him. "What do you think businesses, companies, and organizations of today need to do to overcome the obstacles that they face?"

Like most students, he was startled at first to find that it was finally time for him to speak, but despite being surprised, the young man wasn't nervous for even a fraction of a second.

"Agility and innovation—those are the only two things that they need to focus on," the student said, with exemplary brevity.

"Agility and innovation. Very good!" I replied, appreciating his answer even though I didn't necessarily agree that those two were the *only* things that needed to be focused on. However, I didn't even ask him to elaborate on the point that he had made or bother countering his answer because he didn't look like he was in the mood to elaborate or argue over the statement that he had made.

"I was about to say the same thing!" one of the more studious girls seated at the back of the class said.

"Oh, yeah?" I replied, without the slightest bit of sarcasm in my tone.

My student nodded, not knowing any other way to respond.

"So, what do *you* propose should be done to increase agility or innovate more efficiently?" I asked her inquisitively.

"More than anything else," she said, "I think that if the businesses, companies, and organizations of today *really* take the time out to listen to and focus on the requirements and preferences of customers, that would suffice for the innovation aspect.

"Even when we talk about some of the greatest companies in recent times, such as the Nokia Corporation and Kodak®, I think that, unfortunately, they didn't focus enough on their customers' needs or go sufficiently out of their way to find out what it really was that they wanted. In my opinion, the problem with both of these industry giants was the same: They enjoyed success while it lasted and continued to live with the outdated belief that they'd be able to make progress and succeed even though they barely changed anything about the ways in which they carried out their processes, activities, or operations. As a result of this, it was only a matter of time before their demise."

"Don't you think they tried making things different?" I asked her, just to find out her point of view on innovation.

"I'm sure they did," she responded. "That's probably the only reason why they were successful for as long as they were. But with that said, there weren't really any *remarkable* changes. All they essentially did was tweak a thing or two in hopes that their customers would continue to be satisfied and convinced with what they were being offered."

As unfortunate and harsh as everything that my student said sounded, I couldn't agree more. In my opinion, these companies really could have performed a whole lot better if only they had done proper research on the market and had tried to not only understand the needs and requirements of their own customers but also learn crucial information about potential customers and what they were looking for when they were shopping for new products or services.

Even though the solution that my student had offered after making extremely bold statements was very general, the fact of the matter was that her statements had inspired other students to join the conversation as well. Nearly all of the students present in the classroom soon took part in the ongoing discussion.

During the time that remained, my students shared their thoughts about the current situation in the corporate world; the reasons for the lack of responsibility that leaders and managers of businesses, companies, and organizations of the VUCA world were displaying; and their own million-dollar ideas about how to foster creativity and promote innovation.

Since I could understand how much courage it takes for some students to share their thoughts and opinions in front of the entire class, I appreciated and acknowledged the effort that every student was putting into the discussion. Being their professor, I also believed that it was my duty and responsibility to correct them whenever they said something that wasn't right or thought of solutions that were headed in the wrong direction, and the students appreciated my help.

More than anything else, however, I could tell that my students liked the deal that we had made at the very beginning of the class. Since no one was being condescending towards anyone else, most—if not all—of my students didn't find the need to fear sharing any of their thoughts or feelings. For once, I saw my students truly feel connected within the learning process and know that it really doesn't make a difference if someone doesn't know something and someone else does—even if they're all in the same class and have access to the same information as everyone else.

As clichéd as it may sound, time really flew by when everyone in the class started participating. In fact, most of the students were actually surprised when the bell finally rang. There was so much positive energy in the classroom for that hour that the students looked like they didn't want to leave. The expressions on their faces revealed that they had finally truly enjoyed the class. My students learned a lot during the conversation that ensued in class, which was similar to the times that I would casually tell Bill everything that I thought he needed to know about a certain topic or concept that he was unfamiliar with. Since we were already on the topic, I was also able to share with them some of the knowledge that Scott had shared with me. My students would obviously be interested in finding out how agility could be learned, and I wasn't sure whether I'd get a chance to tell them all of this again, considering that we didn't have much time left before finals week. Once I was out of the class, I headed back toward my office. Once again, thoughts of the phone conversation that I had with Bill that morning started circling in my mind. As concerned as I was about him, I tried not to call him up and make things even more difficult for him as he would probably be at work at that time. Besides, there were now only a few hours left before our meeting that day. Since I knew that we would be meeting in a couple of hours regardless of whether I called him or continued to panic throughout the day, I decided that it would be best if I kept myself busy with other tasks and tried to divert my attention from Bill and the conversation that I had with him earlier in the day.

Even though I really didn't expect myself to get distracted by work, I was surprised to find that it actually did make a difference. Of course, I couldn't forget about Bill entirely, but the anxiety that his phone call had caused somehow became more manageable when I tried to busy myself with preparations for lectures and grading my students' papers. In fact, since I subconsciously knew why I wanted to keep myself busy, I realized that I was actually working more attentively than usual.

I was able to work without any breaks for about two hours. When I finally checked the time, I was quite relieved to see that it was 4 p.m. *Just two more hours to go,* I thought to myself.

Knowing that procrastinating would eventually lead to overthinking the situation, I went straight back to work with the same amount of concentration. This time, however, I couldn't work attentively for more than a few minutes. Almost immediately after I had started working again after checking the time, my concentration was interrupted by a phone call.

It was Bill.

"Hi, how are you doing?" I said, picking up the call as soon as I could, while trying not to make the conversation awkward for my worried friend.

"Hey, professor. I'm sorry if I got you worried earlier," Bill's voice replied. "Just wanted to confirm that you'll be available in the evening. I really need to speak to you about some important stuff."

Even though Bill was more apologetic than ever before, the way in which he was behaving bothered me a lot. I could tell that Bill was deeply troubled by something, but I couldn't figure out what it was. Regardless of all of that, however, I knew that I had to do something to help him. Bailing on Bill at a time when he was so desperate to meet and have a proper discussion was out of the question. Besides, Bill had fortunately called me on a day when I didn't have much planned for the evening. I could easily go and meet him for as long as he wanted.

Trying to keep my composure, I finally responded to Bill.

"Don't worry, there's not much that I had to do this evening anyway. I'll definitely be there!" I said.

"I'll be waiting, professor. I honestly don't know what I've done to deserve a friend like you. Thank you so much," Bill replied. I could tell by his voice that he was finally starting to feel relieved.

I, on the other hand, was more worried than before. I wanted to tell Bill how I had been continually thinking about the conversation that we had that morning. Revealing that information, however, could make things much worse than they already were for him.

For some reason, Bill kept trying to cut the conversation short. I respected his decision and the phone call was over in a little over two minutes. That phone call, however, marked the end of my productivity for the day. Nothing I did would be enough to help me to stop thinking about Bill and what was bothering him so much. Even though I knew that he wanted to discuss the entire situation with me at length when we finally met (in a little less than two hours), the fact of the matter was that I was deeply disturbed by the fact that he wasn't openly talking about his situation on the phone. Just like earlier that day, my mind started imagining the worst possible scenarios—the only difference was that this time it wasn't possible to bid them farewell.

Since I wasn't able to concentrate on anything in my office, I decided to step outside and take a walk on the campus. To my disappointment, that, too, didn't amount to much. Even though I did get the chance to speak to some students and other faculty members as I paced past the buildings, I wasn't able to stop thinking about the conversation and anticipated meeting for long.

Since the little restaurant was nearly a 40-minute-long drive away from the campus, I decided that it would be best to leave for our meeting spot around 5 o'clock. Taking my chances and getting stuck in traffic was the last thing that I wanted to do on that particular day. Having no doubts that I'd reach there later than Bill on that day, too, I drove as fast as I could to make it to the little restaurant on time.

To my surprise, Bill was nowhere in sight when I entered the little restaurant at a few minutes to 6. Even though this young man was more punctual than anyone I had ever met before, I knew that his new workplace was quite far from the restaurant.

"He should be here any minute now," I said to the waiter when he asked me why my friend wasn't there yet.

Minutes turned to nearly half an hour, and Bill was still nowhere in sight. Throughout that time, I had tried not to call him because it might distract him while he was driving. When it was finally 6:30 p.m., I knew that I had to contact him, one way or the other. Worried sick, I gave Bill a call a few minutes later.

The call was not answered, naturally leaving me more worried than before. A few seconds later, however, I received a text message from his number.

"Be there in 10. Sorry for the delay," it read.

I knew that responding wouldn't be of any use because he was definitely driving and wouldn't read it until he reached the restaurant. Reading his text message, however, did cause some of my worry to fade. I was just glad to know that I'd be meeting my friend in a few minutes.

The tall waiter who served Bill and me every time we went to the little restaurant noticed that I was troubled by something. As a kind gesture, he brought me a serving of his favorite appetizer, on the house.

Staying true to his promise, Bill finally arrived a few moments later.

"Traffic?" I asked inquisitively, as I got up from my seat to greet him.

"Delayed at the office—I didn't have a choice," he replied.

It had only been a little over a month since Bill had begun his new job, which is why hearing that he was being asked to do overtime already came as more of a shock than it should have. Since it was too early on in the conversation to bring that point up, I decided to save it for later. Besides, we had much more important things to discuss during our meeting and we had already lost a lot of time.

Bill and I took our seats and started off the conversation with casual greetings.

"Do you have any idea how worried I am about you?" I finally said, after we were finished greeting each other.

"I actually do," Bill replied as he picked up some of the appetizer from the table.

"What's going on, Bill? I can't tell you how worried I've been since you called me in the morning."

"What do you think it is, Joe?" Bill replied, looking me straight in the eye. The way he responded made it evident that he wasn't in a good mood at all. Never before had Bill spoken to me as sternly as he did that evening.

"It's the new job," Bill finally continued, taking another bite of the appetizer after I hadn't responded.

"I had a feeling that you'd say that," I told my student.

All he did in return was smile.

"You've barely been there a month," I continued. "What's wrong?"

"Everything."

Considering the way in which the conversation was proceeding, I concluded that it would be pretty difficult to have him open up and actually start talking about what was wrong.

Fortunately, it wasn't long before he proved me wrong.

"You know what, Joe? There have actually been times when I wondered whether I made the right decision when I took this job," Bill said. "I can't even decide which one I should call the lesser of two evils."

That is never a good thing to hear from someone who you know for a fact is focused and energetic, with a lot of potential. Having been a professor and connected with the corporate world for quite a number of years, I had heard that statement being repeated far too often. There was always a trend visible in people who felt this way about themselves. Once they feel that their potential isn't being utilized and that their efforts aren't being recognized or acknowledged, people who feel that way stop putting in effort and let their minds rust because they lack the drive and motivation to continue working the way they once did.

What made everything worse this time around, however, was that the person who was saying these words was a lot more than just a student who I had once taught. Bill had grown into a friend who I cared about just like family. Knowing how much Bill was really worth and hearing that, once again, he wasn't being appreciated and given the amount of recognition that he truly deserved for all of the efforts that he had tirelessly put in broke my heart. Besides, no one knew better than I did that Bill was skeptical about his new job right up to the day before he started working there. Being treated unjustly at his new workplace, too, could make him lose all hope in himself.

Since I knew how excited Bill had been about starting his new job and finally being freed from the shackles of his previous toxic workplace, I knew for a fact that he would be giving it his all. Besides, Bill wasn't the type of person to hold back on putting in the required amount of effort—and more—for anything. And this was especially true for something that he was excited about.

Bill still hadn't said much about what exactly the problem was. I, therefore, decided not to let negative thoughts take over my mind and thought that it would be best if I let my friend do the talking before I jumped to baseless conclusions. Since I knew that Bill wasn't in a good mood, I decided that ordering some food would be a better option. That might even give Bill the chance to relax a bit. Perhaps then he would start talking about the problems that he was facing at his new workplace by himself, without my having to force him into speaking and ultimately worsening his mood.

I summoned the tall waiter who had brought me the free appetizer and asked him for more of his recommendations. Although the waiter was kind enough to give us a practically endless list of items that he thought we would like, Bill wasn't interested in anything at all.

"I'm really not in the mood for much," Bill said, when I asked him what he would like to have. In fact, he hadn't even opened the menu once since he had sat down across the table from me.

"Come on, Bill," I said. "It's been a long day. You'll feel better after a light meal."

"I'll have whatever you're having," my uninterested student replied.

Since the weather was pretty chilly, I just asked the waiter to bring two soups of the day for me and my friend.

"Gladly," our courteous waiter smiled. "Anything to drink, sir?" he asked my friend.

"Just water," Bill replied, faking a smile at the waiter.

"All right then. Two soups and water," our waiter repeated our order and left as we nodded. My student was glad that the waiter had left us alone and sunk his head into his palms.

"So," I said to Bill, when we were left alone at our table, "you were telling me about your new job."

I immediately regretted framing my statement the way in which I did because I wasn't sure how he would react to it. Fortunately, his response wasn't as bad as I had anticipated based on his mood that day.

"That's right," Bill replied, lifting his face from his hands to look at me. "Don't get me wrong, professor, I don't mean to sound ungrateful or anything, but I am honestly having my doubts about how long I'll be able to stay at this place without losing all of my sanity."

Even though I started to get an idea of what Bill meant when he said this, I tried my best not to respond or give my opinion and let him do the talking for as long as possible instead. Much like many times in the past, that technique proved to be successful. When I didn't respond for some time, Bill resumed talking about his workplace by himself.

"You see, Joe," Bill continued talking, as he looked at nothing in particular, "I haven't been able to put my finger on the exact problem over there. But it's just so similar to everything that I was going through at my former job."

"Does the fact that you're staying overtime already have something to do with it?" I asked Bill.

"I don't even know, Joe," he said as he looked at me. "I think I should have expected overtime, considering the fact that it's a startup and all. But there's a lot more to it."

The more Bill struggled to explain the problem that he was facing, the more I understood what the matter was. At his former workplace, Bill had been complacent for a very long time, which is why it had become difficult for him to understand the severity of the problem there. This time, however, Bill was a lot more mature and knew a lot more about how he should be treated at work. Besides, he now also knew the difference between a business, company, and organization that is truly agile and innovative and one that is not.

From his previous experience, Bill already knew how deleterious it can be if the leaders and managers at a company believe that they are the only ones who are capable of making sane and practical decisions regardless of whether they are truly in line with the vision and mission of the business, company, or organization where they work. At his previous workplace, Bill had met people of that sort far more often than he should have. Initially, I thought that he was only feeling skeptical about the leaders and managers at his new workplace, and that perhaps he was drawing unnecessary parallels between the new people that he met there and those who he had to interact with on a daily basis at his previous job. However, when Bill started trying to tell me more about the situation at his new job, everything started falling into place.

"It's like they have never heard of the concepts of innovation or agility, Joe," he finally said. "It feels like I'm back to square one, except that this time, the people don't even have as much experience as those at my previous job did. And you know what the worst part is? They use the fact that they're working in a startup as their excuse for practically everything under the sun! No interpersonal skills? It's a startup. No innovation? We'll get there. No team management? What else did you expect at a startup?"

Bill was politely interrupted by our tall waiter who had brought our order.

"Sorry to interrupt the conversation that you guys are having," he said with a nervous smile on his face, hoping that we wouldn't mind the bad timing.

"Watch out, the bowls are hot," said the tall man, as he placed the soup before us. Just like most of the items on the menu that we had tried, the soup, too, looked extremely appetizing. I, for one, couldn't wait to taste it.

"Let me know if you need anything else," continued the tall man as he put a large bottle of water on the table and walked away.

Bill looked more uninterested than ever. In fact, he didn't even take a look at the soup after the waiter had placed it in front of him.

"They're living under this illusion that just because they are working at a startup, they'll be able to learn anything and everything without ever putting in any effort. And yet, again, they feel like everything that I'm doing is wrong," Bill continued exactly where he had left off.

Bill took a small pause and tried some of the soup. His expressions were proof that he loved it, but he didn't say anything in appreciation or acknowledgment of that fact. Instead, he continued talking after just one spoonful.

"The only *right* way of doing things is doing them their way," he said. "None of them are ready to acknowledge that other people, too, can have a good idea or a different style of carrying out a certain process or operation every once in a while. I get told off for the stupidest of things at that place!"

Being made to feel as if you aren't able to do anything correctly or that you aren't a competent employee just because you like doing things a bit differently from everyone else is one of the worst things that can happen to anyone. But what made it even worse for Bill was that he was actually looking forward to this new job, after spending far too many years at a company where he wasn't appreciated enough and his efforts weren't being recognized. Moving from such a place and ending up in a company that is even worse can leave an everlasting impression on a person's mind. The fact that he was at a startup now after leaving a company that was actually established for quite a number of years wasn't doing much good for his cause either.

I tried explaining to Bill that none of this was his fault, and that it was more a problem of the leaders and managers of the workplaces where he had unfortunately been working, but I wasn't really able to find the right words. For the longest time, I looked for the right words to say to Bill, not only to comfort him and make him believe in himself but also so that he wouldn't take what I was saying negatively, or feel as if I was just being supportive to someone who is hopeless. Unfortunately, however, as expected, Bill had already started losing hope in himself and felt as if the problem was really with him instead of at the places where he was working.

"I feel as if I can't do this anymore, Joe," Bill pushed his soup back towards me and put both of his elbows on the table before his head sunk into his palms once again.

"I just can't do this," his voice started shaking.

"Hey, there," I said to Bill. "Do you really think that this is your fault, young man?"

"Who else could be at fault?" Bill said.

I, too, pushed my bowl of soup away from myself.

"Look at me, Bill," I said to Bill. He unwillingly obliged, with no expression on his face.

"First things first, you know that you weren't at fault at your previous job, right?" I asked.

The only thing that Bill did in response to my question was nod. No words were said, and there was still absolutely no expression on his face.

"Then what makes you think that the situation is any different and that you're the one at fault at your new job?" I asked Bill.

As expected, he didn't have too much to say. He didn't exactly agree with my viewpoint at that moment, so he just tried avoiding the question for as long as he possibly could.

"Don't you think it's a little unreal for two of my bosses at consecutive jobs to have the same things to say about me? I'm actually quite convinced that there is something that I'm doing wrong."

I had seen Bill go through this phase not too long ago as well, so I knew that all I really had to do was let him express his feelings before I tried putting the pieces of the puzzle together for him. Before he resigned from his previous workplace, Bill had felt the exact same way and wasn't ready to accept the fact that he was planning on leaving a toxic workplace due to problems with the company. For the longest time, he kept putting all of the blame on himself and believed that he wasn't succeeding or making any progress in his career because he was an incompetent employee who wasn't working hard enough or putting in the amount of effort that was required of him.

Like now, Bill was extremely confused and depressed when he was facing problems due to the lack of proper management at his previous job, and it had taken him quite some time to truly understand and realize that he wasn't at fault. From my last experience dealing with Bill at his lowest, I understood that letting him do all the talking was the best possible solution at this point in time.

I poured my student a glass of water for him to calm down and collect himself. I knew for a fact that he would take a breather after he was done drinking his glass of water and before he started speaking again. However, what happened next what something that I wasn't expecting at all.

"I think I'm going to resign," Bill said.

As much it sounded like an impulsive decision, I secretly supported it wholeheartedly. However, being his mentor and the friend that he trusted most with his life, I had to be completely certain that he was thinking straight and wouldn't end up regretting his decision or hate me for the rest of his life for not talking him out of it at the right time.

As much as I wanted to ask Bill what made him reach this decision, the unfortunate fact of the matter was that I didn't quite know how I should frame the question. Luckily, Bill was in the mood to talk without being asked anything explicitly.

"I know I might not be doing things their way," Bill continued, "and I understand why that bothers them so much. But you know what, Joe? They don't know how to do anything themselves, either. No decision-making skills. No problem-solving skills. Nothing!"

My evidently furious former student poured himself another glass of water before he started talking again.

"Do you remember when I told you about the job offer, Joe? The only reason why I was really excited to start working there was because it is a startup and has great potential. I thought I'd be introduced to a completely different style of thinking, I would get the chance to work together with a team of young and energetic individuals, and I would be able to focus on personal growth and learn like never before. But look at what the reality there is really like!" Bill exclaimed sarcastically before he took a sip of his water.

By the look on his face, I could tell that Bill was also worried about what was in store for him. Once again, he was faced a dilemma that wasn't much different from what he was going through just a few weeks earlier. Bill was once again stuck in a position where anything he did wasn't enough. What made everything worse for him this time around though was the fact that he didn't know what he was supposed to do. To him, it felt like resigning from a new job this early would create a bad impression on his work record and he didn't want to let that happen—after all, he still had to leave a mark in the corporate world and the last thing that he wanted to do at a time like this was tarnish his record and create room for questions in the minds of potential employers.

Since the startup that Bill was currently working at had negligible—if any— interest in innovation and all things creative, I knew that a person such as Bill wouldn't be able to survive there for long anyway. It was better for him to make a decision as soon as possible, before he started finding excuses for himself and ended up needlessly delaying his resignation.

Strategic innovation is essentially the fundamental requirement for the creation of new strategies that will help any business, company, or organization rise to new heights every day. As someone who had recently become interested in innovation and different styles of work, I knew that Bill needed to start working in a place where innovation and creativity are focused on more than anything else.

The reasons why strategic innovation was so important to Bill were not too unrealistic or surprising. Strategic innovation is the perfect blend of traditional and nontraditional approaches that are necessary for the businesses, companies, and organizations of today. In the VUCA world of today, it is almost impossible for individuals in the workforce to grow and become responsible pioneers of change if they are not a part of a company, business, or organization that supports and strongly believes in strategic innovation.

The best part about strategic innovation is that this approach is different from the traditional approach that most businesses, companies, and organizations still use, in many instances. Unlike the traditional approach that people who are not innovative or creative use, the strategic approach to innovation focuses on the end result and the goal more than anything else. Additionally, unlike the traditional approach being used by countless companies, businesses, and organizations of today, leaders and managers who work with the strategic approach to innovation and focus on agility more than anything else are known to identify long-term opportunities and bridge them back to the present in a way that will guarantee success and help the business, company, or organization where they work rise to new heights.

One of the major reasons why people are afraid of using the strategic approach to innovation and agility, however, is the fact that they are deemed as rule breakers or revolutionaries when they use this approach. Although this isn't something negative, in most cases, the fact of the matter is that there are a lot of risks involved in using the strategic approach to innovation. The strategic approach to innovation is, in most cases, deemed synonymous with a rule-breaker approach, and, unfortunately, some people these days are still afraid of being the pioneers of change due to the amount of responsibility that it puts on them.

The rare few companies, businesses, and organizations that do believe in and adopt the strategic approach to innovation end up doing exactly what Bill had been interested in doing during his professional career. These companies, businesses, and organizations seek to create new competitive spaces and fields where they can play and grow through exploration and experimentation. But focusing on what could happen next and exploring new dimensions for expansion are not the only things that these places focus on. In fact, the companies, businesses, and organizations that have adopted the strategic approach to innovation not only seek breakthroughs and play around with disruptive innovations but also make it a point to focus on and build up their core. These businesses, companies, and organizations understand that that innovation—disruptive or otherwise—will be baseless if their core isn't built and focused on the way it should be.

Another great aspect of using the strategic approach to innovation is that it combines discipline with creativity. What this essentially means is that even though the companies, businesses, and organizations that use this approach have the freedom to be as creative as they can possibly be when they are trying to innovate, discipline isn't compromised in the least when this approach is being used. This is another of the many aspects of the strategic approach to innovation that attracted Bill.

Bill was always one of those people who loved being creative and adding a personal touch to everything that he did. Since the strategic approach, too, was all about seeking inspiration for innovation from nontraditional sources, Bill listened intently and was keen to learn more as I told him all of this during our conversation. The strategic style of innovation is all about focusing on the needs and requirements of customers regardless of whether they were articulated explicitly.

Bill was also attracted by the strategic approach of innovation compared to the traditional approach due to the fact that it was more consumer based. Since Bill was all about putting the needs and preferences of everyone else above his own, I knew that he would be perfect in a workplace that used the strategic approach.

Bill wasn't the type of person who could continue listening to his bosses and other leaders and managers regardless of whether they were making the right decisions or not. In fact, that was perhaps the *last* possible thing that Bill could do. Bill believed in originality and uniqueness and was a strong believer in the fact that he needed to put the consumers and customers above any rules and politics that were in effect within the company, business, or organization at which he was employed. Besides, experimenting with entrepreneurial ventures and organizational structures that weren't as common would be even more possible had Bill joined a workplace where the strategic approach to innovation was adopted. This is why I tried my best to share as much information about the approach with Bill as possible.

As important as both strategy and innovation are, there have also been countless examples in the recent past of businesses, companies, and organizations failing due to incompetence and lack of strategic innovation.

I tried explaining the importance of strategic innovation and adopting a mentality that supports creativity to Bill as much as I could in order to change his mind about how he wasn't doing well at his current workplace due to his incompetence.

Everything that my student had told me was enough of a reason for him to quit his new job. Bill wasn't being appreciated for all of the efforts that he was making. None of the work that he did was ever enough for him to be recognized. And since he wasn't really getting what he had joined the company for, I realized that leaving was indeed the best decision that he could make. There was really no reason for him to stay put at this new company in hopes that they will eventually change, in light of their current mindset and supercilious attitude. I knew that staying in that place any longer would eventually make Bill complacent to the extent that he would lose all hope in his potential.

But what will he do next? I wondered to myself.

When I asked Bill if he had any backup plans in mind, he didn't really have anything to say. Since he probably never expected that he would have to leave his new job so soon, getting no response from Bill for that question made me positive that he didn't have any exit strategies or backup plans that he could fall back on in case things went wrong at his new job.

Since I didn't want him to start stressing over applying for a new job once again, I proposed the perfect solution to Bill.

"You know what, Bill? I really think you should resign immediately. In fact, you should hand in your resignation tomorrow. A place like that doesn't deserve you," I said to Bill, in as jovial and convincing a tone as I possibly could.

At that moment, I'm sure Bill thought that I was crazy. The expression on his face changed completely.

"I think that you're forgetting something, Joe. I have bills to pay!" Bill replied, not understanding what was going through my head.

My plan, however, was something that I'm sure never occurred to Bill. With years of experience in the professional industry, I had contacts far and wide. The only reason why I hadn't used these contacts earlier to help Bill find a new job that would appreciate and recognize all of the efforts that the young man before me was tirelessly ready to put in was because I didn't want him to feel like he was incapable of finding the right job on his own. This time, however, I knew that I had to interfere. Bill had already been through a lot during his previous job, and experiencing déjà vu at the startup now wasn't doing him much good. Besides, since Bill was still in his probationary period at his new job, the execution of my plan would be easier. Bill wouldn't even have to serve a notice period when he resigned, and he could start exploring and learning as soon as he quit.

"Trust me on this, Bill. We're going to Europe."

References

1. Sun Tzu. *The Art of War.* Goodreads.com. Retrieved from https://www.goodreads.com/quotes/233643-there-are-not-more-than-five-musical-notes-yet-the
2. NNDB. (n.d.). "Ferdinand de Lesseps." Soylent Communications. Retrieved from http://www.nndb.com/people/720/000028636/
3. History. "Panama Canal." A&E Television Networks, LLC. Retrieved from http://www.history.com/topics/panama-canal
4. Jones, Millie L. (2010, January 28). "William 'Billy' Mitchell—'The Father of the United States Air Force.'" Retrieved from https://www.army.mil/article/33680/william_billy_mitchell_the_father_of_the_united_states_air_force
5. Baker, Newton D. (1921). Quote. DaveEnglish.com. Retrieved from http://www.skygod.com/quotes/airpower.html
6. Scientific American. (1910, July 16). Quote. Retrieved from http://secure.afa.org/quotes/Quotes_81208.pdf
7. Triple Helix Research Group. (n.d.) "The Triple Helix Concept." Stanford University. Retrieved from http://triplehelix.stanford.edu/3helix_concept

8. Leimueller, Gertraud. (2017, February 22). "Developing a National Open Innovation Strategy: Five Lessons Learned from the Austrian Example." (Opinion). European Union. Retrieved from https://ec.europa.eu/digital-single-market/en/news/developing-national-open-innovation-strategy-five-lessons-learned-austrian-example

9. Chesbrough, Henry W. and Appleyard, Melissa M. (2007). Open Innovation and Strategy. *California Management Review, 50*(1), 57–76. Retrieved from https://pdxscholar.library.pdx.edu/cgi/viewcontent.cgi?referer=https://www.bing.com/&httpsredir=1&article=1021&context=busadmin_fac

10. Rosenbush, Steve. (2016, January 13). "GE Digital CEO Bill Ruh Says Corporate Structures Must Evolve with Technology." *The Wall Street Journal.* Retrieved from https://blogs.wsj.com/cio/2016/01/13/ge-digital-ceo-bill-ruh-says-corporate-structures-must-evolve-with-technology/

11. Inkinen, Sam and Kaivo-oja, Jari. (2009). *Understanding Innovation Dynamics: Aspects of Creative Processes, Foresight Strategies, Innovation Media, and Innovation Ecosystems.* Finland Futures Research Centre. Retrieved from https://www.utu.fi/fi/yksikot/ffrc/julkaisut/e-tutu/Documents/eTutu_2009-9.pdf

12. Mui, Chunka. (2012, January 18). "How Kodak Failed." Forbes. Retrieved from https://www.forbes.com/sites/chunkamui/2012/01/18/how-kodak-failed/#73ca9dad6f27

Chapter 9

Searching for Innovation

*Persistence and resilience only come from having been given
the chance to work through difficult problems.*

—Gever Tulley[1]

Needless to say, my former student was startled. To him, my plan of going to Europe on a whim sounded like an impulsive decision that he should steer clear of as much as he possibly could.

"There's someone I need you to meet, Bill," I told my confused and somewhat intimidated former student when he was unable to find the words to respond.

Bill, however, wasn't buying anything that I was saying. Whenever I tried to explain to him that this would be a good decision, he refused to understand and acknowledge the fact that resigning from his current workplace this early and going all the way to Europe with his professor to meet *someone* was in fact the best thing that he could be doing at the moment.

Even though it took well over an hour of trying to convince him, Bill finally, albeit unwillingly, agreed to go with me to Europe.

"You won't regret this one bit. I promise," I told Bill, who still didn't look very happy about agreeing to go with me all the way to a different continent.

"Are you sure this needs to happen right now?" Bill asked me inquisitively.

"Trust me on this. It's the best thing that you could be doing at the moment," I replied, with a warm smile on my face to win his confidence.

"When will we go? Where will we stay? How long will we be there?" Bill started asking me the typical pointless questions that everyone who is trying to back off from a plan asks.

"You don't have to worry about any of that," I told Bill. "I'll make all of the arrangements and let you know within a couple of days. All I need you to do is resign next week. Consider the rest done."

I could tell by the look on his face that Bill still wasn't approving of my plan and was probably thinking of all of the worst situations that could result from it. The entire plan sounded ridiculous to him from the very start, and even though he had agreed, I was certain that he was having second thoughts about going with me all the way to Europe during our entire conversation that day at our little restaurant.

For the next few days, I spent every moment of my "free" time planning for the trip. Countless searches were made for about a week and a half for the best flights and places to stay.

Even though I wanted Bill to meet my friend in Delft, Holland, the only way we could get there with a direct flight was by landing in Amsterdam or via a transfer in London to Rotterdam. Since I had already been to Rotterdam several times before, I decided to book a direct flight, which would land at Schiphol Airport in Amsterdam.

Once all of the arrangements had finally been made, I thought that it would be best to break the news to Bill. Bill, however, ended up calling me before I even got the chance.

"Hey, professor. I listened to you and resigned today. I can only hope that you won't leave me to myself now," Bill said with a small laugh as soon as I answered his call.

"Pack your bags, Bill. We're leaving in five days!" I replied cheerfully to Bill.

Even though I had shared the entire plan with him and everything had been decided upon during our last meeting, Bill was once again taken aback at the spontaneity of the plan.

"Are you kidding me?" was the only thing that Bill was able to ask me.

"Hey, you're the one who didn't want to be left to himself," I laughed.

Bill, however, still wasn't finding any of this funny. To help him calm down a bit, I told him that I'd drop by his house with all of the necessary travel documents. When I finally reached there, Bill still wasn't able to process that all of this would be done so soon.

"Less than a week?" he exclaimed, as I put the documents on his desk.

"I would start packing if I were you," I replied with a smile.

I think it was only when he saw the travel documents in front of him that Bill was truly able to understand that he needed to pull himself together and come to grips with the fact that he had less than a week to get prepared for his trip—five days to be precise.

Fortunately for me, convincing Bill that everything would go just as planned was the only difficult part about the entire trip. Once we landed at the Schiphol

Airport, in Amsterdam, Bill finally started feeling more positive about the entire plan.

"I have a feeling this will end well," he said to me with a smile, once we collected our baggage. "I don't know what I can ever do to repay you, professor."

"Trust me more easily next time, please?" I joked.

Once we left the premises of the airport, I noticed how Bill was surprised to see a whole new type of world that he had never experienced before. Bill had traveled throughout the United States extensively and had even gone to Asia and Africa for training, but Europe was a continent that he had never had the opportunity to visit before. By the look on his face, I could tell that he was very surprised at how different Europe was from the United States. Even though both of these regions are often considered to be similar to each other in many ways, the fact of the matter is that they both have some major differences, which Bill was now learning about firsthand.

Even though Bill didn't explicitly make any requests or share with me his expectations of our short trip to Europe, he had indirectly made it very clear that he wasn't interested in luxury living and wanted to experience the true essence of Europe for as long as he would be there. Since trains serve a lot more people in Europe than in the United States, I decided to give Bill his first real authentic European train experience and booked two seats from Schiphol Airport to the central station in Delft.

Bill was evidently impressed by the services available in the Netherlands. Being accustomed to driving around—often even between cities—in his own car, Bill was loving everything about his European adventure already. Time and again, Bill pointed out how well everything was being managed and how he hoped that the public transportation system would improve in his hometown as well.

It took Bill and me nearly 40 minutes to reach our destination from the airport in Amsterdam, but time flew by so quickly that neither of us noticed. As soon as we got off at Delft Central Station, we were welcomed by my friend Hans.

"You must be Bill," my friend said to Bill, as he extended an arm to greet him.

"That's correct. Nice meeting you, Hans," my excited former student said, with a smile on his face.

"Nice meeting you too, young man," Hans replied, returning the smile.

"I'm sure both of you are hungry," my friend continued. "It must have been a long flight."

"Not really," Bill said, attempting to be formal and create a good impression on my friend.

"Oh yeah?" Hans asked inquisitively.

"He's just being shy," I replied.

"Let's go grab a quick bite. We can get straight to business afterwards," Hans smiled.

Bill had to shyly oblige.

Once we were done eating our food and had had the right number of drinks to wash it all down, Hans took it upon himself to take us around the city and share with us all of the information that he thought we'd be interested in. Needless to say, Hans led the way while Bill and I followed. Since I had already told Hans that Bill had never been to Europe before, he, too, decided to give Bill a proper cultural tour of his city before he actually started discussing what we had traveled all the way to Europe for.

Hans decided that it would be best for him to take me and Bill to the marketplace of the old city of Delft before anything else and to give us a brief introduction to the city, keeping the historical and cultural aspects in mind. As our tour guide, Hans also took it upon himself to explain to us the importance of the city of Delft in the Golden Age of the Low Countries, which are present-day Netherlands and Belgium.

"The Dutch Golden Age is known to have spanned throughout the majority of the 17th century. During this era, Dutch art, the military, science, and trade were acclaimed all over the world, ultimately helping the region gain unprecedented popularity. The first section of the Dutch Golden Age was characterized by the Thirty Years' War, which was primarily fought in Central Europe between the years 1618 and 1648," our friend and voluntary tour guide very kindly informed us.

While we were still walking to the marketplace of the old city, Hans decided that it would be a great idea for him to show us some of the more interesting parts of the city, which have a deep historical connection as well. Hans chose a route through which we would have to pass by the Old Church.

"This protestant gothic church is also known as Scheve Jan," Hans told us. "Just like the Tower of Pisa, the tower of the church has a big bell. Back in the day, the Germans wanted to steal the bells to melt the iron and use the molten element to build tanks. However, they were unable to take the bell out."

Once we finally reached the marketplace after a long and interesting walk full of historical and cultural information, Hans took us to a bakery with a signpost of a book present at its upper corner.

"What's that?" my curious former student asked inquisitively.

"I was hoping you'd ask me that question," Hans answered, with a smile on his face. Hans told us about real examples of innovation in printing presses and how these innovations had resulted in the Bible being translated from Greek and Latin to Dutch.

"Once the people of the Netherlands were finally able to read the Bible in their own language and truly understand all of the lessons that were meant to be learned from it, it was only then that they realized that the church should not be filled with gold and that it should be used to help the poor instead.

"Because of Luther and Calvin," my friend, Hans, continued, "the once Catholic people of Holland became protesters and wanted change and reformation. This led to a political and religious revolution while the King of Spain was ruling our country."

Being a person who had always been interested in discovering and sharing interesting facts with other people, Hans continued to tell us about the start of the era of industrialization and how it was marked by the perfection and large-scale use of windmills. At that point, I would never have guessed that he was telling us all of these stories for a reason.

"Back in those days, windmills were not only some of the primary types of engines used in all kinds of factories, but they were also used to push out the water to the sea and to reclaim land," my friend told us.

The best part about the historically and culturally rich city of Delft was the fact that there was just so much to be learned. Hans showed us the house of the inventor of the microscope, Antony van Leeuwenhoek, and made it a point to explain to us the perfection of the glass production process that ultimately led to the invention of the telescope that was used by Galileo Galilei to prove that the earth revolves around the sun.

"I feel like the Netherlands is still a country that is very innovative," Hans added, once he was done sharing with us different examples of innovation in a bygone era. "Rankings from different sources position the Netherlands as one of the most innovative countries in the world. And the domains and fields that the Netherlands excels at, too, are not limited by any standards. You might find this a tad difficult to believe, but the Netherlands has recently become an agricultural giant." It had been quite a while since Hans had begun taking us around the city and telling us interesting facts about the city where he had lived and which he had loved for quite a number of years. It was evident that Bill was enjoying every moment of his small European adventure. He was amazed at everything from the greenery to the cleanliness and the architecture, and was particularly fond of the fact that every other person in the city traveled by bike. However, I felt that Bill had a question that he wanted to ask the whole time that we were roaming around the city. He hadn't said much besides asking an occasional question or two, but he had this look on his face ever since we had reached Delft, which made it evident that he was holding back on asking something very important that had been was bothering him for quite some time.

And I wasn't the only one who had noticed this. Even though I had already given Hans much more than what would classify as a brief introduction to Bill and friend who I had brought along with me to Europe, Hans still thought of using the typical question as an icebreaker.

"So," Hans finally asked him, as we continued strolling throughout his city, "what do you do, young man?"

It was awhile before Bill realized that the question was directed towards him. And he remained silent for some time after registering the question as well.

"I've recently just been resigning from jobs," Bill said jokingly.

My friend and I laughed heartily. Bill didn't know that Hans already knew some details about his life, which is what made his confidence and lightheartedness on the matter even more smile-worthy. Bill, however, probably thought that that answer was the wrong way to start a real conversation with someone who he had only met a few hours ago. He therefore elaborated on his answer.

"I was working at a company as a sales executive until a few weeks ago. It was the typical job where you have to go around cities providing training, and every boss of yours makes you feel as if you don't know what you're doing," Bill said.

"Once I finally figured out, with the help of Joe here, that this workplace wasn't doing me any good, I decided not to let it take its toll on me any longer and started having frequent conversations with my former professor about agility and innovation and the type of business, company, or organization that would really be a good fit for me. I'm not quite sure what happened afterwards, but there was just too much pressure and I resigned to join a startup," Bill continued.

"Yeah? How did that go?" Hans asked him inquisitively.

"It was a disaster," Bill replied. I hadn't really told Hans much about the startup and Bill's situation over there because I didn't really know much about it myself, which is another reason why Hans was genuinely interested in finding out how that part of the story went.

"I think it was probably even worse than my last job, in many ways," Bill told Hans. "The people over there were living in this bubble where they believed that they would learn everything along the way, but they weren't ready to change a single thing about the way in which they worked. It was ridiculous. These people, too, thought that they were the only ones who knew how to do things, even though they explicitly told me that they're open to ideas and are trying to create an environment that focuses on innovation and creativity more than anything else."

"That's what they all say," Hans laughed.

"I learned my lesson the hard way," Bill said, faking a smile.

"So, how's it going now?" Hans asked Bill.

"Joe suggested that I resign from there, as well," Bill explained.

"I'm very glad you did that," Hans said to me, before turning back to Bill. "You should never stay in a place like that long enough for you to become complacent and start giving up on yourself."

"I guess so," Bill replied.

"And what about yourself? What do you do?" Bill asked Hans. "I mean, there really isn't much that I know about you except for your name."

Both Hans and I realized that this was the question that Bill had wanted to ask all day. Bill hadn't really known why I had decided to bring him all the way to Europe and barely even knew anything about the person that he was supposed to meet. While I'm sure he wouldn't have been so skeptical had he been on a regular trip to Europe, which he had actually planned, neither Hans nor I found Bill's skepticism baseless.

However, before he starting answering the question, Hans smiled.

"Well, I'm sure that Joe here already knows a lot about what I've done and achieved throughout the years," Hans said.

"But there have been failures, too, which I don't regret one bit," my Dutch friend said, with a big smile.

"I'm sure," Bill said, to keep the conversation alive as humbly as he could.

"I think what's important for you to know at this point is that I studied at the Delft University of Technology and received my PhD for my research on Enterprise Design. More than 20 years ago, I wrote a paper with my promoter professor, Jan Dietz, titled 'Organizational Transformation Requires Constructional Knowledge of Business Systems.'[2] And I think that's why your professor thought of bringing you to me," Hans said, with a warm smile on his face.

"That's correct," I added, returning the smile of Hans.

"I knew it," Hans said, patting me on the back. "I presented the paper in 1998 at a conference on the Big Island of Hawaii. It was so much fun working on that."

Once Hans and I had started talking about the reason why we had traveled all the way to Europe, I noticed that Bill was evidently impressed at how professional and experienced Hans was at everything that he did. Not only that, but I could also see all of the worry and skepticism on his face gradually fading away.

Since we had already been touring around the city with Hans for four or five hours, I decided that it would be best if we sat down somewhere to discuss his paper at length. Being the generous person he is, Hans suggested that we should go to his favorite restaurant, Van der Dussen, to get an authentic taste of the Netherlands. Since Bill and I barely knew anything about the city and the country, we didn't have any particular opinion and took Hans' word when he said that we wouldn't be disappointed.

As soon as we entered the restaurant, Bill and I noticed that Hans was just about as popular there as we were in the little restaurant where we had been meeting frequently over the past few months. We were greeted by everyone from the owner to the waiters of the restaurant, and much like the treatment

Bill and I receive at our own hometown restaurant, Hans was given free appetizers as well. Needless to say, it was great to see how restaurant owners throughout the world go the extra mile and try to ensure that their loyal customers are satisfied at all times.

Our waiter at the restaurant in the middle of Delft had very European features and a thick accent. He was quick to bring the three of us menus in English because Hans had told him that his friends don't speak Dutch. Since it was our first time at the little restaurant and Hans was apparently a regular customer, we decided to ask him for his suggestions about his favorites at the restaurant. Much like any other person who is asked for recommendations for food, Hans couldn't really pick only one favorite item and gave us a list of some of the dishes and items on the menu that he enjoyed the most.

Since none of us could decide what we wanted to have, we decided to go for the chef's special for the day. Our waiter had a broad and welcoming smile the entire time. When he felt that we had finished deciding what we wanted to eat, he started collecting the menus from the table. Hans, however, asked him to leave one menu on the table. The waiter politely obliged and walked away with a courteous, "Thank you," as he left with our orders.

Once he had left our table, we knew that we had to get straight to business. Even though Bill was still feeling very shy and was very limited in his speech, especially around Hans, I knew that it was important for both of them to interact with each other as much as possible, which is why I didn't say much.

Ultimately, Bill had to do the talking.

"So," Bill finally said, to break the ice with Hans, "why did you decide to do research regarding enterprise design at the university as an entrepreneur?"

Hans immediately understood that the question was directed towards him and lifted his head from the menu, which he was very carefully browsing through.

"Well," Hans replied, with his characteristic warm smile, "in my view, the traditional knowledge regarding enterprises, which originates from areas and fields such as business administration, management science, and logistics fails to provide the correct understanding for the purpose of redesigning them."

"He's been thinking about innovation since the 1990s," I added.

"That's correct," Hans agreed. "In the 1990s, I saw a promising new kind of understanding brought forward by modeling approaches in the so-called language/action perspective began by American researchers such as Austin, Searle, and Flores. In fact, one of these approaches has been in practice for quite a number of years. It is widely known by the name of DEMO.[3]"

"DEMO?" Bill asked, with a very confused expression on his face.

"That's right," Hans replied. "The Design and Engineering Methodology for Organizations (DEMO) is based on theoretical foundations, such as the system concept and corresponding white-box model. These notions provide a constructional understanding as opposed to the traditional functional understanding of organizations. This white-box rather than black-box understanding of business processes is needed to achieve the promise of the 1990s that the potential benefits of modern information and communication technology for organizations would really be exploited now, since it was fully understood then that IT was only a means to an end—an enabling technology—and that the real issue was the reengineering, the redesigning, or even the redefining of the enterprise.

"Concurrently, it became evident, at least to a number of people, that the traditional knowledge regarding organizations was not appropriate and sufficient. At several places in the world, research groups started to investigate the possible practical contributions of the theoretical achievements of language philosophy. The particular character of this research is commonly referred to as the language/action perspective."

"Wow, that's pretty interesting stuff!" Bill exclaimed, evidently impressed at how comprehensive the topic was. "No wonder you decided to your research and write a paper on it."

"It's just something that I've always been interested in," Hans replied with a smile.

"Good stuff," Bill replied. "But there's a question that I want to ask if you don't mind."

"I'm a professor too, Bill," Hans replied with a laugh. "I can't afford to be bothered by questions."

Bill and I smiled at Hans' statement before Bill finally asked him the question that he had had in mind.

"I'm sorry if this question sounds bizarre," Bill said, "but can you please tell me more about the organization as a white-box?"

Hans had a smile on his face but suddenly became very serious, as if he wanted to tell Bill something important.

"You know what, Bill? People ask questions when they feel like they don't understand something. You see, that's the reason why you should never find your own questions bizarre, stupid, or immature—they will only help you learn something new," Hans said to Bill.

"That's what I keep telling him as well!" I added.

"I'm sorry, I guess it just came out the wrong way," Bill said.

"There's no reason for you to be shy and courteous, Bill. We're friends now," Hans said to Bill, putting an arm around his shoulder. "As for your question, the system concept and the corresponding white-box model have proven to be crucial factors for success in redesigning and reengineering projects. A racing car driver is perfectly able to drive a racing car on the basis of his functional knowledge of cars, that is, on the basis of knowing the effects of manipulating the controls, taking into account various external conditions. A racing car mechanic is perfectly able to repair and tune a car for optimal performance. He does so on the basis of his constructional knowledge, that is, on the basis of knowing how the constituent parts, such as the engine, the gears, and the transmission chains, collectively realize the car's function, and how this is influenced by various external conditions.

"Functional knowledge and constructional knowledge have very different natures. The functional knowledge of a system is founded on a black-box model of the system. The racing car driver knows all the input and output variables, and by manipulating the control variables (which constitute a subset of the input variables), he controls the behavior of the car (i.e., the manifestation of its function in the course of time).

"The constructional knowledge of a system, on the other hand, is founded on a white-box model, that is, on a model that completely and precisely shows the mutual influences among the constituent components. The racing car mechanic knows how the components of the car work, how they interact, and how they constrain each other's operation. The dynamic properties of the components, and the way these components are assembled, determine the possible processes, that is, manifestations of construction and operation in the course of time."

Even though Hans had a very different way of doing things and would use a number of different types of examples to prove his point, Bill was fortunately quick to get the hang of things and understood much of what my friend said without any major problems. As always, however, Bill had many questions, which he didn't hesitate to ask. Besides, since Bill now already had the green light from Hans, and he was informed that he shouldn't hold back on any of the questions that he might have because no question is too immature to be asked, Bill started feeling less shy and became more confident about asking his questions. I, too, supported him because that is exactly what I had brought him all the way to Europe for. I certainly wanted Bill to learn as much as possible from the experience and knowledge of Hans, and I was very glad that things were finally going according to plan.

A while after Hans and Bill had started talking to each other about enterprise design, the waiter came to our table with our orders. There was a wide variety of fish, chicken, and beef on the table, and every one of the dishes looked more scrumptious than the other.

"Bon appétit," our waiter said, as he put the last item on the table and served us our drinks of choice. Hans and the waiter spoke a few words to each other in Dutch, so we couldn't understand them.

"The waiter was telling me that he asked the chef to make a special meal because I brought in my friends from another country," Hans finally told us, with a broad smile on his face as soon as the waiter left the table. "I hope you guys like it as much as I do."

"Fingers crossed," I replied with a smile.

And it really was special. I had heard a lot about Dutch food from many people, but the meal that we had exceeded both of our expectations, by far. The meat was cooked to perfection, and the taste was just right. In fact, both Bill and I enjoyed our meals so much that we were busy devouring the food before us for quite some time before we finally started talking again.

"This is great," Bill finally said. "No wonder it's your favorite restaurant."

"I'm glad you like it," Hans replied.

"I had a question though," Bill said, as he picked up his glass to wash down his food. "What do you think is needed to successfully apply enterprise design in order to achieve organizational transformation and innovation with new IT?"

Bill started twirling his drink in his hand as soon as he had asked the question, just as he had done in countless conversations with me.

"I'm glad you asked that question," Hans said swallowing a bite of his food. "The first methodologies for transforming organizations with information technology were introduced by IT-people. In the early years of automation—the 1970s—a computer processor was roughly considered to be equal to a human processor. Organizations were—just like software—perceived as a limited set of procedures in which events trigger processes to transform data.

"At the same time, the professionals on the organization side, who we will call the O-people from now on, have not been equipped appropriately and have not been powerful enough to offer resistance to the IT-people. The O-people tended to take the authority of the IT-people for granted. Moreover, they were not able to tell exactly what the IT-people did wrong because their own understanding of the design of the enterprise was not complete or accurate.

"The prevailing model of a business system among the O-people is the black-box model. The application of this model has a long-standing tradition, for example, in the fields of management science, logistics, economics, and business administration. The black-box model is very appropriate and sufficient for dealing with management issues and controlling the behavior of a business system.

"But is it also appropriate and sufficient if one wants to change a business system beyond the scope of its achievable behavior, that is, beyond the current ranges of its input and output variables?"

"No, I don't think that that is the case," Bill replied to Hans.

"Transforming an organization means modifying its 'construction,' and success or failure in doing this depends heavily on the degree of understanding about how the organization 'works,'" Hans said to Bill to help him to explain the situation and make him feel more confident in his answer. "Knowledge that is only founded on a black-box model is insufficient and inappropriate for this purpose. What one also needs is constructional knowledge of business systems—that is, knowledge that is founded in a white-box model. Of course, there are several factors that determine the success or failure of a business process (re)design or (re)engineering project, and the way one understands enterprises is only one of them. Still, this is a crucial factor that is frequently not recognized and often even seemingly denied.

"The prevailing model among IT-people, as defined earlier, is the white-box model. Since this type of model appears to be the one needed, it is tempting to let them do the job of (re)designing and (re)engineering the enterprise. Actually, they did and still do this job all over the world, but unfortunately, they often don't do a good job because although they possess the correct type of knowledge, they do not recognize that enterprises and information systems belong to different system categories."

"What do you mean by system categories?" Bill asked Hans, as he continued to twirl his glass in his hand.

"Information systems belong to the category of conceptual or rational systems. The components of a rational system collect, distribute, contain, and derive knowledge about facts about the world. They act upon each other by emitting commands to each other to perform these rational operations. The components operate in a rather mechanical way, that is, a command is a cause for some effect, a stimulus to which there is a particular, well-defined response. This mechanical understanding of how a system works fits perfectly well for rational systems, thus for information systems. The mistake many IT-people make is that they consider an enterprise as a kind of information system, and they consequently apply the rational white-box model to understand the organization. They fail to recognize and appreciate that organizations are essentially social systems, not rational ones."

As the conversation between Bill and Hans proceeded, I couldn't help but be proud of Bill. Even though Bill had only recently resigned from his new job, I loved how he was confidently ready to start afresh and ready to learn instead of letting the opportunity that he had go to waste. Bill was always one to hit the ground running, and even though he was only recently having very negative feelings about himself, he was still able to have a proper conversation with Hans about the things that could help him build a much brighter future than would ever have been possible before.

In fact, I hadn't said much to either of them ever since Bill and Hans had begun conversing with each other as I was having a very positive feeling about the meeting. I knew that it took Bill a lot of time to open up with new people; however, considering how well the meeting was going, I knew that he would be just fine. Besides, Hans wasn't the type of person who would ever be in the least bit arrogant. As long as I had known him, Hans had always been one of the most welcoming and supportive people—and that was especially true when he was dealing with those who were much younger than himself. He always felt that professors and other people who are responsible for mentoring and teaching students and other young people should always ensure that they don't intimidate those who wish to learn from them.

As Hans and Bill were very busy in their conversation about enterprise design, neither of them realized that we had been out of drinks for quite some time. I, therefore, took it upon myself to summon the waiter and ask him to bring us another round. It was only then that Bill realized that he was slowly twirling nothing but two melting ice cubes. "I'm sorry," Bill said, with a nervous smile on his face as he put the empty glass back down on the table between us. The polite waiter, too, nodded with a smile, took Bill's empty glass, and left to bring us more drinks.

"I have another question, Hans," Bill said.

"Ask away. That's what I'm here for," Hans and fellow professor responded.

"Well, it's not exactly a question but more of something that I'm confused about. I don't quite understand how one can 'see' and discuss the construction of an organization."

"For the purpose of studying systems, or, say, for analyzing their external behavior or their internal processes, we need to model them, that is, to conceptualize the properties in which one is interested while abstracting from all other ones, and, preferably, to formalize the conceived model. There are several well-known types of models, including the two extremes—the black-box and the white-box.

"The black-box model deals exclusively with the external behavior of a system, that is, with the effects of the activity and with the mutual influences between the kernel and the environmental elements—both as far as they are considered interesting, and both in an aggregated form. This is effectuated by conceiving of a number of input and output variables, each of which has its own value range.

"The relationships between the input and output variables are determined by the so-called transfer function. The knowledge that one acquires about a system by applying a black-box model is called functional knowledge. As I said previously, this kind of knowledge is necessary and sufficient if one wants to 'use' the system, that is, to control its external behavior. Behavior then is defined as the manifestation in the course of time of the transfer function.

"The behavior of a system is also defined as the time series of the values of the output variables. The black-box model best fits the teleological system definitions. If the number of input and/or output variables is large, the transfer function may become complex and difficult to understand.

"To manage understanding in such a case, the technique of functional decomposition is applied. Mathematically spoken, the transfer function is then rewritten as a convolution of partial functions. The practical significance is that for each of the output variables, a separate subsystem is conceived that can be studied and further decomposed on its own. The black-box model of a racing car, for instance, could usefully be decomposed into a driving subsystem, a brake subsystem, a steering subsystem, etc. The technique of functional decomposition can also be applied in the reverse direction, thus for functional composition.

"Functional decomposition is a very effective technique for understanding the function of complex systems. The knowledge of a system thus acquired, however, is still functional knowledge and that should not be mistaken for constructional knowledge. The result of functional decomposition does not tell you anything about the workings and the construction of the system. To check this, ask a racing car mechanic to disassemble a car into its functional parts!"

Bill was listening very intently to Hans as he shared one example after the other with him. However, after many conversations and meetings that I had with Bill over the last few months, I knew that even though he understood most of what Hans was saying, he still had many questions in his mind that needed answering.

"So how should I conceive the white-box perspective on organizations?" Bill finally asked, with an inquisitive look on his face.

"I had a feeling that you'd ask me that," Hans said. "The white-box model fits best with the ontological system definitions. It deals with its internal operation, with the working principle of the elements, and with the way in which the system is constructed. One can conceive of the constructional composition of white-box models as the counterpart of the functional decomposition of black-box models. Examples of the constructional subsystems of a racing car are the chassis, the radiator, the wheels, and the battery. Constructional composition always adheres to the definition of subsystems. This cannot be said of functional subsystems. Actually, the term 'subsystem' in that case is a misnomer because one cannot be sure that a functional subsystem is a system at all, according to our definition."

As soon as Hans said this, I saw a smile form on Bill's face. It was one of those smiles that he always had before he asked a witty question. This time, however, I had a feeling that he was somehow relating everything that Hans was saying to his previous workplaces. His last two jobs had both been complete disasters, and he was probably wondering what Hans would have to say about the company and startup where he worked. It was, however, probably still very early on in the conversation for Bill to start complaining to his new friend about how he felt that he was treated unjustly, and how both of these places were making things worse for themselves by not listening to constructive criticism and having a pessimistic point of view about everything.

"So why do so many transformation and innovation projects fail?" Bill asked Hans, as the smile on his face continued.

Hans smiled. Just like me, Hans probably understood completely what Bill was thinking when he asked that question.

"Well one of the reasons is that the current ways of thinking concerning enterprises of both the IT-people and the O-people are not appropriate. The black-box model fails because it is only about behavior, and the white-box model, as used by the IT-people, fails because it applies to the wrong system category. An appropriate way of thinking must encompass a white-box model, but one that applies to the category of social systems," my friend said.

Bill nodded. "I think I am starting to get the idea," he said, "but I still find it a little hard to visualize the construction of an organization. Can you give an example?"

Our waiter came back to the table once again and brought us the drinks that I had ordered. "Anything else?" he asked, once he was done placing our drinks on the table.

"No, thank you," I said with a smile. The waiter smiled as well and left our table.

As soon as the waiter left, Bill instinctively picked up his drink, took a small sip, and started twirling it in his hand once again.

Hans and I, too, picked up our glasses from the table and started drinking from them.

"Let's do a small exercise," Hans suggested, as he placed his glass back on the table. "Start to think of an organization with which you are well acquainted."

"All right, done," Bill replied.

"Perfect," Hans said. "Now think of it in an operation-oriented way, such that you see the activities, the work flows, the people who perform actions, and the equipment they use, as well as the machines that they operate. Now leave out all organizational structures, such as the grouping of employees into departments and business units (or however these groups are referred to in the organization that you have thought of) or hierarchical relationships. Having done this, you only see people, the equipment they use, and the machines they operate.

"Next, leave out all means of communication, information storage, and information processing, such as computers and networks, pencils, paper, and filing cabinets. Having done that, you see a collection of people who talk to each other and who do things with or without machines. The picture of your organization you have created now is called its OER-shape—its primal shape or archetype. 'Oer' is the Dutch word for primal, and I'll explain why I used the Dutch word in just a little while. Notice that in this OER-shape, many employees are no longer visualized as workers who operate and manage the computer software and computer equipment."

"All right," Bill replied, with a curious, yet somewhat satisfied, look on his face. "I think I'm starting to understand where you're going with this."

"Not so fast," Hans said to Bill, with a warm smile. "Let us focus now on the communication between the people and ask ourselves one simple question: What do people do when they talk to each other? Because we dropped all technology, it has become rather easy to discover that the basic meaning of the word 'communication' is the sharing of thoughts between human beings.

"Because we are interested in business processes, we pay no attention to communication that is not directly relevant for performing business activities. This sharpens the picture of the organization further: We only see people who communicate about some world they share in common and who only execute actions that affect changes in that world. We call this collection of communicating people the subject system. The word 'subject' emphasizes the important distinction between the people talking and the things they talk about, and it also stresses that these people are human individuals, not artifacts.

"In addition, it appears to be very convenient to abstract from the individual subjects and instead concentrate on the kind of things they do and communicate about. Such an abstracted role of a subject is called an actor. Every distinct actor role can be performed by one or more subjects, and every subject can perform one or more actor roles."

"Okay," Bill said "I'll admit that I'm starting to get just a tad confused now. Just now you said that we needed to focus on communication—the language and action perspective."

"That's correct," Hans replied.

"What I don't understand in all of this is how communication and organization are related," Bill said, as he continued twirling his now half-empty glass in his hand.

"That's right, Bill," Hans said. "The communication that is left can be divided into two kinds—namely, informational and performative. What I mean by informational communication is the dissemination of knowledge about the object world. But this does not change the object world.

"Performative communication, on the other hand, consists of requests and promises, of statements and acceptances, as well as examples of declinations of requests and rejections of stated results. The distinguishing property of performative communication is that it aims at bringing about changes in the object world. In performative communication, the subjects are engaged in mutual commitments. With the notion of commitment, we are at the heart of the category of social systems, of which organizations are a special kind. A social system is a system in which the elements are social subjects, that is, human beings who enter into and comply with commitments. This is the working principle of social systems, thus also of organizations. The entering into and complying with commitments takes place on a background of shared norms and values and is directly related to the notions of authority and responsibility. Every subject is allowed only to enter into—and consequently comply with—commitments for which it is authorized, and it can only be held responsible for those commitments."

Hans took a small pause to take a sip of his drink and asked Bill if he was following his line of thought. Once Bill nodded, Hans put his glass back down on the table and continued talking.

"Changes in the object world are brought about by executing particular actions. It is useful to distinguish between two classes of actions: material actions and immaterial actions. Examples of material actions are the manufacturing and the transportation of goods. Examples of immaterial actions are making a decision, passing a judgment, and determining a position. The problem with immaterial actions is that the results cannot be observed; they can only be made manifest through communication. Let us therefore look more closely at the relationship between action and communication."

As time continued to pass, my friends and I noticed that the number of people in the restaurant continued to increase.

"This place looks like it's pretty popular among people here," I finally said.

"It's my favorite, after all," Hans joked.

"I knew you'd say that," I said with a laugh. "But it really isn't surprising at all that so many people come here. The food's great and they have amazing music!"

"That's right," Hans said. "My friends, Professor Jan Dietz and Professor Jan Hoogervorst, and I really like to have our discussions at this restaurant. The combination of a good glass of wine and food is excellent."

Bill and I started laughing.

"We have a favorite restaurant back home, too," I said. "We're treated like royalty over there as well."

The lighthearted conversation about our favorite restaurants continued for quite some time before my friends started talking about enterprise design and discussed with each other their points of view on the organizations of today.

"It appears that an action is always preceded by a conversation and that it is succeeded by a conversation," Hans said. "Both conversations are performative and are carried out by the same actors. The aim of the first conversation is to reach agreement about a future action to be executed by one of the actors, whereas the aim of the second conversation is to reach an agreement about the result of that action. This pattern of a conversation before an action, the execution of the action, and a conversation after an action, is called a transaction. The three phases of a transaction have been named order phase, execution phase, and result phase.

"The order phase, or O-phase for short, of a transaction starts with a request from one of the actors to another. The requesting actor is called the initiator of the transaction, and the receiving actor is the executor. The order phase ends successfully with the promise of the executor. It may, however, also end unsuccessfully. But, in either case, there can be a lot of communication back and forth before it ends.

"The execution phase, or E-phase for short, consists of achieving the material or immaterial result the actors have agreed upon, by the executor. It may, and often does, involve the initiation of other transactions of which the results contribute to or collectively constitute the final result. The result phase, or R-phase for short, begins with the statement by the executor that the agreed upon result has been established and ends successfully with the acceptance of the result by the initiator.

"Like the other conversation, this conversation may have an unsuccessful termination, and there may be a lot of communication back and forth before it terminates. The first letters of the phase names constitute the word 'OER,' which has, in the Dutch language (as was mentioned previously), the meaning of primal, or original. It is important to note that the result of a transaction is not achieved after the action has been executed but only when the result has been accepted by the initiator. This necessarily holds for immaterial actions, but it also appears to hold for material actions as well. One may easily find examples in many organizations where the physical establishment of a change does not count as a new fact, but the authorized statement of it followed by the corresponding acceptance is what makes it be considered to be a fact. Once more, this illustrates that an organization is essentially a collection of social individuals—human beings who enter into and comply with commitments to each other. What these subjects constitute in their communication is what really counts."

Bill put down his glass, which was, again, nearly empty.

"Do I understand correctly that communication comprises the construction of a business process and thus the enterprise?" he finally asked, evidently not certain whether that was a good question to ask.

"Yes, Bill," Hans replied. "The transaction concept is the universal building block of every business process. Conversely, a business process is a coherent structure of transactions. The most important thing to keep in mind about business processes is that they are sequences of commitments between authorized and responsible social individuals. A business process cannot consist of less than a transaction, although the complexity and duration of transactions may vary largely.

"The 'realization' of a transaction can be widely dispersed across organizational structures and physical locations, and several persons, several pieces of equipment, and several machines may play a role in its completion. The foremost advantage of this way of thinking is that it allows one to abstract from all the details in which one can easily get lost in transforming the enterprise, while keeping a clear view of what is essentially going on. "

"I think I understand that now," Bill said. "But how can the DEMO approach that you spoke about earlier help in transforming organizations?"

"Let me explain," Hans replied. "Understanding the structure of business processes, which is clearly distinct from the 'realization' of the informational processes, is a prerequisite for designing and engineering them. Because of its firm theoretical foundation, all relevant notions, such as the notion of the business process itself, can be defined clearly and precisely. It has also been shown that this framework can help to effectively deliver products and services to the marketplace. And this doesn't only hold true for information systems.

"Organizations, too, are entities that can be redesigned and reengineered. Actually, an organization is also an artifact, albeit a special one, namely, one of which the elements are subjects—human beings in their role of social individuals. Organizations work because these subjects enter into and comply with commitments to each other. Anyone who understands this working principle, and who also understands that the business transaction is the atomic building block for constructing business processes, is well-equipped to work as a real enterprise engineer."

"Wow. I never really thought of enterprise design that way," Bill replied. "Thanks a lot for all of your insights."

"No problem," Hans said politely, as he nodded slightly. "But there's something else that I'd like you to know as well, Bill. Next to enterprise design, there is a need for enterprise engineering, which is basically all about how you're supposed to realize the design continuously. Since both of you are planning to stay in my country for some time, I'd like to invite you both to come along with me to Antwerp tomorrow. I want to show you how to realize evolvable software."

I was just as surprised as Bill when I heard this because Hans hadn't told me that going to Antwerp was a part of his plans. However, as learning more from the experience and gaining from the knowledge of the professional before us was the primary reason why we had flown all the way to Europe in the first place, we decided that it would be best if we were to accept the offer and seize the opportunity to learn from someone who was so passionately and readily willing to not only teach my student but also to help me, an old friend of his, learn.

"We'll accept your offer," I said to Hans, as Bill was too startled and shy to agree or decline.

"Perfect!" Hans replied. "Make sure you get a good night's sleep."

"We will," I replied with a smile, before we called it a day.

The next day, Hans came to pick us up from our hotel at around 8 o'clock in the morning.

"You ready, Bill?" Hans asked Bill.

"As ready as I'll ever be, I guess," Bill joked.

"All right, then," Hans said. "We'll be passing through Rotterdam, one of the biggest harbors in the world, and you'll also be able to see the Delta Works."

"What's that?" my curious former student asked Hans.

"It's an infrastructure of dykes and bridges in the province of Zeeland," Hans replied. "It's basically a huge construction project to protect a large area of land around the Rhine-Meuse-Scheldt delta. You'll see all of this on the way to the University of Antwerp."

Once we reached the University of Antwerp, Hans introduced Bill and me to his colleagues at the university—Professor Jan Verelst, Professor Steven de Haes, and Professor Herwig Mannaert. After telling his friends and colleagues his reason for bringing us to the university, Hans continued walking across the campus, and Bill and I followed suit. Hans then went on to explain the kind of research being performed in Antwerp.

"Over here," Hans said, "we explore Enterprise Governance & Engineering, especially the evolvable enterprise—also called Normalized Systems Theory— to provide organizations with much-needed resilience."

"Why did the university start this research?" Bill asked Hans.

"Bill, as you know, the introduction of changes is a major disruption for large-scale software projects," Hans replied. "Change management is an attempt to mitigate disruptions and reduce conflict. However, change management is costly and delays progress. It also inhibits innovation and functionality, result-ing in reduced value and customer satisfaction. Millions of business-critical applications fail to keep up with current technology and deteriorate in func-tionality and performance over time. In addition, the upkeep and maintenance of these applications is costly and risky. This is not new.

"'As far back as the 1970s, Prof. Dr. Manny Lehman proposed his Law of Increasing Complexity, stating, "As an evolving program is continually changed, its complexity, reflecting deteriorating structure, increases unless work is done to maintain or reduce it." [2] 'Normalized Systems Theory . . . [promotes the design] to not only accommodate change, but also to promote change [3] [by eliminating technical debt. This includes continuous change and decreasing complexity].'"[4]

"So, the Normalized Systems Theory is basically about solving a fundamen-tal problem of technical debt in information systems?" Bill asked.

"Yes, indeed," Hans replied. "The Normalized Systems Theory addresses the laws of Professor Meir 'Manny' Lehman, who was the chairman of the Department of Computing at the Imperial College of London. From 1974 on, Lehman worked on eight laws of software evolution. Lehman suggested that there needs to be continuing applications and systems change and growth in order to maintain resilience. Applications change and systems growth will, however, cause a decline in quality as well as increase complexity. And complexity is one of the main reasons for project failure and maintaining the information systems.[5]

"Lehman stated that software does not age with use, but deteriorates from the need to adapt it to the changing technology and or new user requirements. He identified three kinds of information systems: static information systems; parameterized information systems (such as ERP); and environmental information systems, which are the most recent kind. The problem, according to Lehman, is the so-called e-systems, which must be adjusted to the changing environment—for example, new legislations or cloud technology.[6]

"Lehman points out that as an application evolves, all people associated with it—developers, sales personnel, and users—must maintain mastery of its content and behavior to achieve satisfactory evolution. The aging, growth, and increasing complexity of software diminishes that mastery. In practice, this loss of mastery of applications is mostly felt by large organizations such as banks, insurance companies, and government agencies."[7]

"I don't understand this," Bill said. "The oldest software in the world is not in a museum but rather is still used daily on the mainframes of large organizations. At the same time, newly developed software is typically replaced after seven years of use and adjustments, repeating the life cycle all over again."

"You're certainly right, Bill," Hans said. "The Normalized Systems Theory[8] is, therefore, accompanied by a system development methodology and tooling that uses software robots, called the prime radiant. This approach has great promise in reducing complexity and increasing the ability of the organization to successfully grasp business and technical changes without disruption.

"The Normalized Systems Theory has been developed to build systems that are immune to the Increasing Complexity law—in other words, systems of which the impact of changes is proportional to the additional functionality, not to the size of the existing system. As a result, some related properties such as scalability, reliability, and testability can be achieved. Indeed, applications conforming to this theory can become very large, without restraining the adaptability over time. This research is based on applying well-known engineering knowledge from other domains, such as stability from systems theory and entropy from thermodynamics, and has already received several best paper and industry awards."

"But has this research lead to applications in practice?" Bill asked.

"You bet it has!" Hans replied. "To show the feasibility of constructing real-life transaction systems based on extremely fine-grained modular structures, about 30 applications have been developed and maintained in a variety of domains and several European countries, including some of the biggest IT departments in Belgium and the Netherlands. Domains range from administrative systems to management of containerized power solutions on backbone networks and centralized management of dispersed data center corridors.

"Results show that it is now feasible to realize both an increase in productivity by several factors in the development of transaction systems, as well as attain an unprecedented level of control during maintenance. At the same time, performance testing has exhibited excellent results, showing that there is no fundamental trade-off between performance and modularity, as is often assumed. Fine-grained modular structures combined with highly systematic development processes offer both."

Considering the depth of Hans' explanations and the amount of time and patience that he was willing to invest in Bill, I was certain that these two meetings with Hans helped to finally put things into perspective for Bill. Hans was teaching Bill and answering his questions as he would for one of his own students. In fact, there was even a lot that I personally learned from the conversations, so far.

Once Bill and old friend were done asking and answering questions about enterprise design and enterprise engineering, all of us decided to have lunch.

References

1. Tulley, Gever. (2018). "Gever Tulley Quotes." BrainyQuote.com, Xplore Inc. Retrieved from https://www.brainyquote.com/quotes/gever_tulley_559476
2. Dietz, Jan L. G. and Mulder, Hans B. F. (1998). "Organizational Transformation Requires Constructional Knowledge of Business Systems." *Proc. HICCS*. IEEE. Retrieved from https://www.computer.org/csdl/proceedings/hicss/1998/8245/05/82450365.pdf
3. Dietz, Jan L. G. (2001, January 15). DEMO: Towards a Discipline of Organisation Engineering. *European Journal of Operational Research, 128*(2), 351–363. Retrieved from https://www.sciencedirect.com/science/article/abs/pii/S0377221700000771
4. Manganelli, Joe and Mulder, J. B. F. (2017). "Thoughts on Application of Evolutionary Software Development for Complex, Large-Scale, Integrated, Open Systems." In: Aveiro et al. (eds.). *Proceedings of the EEWC Forum 2017*. Antwerp, Belgium (09-May-2017 to 11-May-2017). CEUR Workshop Proceedings. Retrieved from http://ceur-ws.org/Vol-1838/paper-06.pdf. The material in Joe Manganelli and Hans Mulder's article regarding the work of Prof. Dr. Meir "Manny" Lehman has been previously published in the following: [2] Lehman, Meir M. (September 1980). "The Law of Increasing Complexity." *Proceedings of the IEEE 68*(9), 1068 and [3] Mannaert, Herwig and Verelst, Jan. (2009).

Normalized Systems: Re-creating Information Technology Based on Laws for Software Evolvability. Koppa. ISBN 978-90-77160-00-8.

5. Ibid.
6. Ibid.
7. Ibid.
8. Eessaar, Erki. (2014). On Applying Normalized Systems Theory to the Business Architectures of Information Systems. *Baltic J. Modern Computing, 2*(3), 132–149. Retrieved from https://www.bjmc.lu.lv/fileadmin/user_upload/lu_portal/projekti/bjmc/Contents/2_3_2_Eessaar1.pdf

Chapter 10

Moving to the Age of Agility

My friends and I collectively decided that we should have lunch at a small local restaurant in Antwerp—a restaurant that would be able to give us a true taste of Belgium. Bill and I had only been in the country for one day, and there was a lot of local food that we hoped to try.

As expected, the conversations during lunch, too, revolved around enterprise design and engineering. There were talks about agility and innovation, and my old friend, Hans, took every opportunity to share insights and important information with Bill about the things that he thought Bill should know when he starts to look for a new job.

"What do you know about the Information Age?" Hans asked Bill.

As soon as Hans asked him this question, Bill turned towards me because he and I had previously discussed the Information Age, during several conversations, and we had already shared with each other what we thought about it. Bill was evidently interested, and I must admit that I was as well.

Not knowing how else to respond, Bill replied using the typical definition that comes to the mind of every person whenever they think of the Information age.

"I don't know which answer you're looking for," Bill replied. "I guess all I really know about it is that it is the age when industrialization had its greatest effect, and there was a prominent and extremely substantial shift in the way in which the processes, operations, and activities were being carried out in our businesses, organizations, and companies."

Hans said nothing in return and started fiddling with the menu on the table before us.

"I mean, I know that the answer that I gave you probably wasn't the one that you were looking for, but I really don't understand what you wanted to me to say," Bill said, faking a smile.

"That's not it," Hans replied. "In fact, there's really no other way in which I'd probably be able to answer that question either, if someone were to randomly ask me a question like that at a lunch table. The only reason why I asked you this question was to hear what you think about the Information Age."

"I guess you got your answer then. But I don't feel as if that definition still applies today," Bill added, as an afterthought.

"I was just about to say that as well," Hans replied. "In fact, I feel as if everyone around us, for some reason, refuses to acknowledge the fact that today's day and age is something far more advanced than what the traditional definition of the Information Age describes. The characteristics of our time and the features and abilities of the companies, businesses, and organizations of today are so different from anything in the past. Besides, being perpetually stuck with that mindset really won't do justice or help us find solutions to the problems and challenges that our businesses, companies, and organizations are facing in today's day and age."

The discussion between Bill and Hans really got me thinking about a lot of things as well. To share my opinion on this topic, I told my two friends that I had recently read a book[1] that defined our current day and age as the "Age of Interactions." Needless to say, both Bill and Hans were extremely interested in hearing more about this definition and why one would reach that conclusion.

"What's the most prominent change that you think the Information Age was able to bring?" I asked Bill and Hans.

"Hyperconnectivity," both Bill and Hans replied together.

"That's the first thing that always comes to my mind as well whenever I think of an answer to that question," I replied. "The technologies that have become widely available to the masses in the wake of the Information Age and hyperconnectivity have made room for quality interactions that wouldn't have been possible in the past," I told Bill and old friend.

Both of my friends were evidently interested in the propositions made by David Alberts, author of the book that I was quoting. Alberts had also claimed that unlimited possibilities had been unleashed as a result of these technologies, hyperconnectivity, and the interactions that had become possible in the wake of the Information Age. However, continuing to call every era even decades after the commencement of the Information Age by the same name was something that the author of the book was simply unable to wrap his head around—much like everyone who I was sitting with at that table at a little local restaurant in Antwerp.

"The challenges of the Volatile, Uncertain, Complex, and Ambiguous (VUCA) world of today are nothing like they used to be in the past," I reiterated to both Bill and Hans. Both of them nodded in approval of my opinion. "In fact, I think it's even fair to say that the challenges that we are facing in our businesses, companies, and organizations today are a result of the increasing complexity and all of the new technologies, thoughts, and ideas that have consumed our corporate settings."

This really got both of my friends thinking.

The fact is that no matter how volatile, uncertain, complex, and ambiguous our work environments and the corporate world in itself have become, the widespread availability and use of technology has allowed people to connect with each other in ways that would never even have been imagined in the past. The introduction of new ideas and industrialization has paved the way for a lot more than just new and improved business processes. Opportunities that were lost in the past are now no longer something that needs to be worried about since hyperconnectivity has caused a substantial difference in the number of opportunities that people can now benefit from.

As is seen in the case of every change, however, the Age of Interactions as well was bound to come with its fair share of problems, complexities, and limitations. It should, however, be noted that the complexity of the Age of Interactions is not something that could have been avoided even if one tried because the challenges that we face in our business environments today are, in fact, based on many different factors. Not only have natural disasters such as earthquakes, tsunamis, and floods contributed to the problems and challenges that we face, but there have also been inevitable factors such as instability, terrorism, and conflicts, which have made things much more challenging for the businesses, companies, and organizations of today.

Factors as great as the ones mentioned above are certainly not something that can be controlled by a single actor, or even by a small set of actors who are very capable and know exactly what they are supposed to do. The nature of the challenges and factors that are involved in the complexities that our businesses, companies, and organizations face in the world today is in many ways different from those of the past. Responding to the challenges of today is, therefore, not something that can and should be taken care of by just a handful of entities or actors. In reality, the challenges of today can only be responded to effectively if a large collection of heterogeneous actors or entities works together to find a solution.

As I discussed all of these ideas with my friends, they were not only evidently impressed, but they also found themselves agreeing with nearly every word that I said. The Information Age and the Age of Interactions were meant to reduce uncertainty in our environments and corporate settings. Although this has proven to be the case in certain situations, the technologies and advancements that have made it possible are also the reasons why hyperconnectivity has become the latest talk of the town. Although the transfer of information has become much easier now than it ever was in the past, the fact of the matter is that we are now living in an era of constant communication and continuous connectivity. Both of these consequences of the Age of Information may have created room for many developments and solutions; however, they have also given rise to new problems.

My friends and I were busy having a very intense conversation about the Age of Information and its consequences when the waiter came to our table with the best local dish that he thought we'd be interested in. Much like the experiences that Bill and I had in the Netherlands, the food was amazing and cooked to perfection. I wasn't planning on staying in Europe for too long because I had to get back to my university lectures, and I had many other important tasks awaiting me at home, so I needed to savor every bite.

We took our time with the meal, but once we finished eating, we knew that it was time for us to get back to business. The conversation about the corporate world began right where it had left off before we were presented with our meals.

"Professor Joe and I have had several conversations recently about the corporate settings of today," Bill started telling Hans. "It's almost impossible to make predictions about anything, considering the situation that we're in nowadays. The ability of a business, company, or organization to survive, its efficiency, and its effectiveness must all be kept in check with certain boundaries and limitations. We were discussing how the businesses, companies, and organizations of today, as well as those of the future, will always have to achieve and maintain success in light of new circumstances that are more diverse and unique than those which the leaders of these places are used to. They will also have to constantly analyze and refine the ways in which they carry out their processes because goals, objectives, targets, tasks, and purposes will no longer be the same for years on end."

Bill took a pause to pour himself, as well as the rest of us, some water from a large bottle that the waiter had brought and placed on our table. After he drank an entire glass of water in one go, Bill continued summarizing the countless conversations that he and I had recently shared back at home.

Bill explained to Hans how we had both spoken to each other about how the businesses, companies, and organizations of the VUCA world of today have so much more to keep an eye on than those of the past. Bill told Hans that we had had conversations about the unknown features and unpredictable states that have almost become characteristic of the businesses, companies, and organizations of today.

"Even though the technological advancements and industrialization may be able to reduce uncertainty in very specific situations, I don't think that the corporate environment of today will ever try to fall back on the traditional strategies and approaches that have now become obsolete. We have no option but to increase our agility."

"We have no option but to increase our agility," Hans repeated in approval and appreciation of the wise words that Bill had said. "And to move to the Age of Agility," I added.

Even though Bill had said those words much like an afterthought, I couldn't help but be proud of Bill and the words that he was saying so confidently in front of someone who had so much experience. Although he remained quiet for the major part of the conversation just to see what Bill had to say, Hans, too, was evidently impressed at the intellect of Bill.

There was another small pause during which not much was said. In order to break the silence, I continued telling Bill and Hans about more things that I had learned from the book that I had been quoting earlier by David Alberts.[2]

"The situations that we're facing in the corporate world these days are being referred to as complex endeavors," I told my friends. "These situations manifest themselves in the VUCA corporate scenario of today and are characterized by their multidimensional effect spaces, multifaceted nature, and their complex components.

"Since practicality comes into play in these situations, the potential number of interactions in complex endeavors is impossible to count, and knowing about all of the interactions that occur in a specific setting is impossible as well. The interactions that can occur within a given amount of time during complex endeavors are, for the most part, known to be dynamic and unpredictable. Since it is impossible to predict with certainty the number and nature of the interactions that occur within complex endeavors, it is not possible to manage the risks and uncertainties of these situations or settings either."

As I explained all of this to my friends, I felt as if I was being just a tad selfish and that I was placing myself in the spotlight for too long because this was essentially supposed to be a conversation—and trip—during which Bill would become more confident in his decisions and truly understand how he can survive in the utterly confusing and chaotic corporate world of today. Fortunately, I didn't have to continue talking about what I had read in David Albert's book for too long because Bill and old friend joined in the conversation and started offering their opinions.

"I'm not quite sure why that's a problem," Hans and fellow professor said. "I feel that change is constant. Something like that will obviously bring with it opportunities as well as limitations and challenges."

Hans took a small pause to drink some water before he continued. "And that's why we have no choice except to move to the Age of Agility, as Joe suggested."

Bill nodded at the last words that Hans said.

The funny thing about agility is that in today's time, it is perceived as an unattainable notion or idea that is only within the reach of those with mystical powers or the best of the best. As much as we love relying on that definition of the concept, it couldn't be more wrong. Agility, much like a lot of other qualities and characteristics, is something that needs to be worked on by individuals and teams for years—but that still doesn't mean that it is something that can be "mastered" as we use the word.

As a matter of fact, agility comprises an active component and a passive one. Although passive agility is simply the term that is used when a business, company, or organization possesses the right characteristics and abilities to continue carrying out its processes, operations, and activities effectively, even in the midst of changes and unusual circumstances, active agility has more to do with the ability of the said business, company, or organization to take the steps that are required or respond whenever need be. These steps or the response that is expected of any business, company, or organization that claims to be actively agile can vary from taking an action to taking one, changing the way in which processes are carried out, changing the approach used for management, or even changing the overall perception of governance within the business, company, or organization that is being defined as agile.

But that's not all.

In certain cases, a business, company, or organization may never be able to adapt properly or be considered truly agile unless the definition of success—or the way in which it is perceived—is changed from the core.

"One thing, however, that people generally disregard these days is that being forced to change and changing for the sake of change isn't what can be defined as agility," Hans continued.

"For any business, company, or organization to be considered agile, effectiveness is a prerequisite," I added.

Bill was nodding and looking back and forth between Hans and me throughout the course of the conversation. One thing that remained constant was that he kept twirling his glass, even as he looked at both of us and offered his opinion intermittently.

"The capabilities and behaviors of any business, company, or organization can't be deemed agile unless they have the capacity to help maintain or improve the measure of value of the given entity. In fact, some may even go as far as demanding proof of improvement before the entity is considered agile," Bill stated.

The measures that are set to determine value are enough for one to get a clear picture of the perspective, vision, and values of any business, company, organization, or any other type of entity that exists. These measures are also naturally able to give one a complete picture of the interests of the business, company, or organization in question because they ultimately help people understand the state that the given entity essentially desires to reach or attain.

Since business environments (especially those of the world we now live in) are prone to change quite frequently, it is not only absurd for one to think that the same strategies and activities will yield the same results that they did in the past, but it also unfair for one to believe that the standards and ideas that any business, company, or organization has for success will not change. Circumstances are constantly evolving, and our environments are now subject to more changes than ever before. The goals of any entity will, therefore, not only change constantly, but they will also seem to become even more difficult to attain, with time.

Unfamiliar situations as well are something that will be more prominent, and businesses, companies, and organizations of today and those of the future will increasingly find themselves in such situations. The unpredictability and uncertainty of complex endeavors and the VUCA corporate world, in general, necessitates that people and entities will find themselves in more and more unfamiliar situations that they may or may not know how to react to effectively. What should and *must* be relied on in such cases, too, is agility.

As broad as the entire concept is, agility can be applied to anything—from individuals to businesses, collections to companies, nations to governance, command to management, organizations to tactics, and more or less any entity or domain in existence. However, as important as the concept and its manifestation may be, the most prominent prerequisite for agility and developing this characteristic is responsiveness.

To be deemed responsive, any entity—regardless of whether it is a business, company, organization, or even an individual—must be able to recognize prominent changes within the environment, in a competitor, or within oneself in a timely manner. But that's not all. Since one really can't be called responsive without proposing or at least recognizing a plausible solution, thinking of an effective and appropriate response as well is part of the process. Comprehensive and mindful awareness of the environment—both within and surrounding the entity—is key.

Agility has been conceived of as an unrealistic notion for far too long. However, mindful analysis reveals that it may be difficult, but it certainly isn't something that is innately unachievable. The characteristics can be learned and adopted, the skills can be developed, and the right results can be attained with the right amount of persistence and motivation.

Since I knew that Bill had already learned everything that was important for him to know, I was finally at peace. I knew for a fact that the lessons my friends and I had taught him during our local and international meetings would stick with him for the rest of his life. I knew that Bill was now not only equipped with all the knowledge that was important, but that he also had learned everything he needed to about steps that he would have to take to reach his ultimate goal. I knew that it was time for me to let him explore and broaden his horizons.

Once we were done with our meals and drinks, I took out a notebook and pen from my bag—an action that surprised both Bill and Hans, equally. Initially, they thought that I had just remembered some very important business that I had to take care of; however, both of them changed their minds once I had flipped to an empty page and started drawing boxes.

"What are you doing?" Bill whispered, so quietly that I had to read his lips to decipher what he was saying.

"Dynamic strategy," I stated, as I wrote the words on the top of the page. Unsurprisingly, that was enough for them to understand what I was doing.

Once I had drawn half of the figure and Bill still didn't know what was going on, I decided to be a good friend and help him out. "Enterprise Agility Model," I whispered back to my student, who still looked very perplexed.

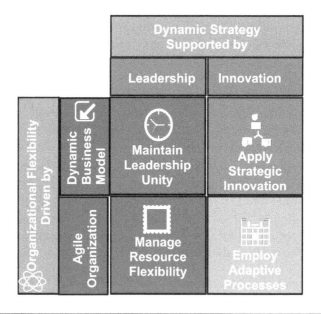

Enterprise Agility Model

The agility model appears to be a very simple figure with just a few boxes, which is probably why Bill wasn't readily giving it the importance that it deserved. Even though it looks relatively simple, the agility matrix is, indeed, one of the most comprehensive matrices of the corporate world and has treasures that leaders and managers in the businesses, companies, and organizations of today can learn from.

Once I was finished drawing the matrix, I handed the notebook over to Bill.

"Dynamic strategy and organizational flexibility," I said to Bill. "These are two of the most important aspects of any entity that wishes to succeed in the corporate world of today. Although that may sound pretty straightforward, the fact of the matter is that these are the very things that businesses these days need the most help with. Executing dynamic strategy means that you're constantly focusing on organizational challenges.

"Look closely at the agility model that I've drawn for you. Dynamic strategy is essentially divided into two core areas, namely, leadership and innovation. Similarly, organizational flexibility is divided into two core components—that is, organizational and business models. What you need to understand here is that organizational flexibility and dynamic strategy work hand in hand for the success of the business, company, or organization. And organizational flexibility needs to have more than one way to achieve a desired result."

Bill listened intently and studied the entire model several times while I explained it to him, pointing at each term with my pen as I spoke about it.

"Now, as the model suggests, any entity in the corporate world of today comprises four key components. If you focus on leadership while working on creating a business model that will work for your entity, regardless of whether it's a business, company, organization, or any other type of entity, you will essentially be working on the area of leadership unity and culture that you see right here. The flexibility of the business model is very important. When a business model is failing, the company must be able to find a new model or way of operating in the face of change," I said and pointed to the first of the four key components of the Enterprise Agility Model.

"Now, you might have already realized that leadership unity and culture are pivotal to any entity in the corporate world of today. Agility isn't really possible if the culture in your business, company, or organization isn't supporting it. I'm sure that you have already seen this firsthand in both of the places where you most recently worked. Additionally, you don't only need to have leaders, but also *leadership,* that supports the idea of agility. If your workplace is filled with arrogant leaders who think that they know better than all the rest, there is no way that your company, business, or organization will be able to rise above the challenges that are bound to come its way."

Bill nodded in agreement. Since Bill had already experienced this, there was no reason why he would need further explanation about the first part of the agility model.

"The second core constituent of the agility model is the strategic aspect. This aspect is key when you're interested in making your business model one that is bound to survive through the challenges and limitations of the current setting—something that is innovative and creative. Again, it is impossible for any entity, regardless of whether it is a business, company, or organization, to succeed without the right dynamic strategies that are in line with their vision and the corporate environment."

I could tell by the look on Bill's face that he was becoming very interested in everything that I was saying to him. And this reaction of Bill wasn't surprising in the least. The agility model was, in essence, a concise yet very informative summary of everything that Hans and I had been telling him throughout all of our conversations over the last few months.

The third and fourth sections of the agility model are based on how the organization can become more flexible and agile in light of leadership and innovation. I explained to Bill how businesses, companies, and organizations in the VUCA world of today need to embrace flexibility and become more adaptive to ensure that they could overcome any and all problems and challenges that come their way.

Bill may have ridiculed the matrices and models that I told him about in the past (all, of course, in good humor), but the agility model was something that he was responding to completely differently. I explained to Bill how the agility model was perhaps one of the most important tools that the businesses, companies, and organizations of today's world could rely on. I could tell by the look on his face that Bill knew that this was one of the things that he would absolutely have to remember and return to for the rest of his life. Throughout my conversations with him, I had seen Bill grow more patient and more grateful for all of the knowledge that my friends and I were readily providing him with.

Our meeting with Hans ended on a very good note at the little restaurant, and he understood that his job was done as well. When they saw that we were about to leave, the waiters and owner of the restaurant came to our table to ask us if everything was all right and whether we enjoyed the meal. Seeing Hans being treated like royalty was a very uplifting sight.

"It's probably the best thing I've had on my trip!" Bill exclaimed. I can testify to the fact that he wasn't lying.

A smile appeared on all faces before we finally said our goodbyes—goodbyes that were interrupted by a phone call.

"Hi," I heard Bill say on the phone. His voice was equally tense and anticipatory.

"Yes, this is Bill," he said, after a small pause.

Even though I should have expected it, what happened next was something that I couldn't make sense of at the moment. A broad grin then appeared on the face of Bill. The next thing I saw was that he seated himself back down on the chair where he had been sitting at our table. Both Hans and I looked at him in amazement.

"I'll be back and available next week," Bill continued on the phone. "I'm actually out of the country at the moment."

Bill's conversation on the phone continued for a few more minutes, but I knew exactly what had happened. Hans, however, still looked at Bill with the same amount of curiosity and skepticism as he did earlier.

Bill put both of his elbows on the table and held his face in his palms as soon as he hung up. Since I already knew what had happened, I leaned in and hugged Bill, patting him on the back.

"Congratulations," I said to him. It was only then that Hans understood that the phone call was to arrange a meeting with a well-known company executive regarding a potential job offer.

"You knew about this? Wait—you did this!" Bill sprung off of his seat to hug me back.

"I tried," I responded with a warm smile.

Bill had been invited to the office of none other than my friend, Steve K., who I had spoken to about Bill, at length. My friend had been so impressed by the intellect and potential of Bill that he had promised to help me—and him—out whenever he got the chance. The phone call was the manifestation of my friend keeping his promise. Hans, too, congratulated Bill.

Throughout the ride back to Delft, the happiness on the face of Bill was evident. For the longest time ever, Bill couldn't even find the right words to say. Both Hans and I knew all of the emotions that he was probably experiencing, which is why we didn't say much to him. We were just glad that all of our efforts had come to fruition.

After awhile, Hans, Bill, and I finally found ourselves with some spare time to talk about more lighthearted topics—the weather, the food, the local traditions and customs. We tried our best to talk about anything and everything that was unique to the Netherlands. *What a conversation that was!*

Bill told us that he would like to make the most of the opportunity that his current location afforded him and book a flight to Ireland to meet and spend a few days with his relatives. Besides, he now had something to celebrate with his family.

It was only when we finally reached the Delft Central Station that I decided to remind Bill about something.

"I'm sure that you didn't remember this because of all of the excitement, but I'm heading back home today," I said to him.

"I completely forgot!" Bill's jaw dropped. I took the opportunity to continue talking.

"The only reason why I brought you all the way to the Netherlands was to meet Hans and learn from him. Now that we've taught you everything that we thought was important, I think it's best if we leave you to explore on your own. And, yes, Hans knew about this all along."

Unable to think of the right words to say, Bill came forward and hugged me in the middle of the train station for a good minute or more.

"You're welcome," I said, patting him on the back.

Bill looked me straight in the eye, still unable to respond with words.

"I . . . thanks professor," he finally said.

"I don't know what I've done to deserve a friend like you, but I couldn't be more grateful, honestly," he said, before coming forward for another long hug.

"Hey, it's just my job," I laughed. "Now hurry up. I don't want to miss my flight because of this."

Unfortunately, the time had come to say goodbye to Hans. He had to return for an important meeting. We thanked him profusely for all his help.

Bill and I took the train back to the Amsterdam Schiphol Airport, where we arrived a little over two hours before my flight's departure time.

"Guess we made it," I said to my still awestruck former student.

"I still don't know what's going on," was all he had to say for both of us to start laughing.

Bill and I spent a few minutes trying to digest the situation before a screen revealed that I could check in for my flight.

"Well, I guess this is it," I said to Bill.

"I can never thank you enough for this," Bill replied, hugging me tight one last time.

I could tell by the look on his face that all of the conversations that I had had with him—especially the ones in the Netherlands—had changed him immensely and made him grow as a person. As he stood before me waiting for me to head to the counter to check in for my flight, I was immediately reminded of our *first* meeting at the airport a few months ago—the first time I had seen him since he had graduated. Bill had not only grown into a visibly more confident individual but also into a friend who I knew I could rely on for the rest of my life.

And the gratefulness on his face wasn't hidden either. Something about his expression gave away all of the emotions that he was feeling at that moment—emotions that he couldn't process but was still grateful for.

I extended a hand to him for a final handshake at the airport. It was at the moment when he followed suit that it struck me how I had probably changed his life forever.

"I'll see you at the restaurant back home," I said with a smile before I headed toward the counter. Bill smiled and nodded slightly, as he waved goodbye to me.

"Guess I'll look at my options for traveling to Ireland," Bill replied not knowing how else he was supposed to respond at this moment.

"Don't miss me too much," I shouted jokingly, as I turned to the counter. Seeing Bill laugh heartily at my terrible attempt at a joke is the last memory I have of him at Schiphol Airport on his little trip to the Netherlands—his trip in search of agility.

References

1. Alberts, David S. (2011). The *Agility Advantage: A Survival Guide for Complex Enterprises and Endeavors* (CCRP Publications Series). Washington (DC): DoD Command and Control Research Program.
2. Ibid.

Index

A

Age of Agility, 33, 35, 36, 223, 227
agile, 5, 8, 10, 11, 26, 34, 37, 44, 50,
        53, 54, 84, 91, 95, 105, 106,
        108, 110–116, 130, 133, 134,
        147, 150, 156, 160, 190, 228,
        232
agility, 6–8, 10, 11, 20, 21, 27, 33,
        35, 36, 39, 47, 50, 51, 53, 61,
        62, 69, 71, 91, 92, 110, 111, 113,
        130, 133–137, 142, 147, 150,
        155, 157, 161–163, 165, 176,
        182–185, 190, 194, 204, 223,
        227–232, 235
agility matrix, 230
agility model, 230–232
ambidextrous, 118–120

B

best practices, 3–5, 44
black-box, 207–213
business mission, 18
business model, 10, 51, 120, 148, 149,
        175, 231, 232

business process, 8, 52, 119, 162, 207,
        210, 214, 216, 217, 225

C

challenge, 4, 7, 8, 16–20, 23, 32, 33,
        37–39, 52–54, 61, 79, 80, 82,
        91, 98, 137, 162, 167, 224, 225,
        227, 231, 232
change, 1, 3, 5–8, 10, 11, 15, 19,
        20, 26, 33, 35–39, 43, 44,
        46, 49–56, 58–69, 71, 72,
        74, 79, 80, 82, 84, 86, 89–93,
        95–98, 102, 106, 110, 111, 115,
        117–119, 121, 122, 127, 133,
        135–150, 154–156, 162, 163,
        167, 171, 174–177, 180, 182,
        184, 194, 195, 203, 204, 209,
        214–216, 218, 219, 224, 225,
        227–229, 231
change management, 5, 49–55, 63,
        66, 97, 218
chaos, 41, 46, 51, 55, 74
communication, 4, 8, 26, 32, 64, 97,
        98, 120, 207, 213–216, 226
competitiveness, 166, 171

creativity, 18, 44, 50, 102, 106, 119,
    139–141, 143–145, 148, 161,
    162, 164, 166, 184, 193–195,
    204
culture, 19, 20, 43, 51, 53, 61, 66, 71,
    92, 118, 142, 165, 231

D

decision, 5, 7, 8, 16, 18, 19, 22, 23,
    28, 31, 37–41, 43–46, 51–54,
    56–58, 60, 62–65, 71–76,
    78–82, 89–92, 95–100, 103,
    104, 113, 118, 121, 122, 124,
    125, 131, 137, 138, 153, 158–
    160, 163, 165, 168, 174, 178,
    186, 188, 190, 192, 193, 195,
    199, 215, 227
DEMO. *See* Design and Engineering
    Methodology for Organizations
Design and Engineering
    Methodology for Organizations
    (DEMO), 206, 217
disruptive innovation, 171–174, 176,
    194
Dunning–Kruger effect, 76, 77
dynamic strategy, 136, 230–232

E

enterprise, 11, 39, 44, 205–211, 213,
    215–218, 220, 223, 230, 231
environment, 4, 6, 9, 14, 18, 19,
    37–39, 43–46, 50–54, 57–63,
    65–69, 71, 72, 79, 82, 84–89,
    91, 95–98, 104–108, 110,
    112–116, 122, 125, 128–130,
    135–138, 141–144, 147, 149,
    150, 155, 160, 161, 164, 166,
    175–178, 182, 204, 219, 225,
    227, 229, 232
evolution, 19, 36, 219

F

flexibility, 8, 47, 82, 115, 137, 231, 232
functional decomposition, 212

G

goal, 3, 10, 14, 17, 19, 25, 42, 52, 53,
    68, 78, 79, 82, 87, 91, 96, 108,
    112, 116, 124, 127, 130, 156,
    161, 194, 226, 229, 230

H

holacracy, 121, 123, 124, 126–130
holistic, 39, 41, 47, 50
HR. *See* human resources
human resources (HR), 148–150
hyperconnectivity, 224–226

I

implementation, 66–69, 96, 121,
    124, 135, 164, 176
incremental innovation, 171, 172
Information Age, 33, 36, 39, 95,
    223–225
information technology (IT), 1, 3–11,
    13–23, 25–33, 35–47, 49–69,
    71–93, 95–103, 105–131,
    133–150, 153–195, 199–207,
    209–220, 223–234
innovation, 3, 4, 13, 25, 26, 28,
    36, 44, 50, 92, 106, 118–120,
    139–148, 156, 157, 160–167,
    170–177, 182–184, 190, 193–
    195, 199, 202–204, 206, 209,
    213, 218, 223, 231, 232
innovation environment, 166
innovation hub, 92, 139–148, 156,
    157, 182, 183
innovation model, 167

intelligence, 26, 30, 31, 96, 97
IT. *See* information technology

K

knowledge, 8, 25, 26, 28, 36, 42, 97,
    115, 140, 145, 161, 168, 171, 185,
    205–212, 214, 217, 219, 230, 232

L

leadership, 3, 4, 33, 37, 41, 43–45,
    57, 60, 65, 71, 72, 76–78, 91,
    92, 95–98, 126, 133, 135, 140,
    141, 143, 231, 232
linear approach, 45, 46, 54, 172
linearity, 45–47

M

M&As. *See* mergers and acquisitions
mergers and acquisitions (M&As),
    40, 71, 72, 117

N

normalized systems, 218, 219

O

open innovation, 164–167
organization, 3–10, 20, 21, 26, 27,
    36–39, 41–45, 47, 50–54,
    57–69, 71, 72, 74, 76, 78, 79,
    81–85, 87–92, 95–98, 104–108,
    110–130, 133–150, 155–157,
    160–169, 171–177, 181, 183,
    184, 190, 193–195, 204, 206,
    207, 209–219, 223–226, 228,
    229, 231, 232
organizational learning, 26
organizational performance, 7, 53

P

performance, 7, 9, 10, 19, 53, 54, 79,
    82, 87, 143, 208, 218, 220
performance goal, 53
prioritization, 18
problem-solving process, 167–170
problem-solving skills, 193

R

resilience, 10, 29, 199, 218, 219
responsiveness, 8, 26, 47, 229

S

scenario, 19, 35, 37, 46, 47, 55, 68,
    82–91, 98, 186, 227
scenario planning, 83–85, 87–91
S-curve, 19, 27
shareholder, 53, 71
situation, 4, 5, 8, 17, 18, 21, 25, 26,
    41–43, 45–47, 53, 58, 66–68,
    72, 73, 75, 78, 80, 81, 92, 98,
    101, 103, 116, 127, 138, 170, 173,
    179, 184, 186, 190, 192, 200,
    204, 209, 225–227, 229, 234
skill, 7, 20, 21, 27, 32, 37, 41, 59, 89,
    97, 98, 105, 108, 114, 164, 176,
    177, 190, 193, 229
strategic innovation, 118, 193–195
strategy, 2–10, 13–16, 18, 20–29,
    32–35, 45, 52, 54, 55, 58, 71,
    76–79, 81–85, 90, 91, 96, 100,
    105, 118, 121, 125, 131, 136,
    139, 144, 148, 162–166, 176,
    193, 195, 196, 227, 229–232
subsystem, 212
system(s), 4, 36, 41–47, 50, 63, 97,
    106–108, 119–130, 136, 161,
    165, 166, 176, 201, 205–215,
    217–220

T

technology, 2, 8, 33, 59, 66, 96–98, 120, 121, 149, 161, 162, 167, 173, 175, 205, 207, 209, 214, 218, 219, 224, 225

transformation, 6, 33, 36, 49, 50, 53, 55, 64, 66, 92, 93, 95, 135–145, 147–149, 165, 205, 209, 213

Triple Helix, 164

V

value, 3, 6, 15, 20, 26, 41–43, 53, 62, 107, 149, 167, 171, 211, 215, 218, 228

vision, 3, 5, 10, 14, 16, 26, 39, 41–43, 51, 53, 61, 62, 68, 82, 83, 87, 114, 163, 168, 190, 228, 232

Volatile, Uncertain, Complex, and Ambiguous (VUCA), 37–39, 45–47, 54, 69, 79, 85, 88, 89, 95, 96, 98, 114, 136–138, 140, 147, 150, 155, 161, 164, 166, 168, 174, 181, 184, 193, 225–227, 229, 232

VUCA. See Volatile, Uncertain, Complex, and Ambiguous

W

white-box, 207, 208, 210–213